The Reproduction of Mothering

The Reproduction of
Mothering

*Psychoanalysis and the
Sociology of Gender*

NANCY CHODOROW

UNIVERSITY OF CALIFORNIA PRESS
Berkeley • Los Angeles • London

For
Leah Turitz Chodorow
and
Marvin Chodorow

University of California Press
Berkeley and Los Angeles, California

University of California Press, Ltd.
London, England

ISBN 0-520-03133-4
Library of Congress Catalog Card Number: 75-27922
Printed in the United States of America

1 2 3 4 5 6 7 8 9

Contents

v

Preface

This project owes its existence to the feminist movement and feminist community and its origins to a group of us who, several years ago, wondered what it meant that women parented women. Many of my ideas were first developed with the members of the mother-daughter group.

Friends, colleagues, and teachers have given important advice, encouragement, and criticism during the years I have worked on this book. Many people carefully read drafts at various stages and gave me extensive, thoughtful criticism. I want especially to thank Egon Bittner, Jay Cantor, Margaret Cerullo, Rose Laub Coser, Barbara Deck, Barbara Easton, George Goethals, Rosabeth Moss Kanter, Michelle Zimbalist Rosaldo, Lillian Breslow Rubin, Neil Smelser, Judith Stacey, Barrie Thorne, Gwendolyn Wright, and Eli Zaretsky for their important, generous assistance and support. Discussions with Samuel Bowles, Herbert Gintis, Heidi Hartmann, Nancy Jay, and Abigail Wolfson helped me to clarify and solidify my ideas. William Friedland and John Kitsuse also made helpful suggestions about the manuscript.

I benefited from the special expertise of many people. David Plotke was a valuable intellectual and political critic, as well as an extraordinary editor. Eileen van Tassell contributed extensive comments and suggestions to the sections on biology and saved me from several mistakes. Egon Bittner taught me how to think about and write theory. Several people taught me about psychoanalytic theory and the importance of its clinical foundations: George Goethals, Ilse K. Jawetz, Malkah Notman, Bennett Simon, Edmund C. Payne, and Paul L. Watson. Caryl Hashitani gave me excellent research help.

Diane Ketroser did expert work typing the manuscript. Judith Burton did the mammoth and thankless job of compiling and typing the book's footnotes and bibliography.

Michael Reich has been throughout this project unendingly encouraging. He has read and discussed with me at length countless drafts of sentences, paragraphs, and chapters, and the final product bears the mark of his careful and critical intellect. His supportiveness and nurturance undercut one main argument of this book.

I did not take everyone's suggestions and did not always learn well. Final responsibility for this work is of course my own. I was supported during parts of the writing by a National Science Foundation Pre-Doctoral Research Fellowship, a National Institutes of Mental Health Dissertation Fellowship, and faculty research funds granted by the University of California, Santa Cruz.

I would like to forewarn readers about language. This book is meant for people concerned with the family and sexual inequality, many of whom will not have a background in psychoanalysis. It also is meant to invite reflection by those in the psychoanalytic field itself, to encourage them to focus on the sociological and structural foundations of what they observe mainly in individual clinical manifestations. Such a dual goal is difficult. Anyone familiar with Freud's more technical writings, let alone with psychoanalytic writing since Freud, knows that psychoanalytic language is convoluted and self-enclosed. Translation from this language is difficult. Since most psychoanalytic dialogue takes place among those who have already had several years of psychiatric or psychological clinical practice and study, there is not great incentive to simplify. I have tried to overcome these problems, and to make this a sociological work, while retaining the subtlety and complexity of the psychoanalytic description.

PART I:

Setting the Problem: Mothering and the Social Organization of Gender

1
Introduction

Women mother. In our society, as in most societies, women not only bear children. They also take primary responsibility for infant care, spend more time with infants and children than do men, and sustain primary emotional ties with infants. When biological mothers do not parent, other women, rather than men, virtually always take their place. Though fathers and other men spend varying amounts of time with infants and children, the father is rarely a child's primary parent.

Over the past few centuries, women of different ages, classes, and races have moved in and out of the paid labor force. Marriage and fertility rates have fluctuated considerably during this same period. Despite these changes, women have always cared for children, usually as mothers in families and occasionally as workers in child-care centers or as paid and slave domestics. Women's mothering is one of the few universal and enduring elements of the sexual division of labor.

Because of the seemingly natural connection between women's childbearing and lactation capacities and their responsibility for child care, and because humans need extended care in childhood, women's mothering has been taken for granted. It has been assumed to be inevitable by social scientists, by many feminists, and certainly by those opposed to feminism. As a result, although women's mothering is of profound importance for family structure, for relations between the sexes, for ideology about women, and for the sexual division of labor and sexual inequality both inside the family and in the nonfamilial world, it is rarely analyzed.

This book analyzes women's mothering and, in particular, the way women's mothering is reproduced across generations. Its central question is how do women today come to mother? By implication, it asks how we might change things to transform the sexual division of labor in which women mother.

Historically, the actual physical and biological requirements of childbearing and child care have decreased. But mothering is still performed in the family, and women's mothering role has gained psychological and ideological significance, and has come increasingly to define women's lives.

Two centuries ago, marriage, especially for women, was essentially synonymous with child-rearing.[1] One spouse was likely to die before the children were completely reared, and the other spouse's death would probably follow within a few years of the last child's marriage. Parenting lasted from the inception of a marriage to the death of the marriage partners. Women often died during one of many childbirths.

Although marriage and adulthood were previously coextensive with child-rearing, mothering did not dominate women's lives. A woman carried out her child-care responsibilities along with a wide range of other productive work. In this earlier period, the household was the major productive unit of society. Husband and wife, with their own and/or other children, were a cooperative producing unit. Children were integrated early into the adult world of work, and men took responsibility for the training of boys once boys reached a certain age. Women's child-care and productive responsibilities included extensive training of girls—daughters, servants, apprentices—for work. Women carried out productive and reproductive responsibilities, as they have in most societies and throughout history.

Over the last two centuries, fertility and infant mortality rates have declined, longevity has increased, and children spend much of their childhood years in school. With the development of capitalism and the industrialization that followed, production outside the home expanded greatly, while production within the home declined. Cloth, food, clothing, and other household necessities, once produced by women in the home, became commodities mass-produced in factories. Production outside the home became identified with work as such; the home was no longer viewed as a workplace. Home and workplace, once the same, are now separate.[2]

This change in the organization of production went along with and produced a complex of far-reaching changes in the family and in women's lives. In addition to its diminished role in material production, the family lost much of its educational and religious role, as well as its role in the care of the sick and aged. The family became a quintessentially relational and personal institution, *the* personal sphere of society.[3] Women's family role became centered on child care and taking care of men. This role involved more than physical labor. It was relational and personal and, in the case of both children and men, maternal. The early capitalist period in the United States produced an ideology of the "moral mother":[4] Bourgeois women were to act as both nurturant moral models to their children and as nurturant supporters and moral guides for husbands on their return from the immoral, competitive world of work. The ideology of the moral mother has lost some of its Victorian rigidity, but it has also spread throughout society. Women of all classes are now expected to nurture and support husbands in addition to providing them with food and a clean house.

As women's mothering became less entwined with their other ongoing work, it also became more isolated and exclusive. The Western family has been largely "nuclear" for centuries, in that households rarely contained more than one married couple with children. But these children could be grown, as long as they were not married, and households often contained a number of other members—servants, apprentices, boarders and lodgers, a grandparent—as well. Older children, grandmothers, and other older people living with or near a mother helped in child care. Capitalist industrialization removed grown children, grandparents, and nonfamily members from the household and sharply curtailed men's participation in family life.

Today, homes contain fewer children, and these children enter school at an early age. The household with children has become an exclusively parent and child realm;[5] infant and child care has become the exclusive domain of biological mothers, who are increasingly isolated from other kin, with fewer social contacts and little routine assistance during their parenting time. Participation in the paid labor force does not change this. When women are home, they still have nearly total responsibility for children.

In spite of the vast growth of the state and wage labor, women continue to perform their mothering activities in the family; the rearing of children remains a major familial responsibility. Organized child care and schooling outside the home presuppose and supplement mothering within it. They do not supplant this mothering.

Thus, biological mothers have come to have more exclusive responsibility for child care just as the biological components of mothering have lessened, as women have borne fewer children and bottle-feeding has become available. During the last fifty years, despite the decline in the birthrate, housewives have come to spend more time in child care.[6] Post-Freudian psychology and sociology have provided new rationales for the idealization and enforcement of women's ma-

ternal role, as they have emphasized the crucial importance of the
mother-child relationship for the child's development.

Women's emotional role in the family and their psychological
mothering role grew just as their economic and biological role decreased. We notice women's mothering today because it has ceased
to be embedded in a range of other activities and human relations.
It stands out in its emotional intensity and meaning, and in its centrality for women's lives and social definition.

When we look back historically, we can see both the changes that
have occurred and the tenacity of some ways that gender is socially
organized. Women's productive and reproductive roles have changed,
and the family has changed as well. A century ago, women were legal
nonentities, subsumed under their husband's political and legal status. Today women can vote, and there is widespread recognition that
they should have equal rights under the law. A century ago, few
women could earn an independent living. Today, women are likely
to have jobs, though few are likely to earn enough to support themselves and their children adequately. Women today have two or three
children, and occasionally choose not to have any. The divorce rate
is much higher, and people marry later.

But women continue to mother, and most people still marry.
Women remain discriminated against in the labor force and unequal
in the family, and physical violence against women is not decreasing.
We continue to live in a male-dominant society, even though the legal
bases of male dominance are eroding. These features of our contemporary social organization of gender are common to most other societies and tie us to our preindustrial, precapitalist Western past.

Everyone interested in questions of gender and sexual inequality
and how to change these today must recognize these tenacious, almost
transhistorical facts. Such recognition has led feminists to focus politically on questions of personal life, on women's control of their sexuality and bodies, on family relations, on heterosexual bias and dis-
crimination against lesbians and homosexuals, and on the sexual
division of labor, in addition to questions of equality in the paid economy and polity. Women have learned that fundamental changes in
the social relations of production do not assure concomitant changes
in the domestic relations of reproduction.

This same recognition of the tenacity of sexual asymmetry and
inequality in the face of sweeping historical changes has stimulated
feminist attempts to articulate theoretically the systemic nature of the
social organization of gender, to move beyond descriptive generalizations about sexism, patriarchy, or male supremacy to analysis of

how sexual asymmetry and inequality are constituted, reproduced, and change.

This book is a contribution to the feminist effort. It analyzes the reproduction of mothering as a central and constituting element in the social organization and reproduction of gender. In what follows, I argue that the contemporary reproduction of mothering occurs through social structurally induced psychological processes. It is neither a product of biology nor of intentional role-training. I draw on the psychoanalytic account of female and male personality development to demonstrate that women's mothering reproduces itself cyclically. Women, as mothers, produce daughters with mothering capacities and the desire to mother. These capacities and needs are built into and grow out of the mother-daughter relationship itself. By contrast, women as mothers (and men as not-mothers) produce sons whose nurturant capacities and needs have been systematically curtailed and repressed. This prepares men for their less affective later family role, and for primary participation in the impersonal extrafamilial world of work and public life. The sexual and familial division of labor in which women mother and are more involved in interpersonal, affective relationships than men produces in daughters and sons a division of psychological capacities which leads them to reproduce this sexual and familial division of labor.

I attempt to provide a theoretical account of what has unquestionably been true—that women have had primary responsibility for child care in families and outside of them; that women by and large want to mother, and get gratification from their mothering; and finally, that, with all the conflicts and contradictions, women have succeeded at mothering.

The remainder of Part 1 introduces the main lines of argument of the book. Chapter 2 investigates explanations for the reproduction of mothering based on biology and role socialization. It argues that these explanations are insufficient; psychoanalytic theory can better account for the reproduction of mothering. Chapter 3 examines psychoanalytic object-relations theory as a theory of the reproduction of sex, gender, and family organization.

Part 2 puts forth my reinterpretation of feminine and masculine development. Chapters 4 and 5 show that the early mother-infant relationship creates both a foundation for parenting in children of both genders and expectations that women will mother. Chapters 6, 7, and 8 describe how asymmetries in family experiences, growing out of women's mothering, affect the differential development of the feminine and masculine psyche. Chapter 6 discusses how the early mother-infant relationship differs for girls and boys; chapters 7 and 8 explore gender differences in the oedipus complex. Chapter 9 returns to the early Freudian account, in order to distinguish its useful findings from its methodological and valuational limitations. Chapter 10 continues this critique, emphasizing the importance of parental participation in the oedipus complex.

Part 3 shows how the feminine and masculine development that results from women's mothering also recreates this mothering. Chapter 11 explores women's and men's differential location in reproduction and production, and the contribution of gender personality differences to women's and men's locations in these spheres. Chapter 12 examines the psychological and interpersonal capacities and needs that emerge from women's and men's development, and how these, finally, create women as mothers. In the Afterword, I explore some current contradictions in the organization of parenting and speculate on possibilities for change.

Two contributions to feminist theory have been particularly important to my own thinking and have influenced my presentation here. The first of these formulations argues for the analytic autonomy and social significance of the organization of gender. Gayle Rubin claims that every society is organized by a "sex /gender system" —"systematic ways to deal with sex, gender and babies"[7]—as well as by a particular organization of production. The sex-gender system (what I have been calling the social organization of gender) is, just as any society's dominant mode of production, a fundamental determining and constituting element of that society, socially constructed, subject to historical change and development, and organized in such a way that it is systematically reproduced. A society's sex-gender system consists in "a set of arrangements by which the biological raw material of human sex and procreation is shaped by human, social intervention and satisfied in a conventional manner. . . . The realm of human sex, gender and procreation has been subjected to, and changed by, relentless social activity for millennia. Sex as we know it —gender identity, sexual desire and fantasy, concepts of childhood —is itself a social product."[8]

The sex-gender system is analytically separable from, and it is never entirely explainable in terms of, the organization of production, though in any particular society the two are empirically and structurally intertwined. Developments in the sex-gender system can affect and in different societies have affected changes in the mode of production. In the modern period, however, the development of capitalism, and contemporary developments in socialist societies, have changed the sex-gender system more than the reverse.

Theoretically, a sex-gender system could be sexually egalitarian (and, presumably, generationally egalitarian as well). Hitherto, however, all sex-gender systems have been male-dominated. Moreover, every sex-gender system has organized society around two and only two genders, a sexual division of labor that always includes women's mothering, and heterosexual marriage. Drawing empirically from her analysis of anthropological literature, Rubin suggests that kinship and family organization form the locus and core of any society's sex-gender system. Kinship and family organization consist in and reproduce socially organized gender and sexuality.

The second theoretical formulation of feminist theory that has been particularly important to me both specifies and extends the first, helping to define and articulate the organization of the sex-gender system and sexual asymmetry as it has hitherto been constituted. More specifically, it demonstrates that women's mothering is a central and defining feature of the social organization of gender and is implicated in the construction and reproduction of male dominance itself. Michelle Rosaldo, Sherry Ortner, and I suggest that one can distinguish analytically in all societies between domestic and public aspects of social organization.[9] Mothers and children form the core of domestic organization; domestic ties are based on specific particularistic relationships among people and are assumed to be natural and biological. Because of their child-care responsibilities, women's primary social location is domestic. Men are also involved with particular domestic units, but men find a primary social location in the public sphere. Public institutions, activities, and forms of association link and rank domestic units, provide rules for men's relations to domestic units, and tie men to one another apart from their domestic relationships. Public institutions are assumed to be defined according to normative, hence social, criteria, and not biologically or naturally. It is therefore assumed that the public sphere, and not the domestic sphere, forms "society" and "culture"—those intended, constructed forms and ideas that take humanity beyond nature and biology and institute political control. Men's location in the public sphere, then, defines society itself as masculine. It gives men power to create and enforce institutions of social and political control, important among these to control marriage as an institution that both expresses men's rights in women's sexual and reproductive capacities and reinforces these rights.[10]

Thus, we can define and articulate certain broad universal sexual asymmetries in the social organization of gender generated by women's mothering. Women's mothering determines women's primary location in the domestic sphere and creates a basis for the structural differentiation of domestic and public spheres. But these spheres operate hierarchically. Kinship rules organize claims of men on domestic units, and men dominate kinship. Culturally and politically, the public sphere dominates the domestic, and hence men dominate women.

Societies vary in the extent to which they differentiate the public and domestic spheres and restrict women to the latter. In small gatherer-hunter bands, for instance, there is often minimal differentiation. Even here, however, men tend to have extradomestic distribution networks for the products of their hunting, whereas what women gather is shared only with the immediate domestic unit.[11] Men exchange women in marriage, gaining rights in women that women do not have in themselves or in men, and gaining a position in the masculine social hierarchy.[12]

In Western society, the separation of domestic and public spheres —of domestic reproduction and personal life on the one hand and social production and the state on the other—has been sharpened through the course of industrial capitalist development, producing a family form reduced to its fundamentals, to women's mothering and maternal qualities and heterosexual marriage, and continuing to reproduce male dominance.

All sex-gender systems organize sex, gender, and babies. A sexual division of labor in which women mother organizes babies and separates domestic and public spheres. Heterosexual marriage, which usually gives men rights in women's sexual and reproductive capacities and formal rights in children, organizes sex. Both together organize and reproduce gender as an unequal social relation.

2

Why Women Mother

It is woman's biological destiny to bear and deliver, to nurse and to rear children.

EDITH JACOBSON,
"Development of the Wish for a Child in Boys"

. . . the problem of maternity cannot be dismissed as a zoological fact. . . the theory of cultural motherhood should have been made the foundation of the general theory of kinship.

BRONISLAW MALINOWSKI,
"Parenthood, the Basis of Social Structure"

Mothers are women, of course, because a mother is a female parent, and a female who is a parent must be adult, hence must be a woman. Similarly, fathers are male parents, are men. But we mean something different when we say that someone mothered a child than when we say that someone fathered her or him. We can talk about a man "mothering" a child, if he is this child's primary nurturing figure, or is acting in a nurturant manner. But we would never talk about a woman "fathering" a child, even in the rare societies in which a high-ranking woman may take a wife and be the social father of her wife's children. In these cases we call her the child's social father, and do not say that she fathered her child. Being a mother, then, is not only bearing a child—it is being a person who socializes and nurtures. It is being a primary parent or caretaker. So we can ask, why are mothers women? Why is the person who routinely does all those activities that go into parenting not a man?

The question is important. Women's mothering is central to the sexual division of labor. Women's maternal role has profound effects on women's lives, on ideology about women, on the reproduction of masculinity and sexual inequality, and on the reproduction of particular forms of labor power. Women as mothers are pivotal actors in the sphere of social reproduction. As Engels and Marxist feminists, Lévi-Strauss and feminist anthropologists, Parsons and family theorists point out, women find their primary social location within this sphere.

Most sociological theorists have either ignored or taken as unproblematic this sphere of social reproduction, despite its importance and the recognition by some theorists, such as Engels, of its fundamental historical role.[1] As a consequence of ignoring this sphere, most sociological theorists have ignored women, who have been the central figures within it.

Engels helps us to understand this omission through his emphasis on the shift away from kinship-based forms of material production in modern societies. All societies contain both means of producing material subsistence and means of organizing procreation. Earlier societies (and contemporary "primitive" societies) were centered on kinship relations. Production and reproduction were organized according to the rules of kinship. This does not mean that the relations of production were based entirely on actual biological and affinal ties. In contemporary primitive societies, a kinship idiom can come to describe and incorporate whatever productive relations develop.

In modern societies, ties based on kinship no longer function as important links among people in the productive world, which becomes organized more and more in nonkinship market and class relations. Moreover, the relations of material production, and the extended public and political ties and associations—the state, finally—which these relations make possible, dominate and define family relations—the sphere of human reproduction. Many aspects of reproduction are taken over by extrafamilial institutions like schools. Kinship, then, is progressively stripped of its functions and its ability to organize the social world.[2]

Because of their location within and concern with Western capitalist society, most major social theorists have made the recognition of this major historical transformation fundamental to their theories. They have, as a consequence, developed theories which focus on nonfamilial political, economic, and communal ties and have treated familial relations only to point out their declining importance.* This historical transformation also reinforces a tendency in everyday discourse. Social theorists, like societal members, tend to define a society and discuss its social organization in terms of what men do, and where men are located in that society.

It is apparent, however, that familial and kinship ties and family

---

*Thus, Durkheim describes the shift from mechanical to organic solidarity. Tönnies distinguishes *gemeinschaft* and *gesellschaft* societies. Weber discusses increasing rationalization and the rise of bureaucracy and market relations. Parsons distinguishes particularistic, ascribed, affective role relationships from those based on universalistic, achieved, and nonaffective criteria. Marx gives an account of the way capitalist market relations increasingly dominate all social life.

life remain crucial for women. The organization of these ties is certainly shaped in many ways by industrial capitalist development (though the family retains fundamental precapitalist, preindustrial features—that women mother, for instance). However, as production has moved out of the home, reproduction has become even more immediately defining and circumscribing of women's life activities and of women themselves.

Some theorists do investigate the family. Parsons's concern with the "problem of order" (what accounts for the persistence of social structures over time) and that of the Frankfurt Institute with the reproduction of capitalist relations of production and ideology have led both, in their attempts to understand social reproductive processes, to turn to the family as an area for sociological inquiry.[3] Feminist theorists, including Engels and Charlotte Perkins Gilman,[4] early recognized the family as a central agent of women's oppression as well as the major institution in women's lives. Anthropological theory also, in its concern with societies in which social ties for both men and women are largely defined through kinship, has developed an extensive and sophisticated analysis of kinship and the organization of gender—of rules of descent, marriage rules, residence arrangements, variations in household and family organization, and so forth. Consequently, anthropological theory has informed much family theory, including some feminist theories.[5]

Most of these theories see women's mothering as central. While understanding the importance of this mothering for social reproduction, however, they do not take it as in need of explanation. They simply assume that it is socially, psychologically, and biologically natural and functional. They do not question and certainly do not explain the reproduction of mothering itself either cross-culturally or within modern societies. They understand how women as mothers currently produce men with particular personalities and orientations, and how women's social location and the sexual division of labor generate other features of the social and economic world and of ideology about women. But they do not inquire about how women themselves are produced, how women continue to find themselves in a particular social and economic location.

THE ARGUMENT FROM NATURE

Several assumptions underlie this surprising omission. The most prevalent assumption among nonfeminist theorists is that the structure of parenting is biologically self-explanatory. This assumption holds that what seems universal is instinctual, and that what is instinctual, or has instinctual components, is inevitable and unchanging. Women's mothering as a feature of social structure, then, has no reality separate from the biological fact that women bear children and lactate. These social scientists reify the social organization of gender and see it as a natural product rather than a social construct.

Another explanation from nature is bioevolutionary. This explanation holds that women are primary parents *now* because they always have been. It either assumes that the sexual division of labor—for whatever reason—was the earliest division of labor, and was simply perpetuated; that the sexual division of labor was necessary for species survival in the earliest human communities; or that this species survival division of labor is now built biologically into human sexual dimorphism. In all cases, the implication is that the mode of reproduction of mothering is unchanging, and retains the form of its earliest origins. These accounts argue that women's mothering is, or has been, functional—that children, after all, have been reared—and often imply that what is and has been ought to be—that women ought to mother.

Women's mothering, then, is seen as a natural fact. Natural facts, for social scientists, are theoretically uninteresting and do not need explanation. The assumption is questionable, however, given the extent to which human behavior is not instinctually determined but culturally mediated. It is an assumption in conflict with most social scientists' insistence on the social malleability of biological factors, and it also conflicts with the general reluctance of social scientists to explain existing social forms simply as relics of previous epochs.

In contrast to these assumptions, it seems to me that we must always raise as problematic any feature of social structure, even if—and perhaps especially because—it seems universal. In the case at hand, we are confronted with a sexual division of labor in which women parent, which is reproduced in each generation and in all societies. We must understand this reproduction in order to understand women's lives and the sociology of gender. Why men by and large do not do primary parenting, and women do, is a centrally interesting sociological question.

We must question all assumptions which use biological claims to explain social forms, given the recent rise to prominence of sociobiology and the historically extensive uses of explanations allegedly based on biological sex (or race) differences to legitimate oppression and inequality. That there are undeniable genetic, morphological, and hormonal sex differences, which affect our physical and social experiences and are (minimally) the criteria according to which a person's participation in the sexual division of labor and membership in a gender-differentiated world are assigned, only makes this task more necessary.

A brief consideration of the biological basis of sexual dimorphism suggests the problematic nature of any claim about natural or instinctual motherliness in women. We can begin with the existence of sex differences themselves. Chromosomal differences—XX and XY—begin sexual differentiation. Then there are genital and reproductive differences—the female ability to get pregnant, menstruate, and lactate, the male ability to impregnate—and "secondary" sex differences —men's greater body hair, as well as a sexually dimorphic central nervous system produced by fetal gonadal hormones. The development of genitalia and mature reproductive organs requires appropriate hormonal input prenatally and postnatally, with the exception that without fetal gonadal hormones all fetuses develop an infantile female reproductive anatomy and genitalia. There are statistical differences between average men and average women—men's greater height and higher muscle to fat ratio, for instance. There are hormonal and chromosomal asymmetries, such as women's lesser vulnerability to some genetic defects transmitted on the X-chromosome, and the necessity of fetal androgenization to produce a male morphology. And there may be behavioral differences linked to biology, such as masculine aggressiveness.

But even these facts are not simply biological.[6] People are born with ambiguous genitalia or abnormal chromosomal patterns, yet we always label them as one or the other sex. We define people as male or female according to reproductive organs and capacities, but a woman who has had a radical mastectomy, or total hysterectomy, or who is sterile, is still unambiguously female. A castrated or sterile man, or one whose genitals are amputated or mutilated in anything other than an intended sex-change operation, is still male. On several statistical variables, there may be more difference within each sex than between the sexes. Moreover, the extent of between-sex variation varies among societies, and variation among cultures is often greater than that between the sexes of any particular culture (people of both sexes in one culture may be taller on average, or have more body hair, or higher muscle to fat ratio than people of both sexes in another).

Biological sex differences can be found, but these remain hard to define with clarity. Societies, moreover, make of these biological variations two and only two genders. On the basis of presumed biology, they pronounce all infants male or female at birth, assume that the social fact of two and only two genders is isomorphic with biology, and elaborate their social organization of gender on this basis.

Given how difficult it is to articulate exactly what biological sex differences themselves consist in, it is not surprising that claims about the biological bases of sex differences in *behavior* are difficult to substantiate or even to formulate. We are, of course, biological beings, and our embodiment needs accounting for. Women's physiological experiences—pregnancy, menstruation, parturition, menopause, lactation—are certainly powerful (though it is important to bear in mind that either by choice or involuntarily all women do not have all these experiences). In our society, and in many others, they are also given strong meaning socially and psychologically.[7] There is psychological input into these biological experiences, moreover. Menstruation is affected by stress, women have "false pregnancies," and in societies that practice couvade men's bellies may swell as their wife's pregnancy comes to term. Lactation varies not only with individual emotions and attitudes, but in whole societies the lactation rate can change drastically in a short period of time.[8]

I do not question the reality of these biological experiences. Nor do I mean to raise questions about what constitutes "good-enough parenting" (to vary a phrase of psychoanalyst D. W. Winnicott[9]), or whether children need constant, predictable care from people with whom they have a primary relationship (I believe they do). What I wish to question is whether there is a biological basis in women for caretaking capacities specifically and whether *women* must perform whatever parenting children need.

To evaluate arguments that women's mothering is natural, we must distinguish among a number of issues which are often confused in the literature. First, we should separate child *care* from child*bearing*, nurturing *as an activity* from pregnancy and parturition. Most accounts assume that a child's primary parent, or mother, is the woman who has borne that child. Second, we want to know if there is a biological basis for biological mothers to care for their own newborn and what this consists in. If there is a biological or instinctual basis for parenting triggered by pregnancy, parturition, or lactation, what is its actual timespan? Does it extend into an infant's first months, years, throughout its childhood? Third, given that there are sometimes "substitute mothers," we want to know whether it is biologically more natural for a woman who has not borne the child in need of care than for a man to provide this child care. Do women have an instinctual propensity, or biological suitedness, for mothering which is not triggered by the experiences of pregnancy, parturition, or lactation? Finally, we want to evaluate the biological-instinctual basis for claims that women ought to mother. Such claims, again, could argue either that women are harmed by not parenting, or that infants are harmed by not being parented by *women*.

One explanation for women's mothering is a functional-cum-bio-evolutionary account of the sexual division of labor put forth mainly by anthropologists, who combine a functionalist account of contemporary gathering and hunting societies (closest to the original human societies) and an evolutionary explanation of the "origins of man." These accounts may argue that men's greater agility, strength, speed, and aggressiveness made it natural for them to hunt, and that women therefore gathered and reared children.[10] Alternately, they rely on the demands of pregnancy and child care itself. They argue that lactating women need to be near their nursing infants for a large part of the time, and that women's pregnancy and lactation made it inefficient and/or dangerous to them, to the children they carried in the womb or on the hip, and to the group at large, for them to hunt.[11]

This latter view is most probably correct.[12] Moreover, given the small size of gathering and hunting bands and high rate of infant mortality, it is usually the case that all women needed to be pregnant or nursing throughout most of their childbearing years for the group to maintain itself. Even if, as is likely, some women had the strength, speed, and agility to be better hunters than some men, to allow these women to hunt would not be efficient for the group since the men could certainly not bear or nurse children.

Most evolutionary-functionalist arguments do not argue that women have greater mothering capacities than men apart from lactation, though they may argue (and this argument is questionable as a generalization about all men as opposed to all women) that men's biology is more appropriate to hunting. Rather, they argue that men's not caring for children was convenient and probably necessary for survival in gathering and hunting bands:

With the long years that it takes for the human child to develop and learn adult roles and skills, once gathering and hunting had developed as a major adaptive stance, there was no other way for the division to have evolved except between males and females. There is no need to posit special "killer" or "maternal" instincts in males and females to explain the assignment of these roles.[13]

Children and old people, unlike men, played a major part in caring for children. Moreover, these societies probably spaced childbirths to enable women to carry out their other work.

One major bioevolutionary account argues that women have greater maternal capacities than men as a result of the prehistoric division of labor. Sociologist Alice Rossi asserts that the sexual division of labor was not only essential to gatherer-hunter group survival, but that *because* it was essential, it has become built into human physiology.* Reproductive success went to females capable of bearing and rearing the young, gathering and hunting small game. These capacities (not only maternal capacities, but the manual dexterity, endurance, and persistence required for gathering and for hunting small animals) are now built genetically into women: "[We] *are still genetically equipped only with an ancient mammalian primate heritage that evolved largely through adaptations appropriate to much earlier times.*"[14] I discuss the evidence for maternal instincts in women more fully further on, but in order to further evaluate the evolutionary account it is necessary to address some of Rossi's claims here.

There are two major flaws in Rossi's account. One is that she never provides satisfactory evidence for a maternal instinct in the first place. Rossi refers to common "unlearned responses"[15] to infants in mothers, and to studies showing that the earlier and longer the contact between infant and mother, the greater their attachment at the end of the first month, but the studies she cites investigated only mothers and their own infants. They did not investigate whether other women, men, or children have similar or different responses to infants; whether the maternal responses they discuss are found universally —surely a necessary first step toward arguing for innateness; whether attachment develops between anyone else and infant, given prolonged and early contact. Moreover, Rossi does not provide any evidence or argument that the maternal responses she discusses are unlearned rather than learned. The evidence suggests only that these responses are common to all the women studied. But commonality is not evidence about the origins of such behavior. Rossi also cites studies of monkeys who have been separated from their mothers as evidence of the harm of *mother*-infant separation, without mentioning the difficulties in extrapolating conclusions about humans from studies of monkeys or pointing out that the monkeys were not provided with anything verging on equivalent substitute relationships or care. She asserts, finally, against the anthropological evidence, "that little or no cultural variation can be found in the physical proximity and emotional closeness of the mother and the infant in the early months following birth."[16]

Rossi makes only one claim deriving from maternal hormones. She mentions that infant crying stimulates biological mothers to se-

---

*I discuss this article at some length, because of the centrality of the issue to feminist research, and because Rossi herself has been an important feminist spokeswoman.

crete the hormone ocytocin, leading to uterine contractions and nipple erection preparatory to nursing. However, she neither argues nor provides evidence that this ocytocin stimulation leads to any of the features other than lactation that go into infant care or mother-infant bonding (nor has she looked for studies of ocytocin production in women who are not lactating or in men—a not far-fetched suggestion, since persons of both genders produce some amount of both "male" and "female" hormones).

Second, Rossi's assertion that social arrangements adaptive or necessary for group survival become genetically embedded goes unsupported in her account, and is most probably unsupportable in the unilateral causal form she gives it.[17] If there are genetic bases to particular forms of sociability or human social arrangements, these are of incredible complexity and involve the operation of hundreds of interacting genetic loci. There is no one-to-one correspondence between genes and behavior, as even Rossi herself points out, nor is there evidence that adaptive practices or practices necessary to species survival become genetically programed simply because some such practices may be so.

Thus, we can safely conclude that the bioevolutionary argument stands as an argument concerning the division of labor in gatherer-hunter societies, given the specifically incompatible requirements of child care and hunting, and not as an argument concerning maternal instinct or biology in general.

The account is generalized to other societies, however, as a biological argument. D'Andrade and Barry, Bacon, and Child, and Rossi all argue that differences between men's and women's work are a more or less direct result of physical differences between the sexes. For D'Andrade, male activities "involve behavior which is strenuous, cooperative, and requiring long periods of travel," and female activities "are more likely to involve the physically easier, more solitary, and less mobile activities."[18] For Barry, Bacon, and Child, men's economic tasks are more likely to involve leaving home and to require a high level of skill (they suggest hunting as a good example), whereas women's tasks are nearer to home, "have a nurturant character, and in their pursuit a responsible carrying out of established routines is likely to be more important than the development of an especially high order of skill."[19]

There are two unsubstantiated logical leaps being made here. One is to assume that reproductive differences entail *physiologically* that women rear children, that their ability to bear and nurse children extends to their performing all aspects of child care and being responsible for the raising of older children. These accounts understand the division of labor, which grows out of women's child-*care* responsibilities, as a product of physiology. It is otherwise hard to see what "cooperativeness" or "highly developed skills," as opposed to "routine responsibility," could have to do with physiological differences between the sexes.

Second, these analyses assume that their explicitly argued functionalist account of the sexual division of labor in gathering and hunting societies holds also for other forms of subsistence economies and other forms of production which have a similar division of labor. But it is not at all obvious that a sexual division of labor in which men do not parent was or is either necessary to survival or even more convenient in all nonindustrial subsistence economies. The argument in each case must be made.

Nor can we assume that whole categories of work cannot be performed by child-watching mothers. Along the lines argued by D'Andrade and Barry, Bacon, and Child, and Rossi, Judith Brown argues that the work women with children do must be compatible with the demands of child care. Therefore, women do not do work far from home, dangerous work, or work that is not interruptible. Here she is talking about women with children, and the important issue is child-care responsibilities, not physiology. She points, by way of example, to the reindeer-herding Chukchee, whose herding groups consist of men, boys and girls from about ten, and young women without small children. Chukchee division of labor, she suggests, "is not sexually determined" but "divided according to child-watching and nonchild-watching members."[20]

Recently, however, even this argument has been challenged. Ernestine Friedl suggests that societies organize child spacing and child care to enable women's participation in subsistence activities as much as the reverse. She points to the use of children and old people as child-tenders, to food supplements for mothers' milk, and to

the large number of societies in which women regularly gather wild plants or cultivate crops or engage in trade in locations many miles from home base, and either walk back and forth each day or move out into distant locations for some seasons of the year taking children with them; [and] women who tend large cauldrons of boiling foods over open fires—a dangerous process.[21]

Thus, even accounts of elementary subsistence societies do not demonstrate that women's physiological reproductive functions necessarily entail a sexual division of labor in which women mother. The functionalist argument, moreover, is for the most part an argument from assumed convenience and cultural ideology, and only in rare cases an argument from species or group survival. Originally, and in contemporary gathering and hunting societies, the sexual division of labor in which women mother was necessary for group reproduction, for demographic and economic reasons. As long as basic subsistence was problematic, population small, social organization simple, and women spent much of their adult lives bearing or nursing children, it made sense that they should be largely responsible for older children and more associated with the domestic sphere than men.

However, these same conclusions are offered for situations where these conditions do not hold—for horticultural, fishing, or plow-agricultural societies, where men's work is not more dangerous than women's and does not require long periods of travel from home, where women and men are equally near home and work close to each other. The argument is allowed to stand for industrial societies like ours which do not need this division of labor for physical reproduction. In our society women do not spend most of their "child-bearing years" bearing children, do not have to nurse, and in any case nurse for only a relatively few months. And work activities in the nonfamilial economy are compatible with the requirements of periodic nursing, even if organized and defined in ways which are not (coffee break, for instance, is excusable time off work, whereas nursing is not). It may even be the case today that this division of labor conflicts with the requirements of production, which in most industrial societies seems to be drawing women of all ages into the paid labor force.

It is not enough today to give an evolutionary-functionalist explanation for women's mothering, then, unless we include in our functional account the reproduction of a particular social *organization*, beyond species survival or unmediated technological requisites. This organization includes male dominance, a particular family system, and women's dependence on men's income. We should see the original sexual division of labor as a once necessary social form used by and modified by other social forms as these have developed and changed. The sexual division of labor in which women mother has new meaning and functions, and is no longer explicable as an outcome of biology or of the requirement of survival. The evolutionary-functionalist account does not provide a convincing argument grounded in biology for why women, or biological mothers, should or must provide parental care.

A second argument for women's mothering, put forth by psychoanalysts and assumed by many others—gynecologists and obstetricians, social scientists, physiologists and physiological psychologists—is that women have a mothering instinct, or maternal instinct, and that therefore it is "natural" that they mother, or even that they therefore *ought* to mother. These accounts sometimes imply that it is instinctual that biological mothers mother, sometimes assume that mothers will parent better than fathers or men for biological reasons, sometimes assume that because children need to be cared for biological mothers naturally care for them, and sometimes argue that women "need" to mother.

Psychoanalysts Alice and Michael Balint, for instance, speak of a "need" or "drive" to mother following pregnancy—a "biological" or "instinctual" mother-infant mutuality, an "instinctive maternity"[22] and "interdependence of the reciprocal instinctual aims"[23] in which "what is libidinal satisfaction to one must be libidinal satisfaction to the other [and] the mother and child are equally satisfied in this condition."[24] Therese Benedek speaks of women's "primary reproductive drive"[25] and "instinctual need"[26] to fulfill her physiological and emotional preparedness for mothering. Winnicott suggests that holding the infant physically in her uterus leads to a mother's identification with the infant after it is born and therefore to "a very powerful sense of what the baby needs."[27] Rossi argues that women's maternal instinct has been genetically programmed as a result of past adaptive needs.

Even more speculatively, psychoanalyst Judith Kestenberg argues that maternal feelings develop in early childhood out of undischarged early vaginal sensations. These sensations, because of the "inaccessibility and enigmatic quality of the inner genital,"[28] lead to the wish for a child, an identifiable object which concretizes the vagina, as well as to that intuitiveness which is the basis of motherliness. Kestenberg admits that her account is speculative. Moreover, her methodology is problematic. She postulates the existence of that which wants to demonstrate, "expect[ing] to find a biological substrate for maternal behavior which operates since early childhood."[29] She looks for evidence only to support her position, "turn[ing] to observations of children [the "children" she turns to are all girls] to gather traces of later motherliness."[30] She does not look for "traces of non-motherliness" in girls, nor does she observe boys at all.

Medical researcher Niles Newton argues an even more tenuous case. She suggests that because coitus, parturition, and lactation cannot guarantee successful reproduction without caretaking behavior, and because they are sometimes associated with such behavior, they must therefore biologically cause it: "All three appear, under some circumstances, to trigger caretaking behavior, which is an essential part of mammalian reproduction."[31] This conclusion is unsubstantiated by Newton's evidence *especially* in the cases of lactation and parturition. She argues that parturition makes women more *sexually* responsive, but says nothing about its effects on caretaking behavior.

She shows that on a variety of measures of maternal behavior, the only difference between breast-feeding and nonbreast-feeding mothers was in how often they had their babies in bed with them.

Many commentators believe, then, that some sort of hormonal/ physiological basis for women's mothering exists. At the same time, most qualify their claims, and none provides a convincing argument or evidence for the view that infants need these biological mothers specifically or that women are harmed by not caring for the infants they have borne. (This is not to deny the emotional or physiological experiences of particular women who, for various reasons, may not be able to care for or nurse their infants when they want to nor the effect of this possible distress on their particular infants.) Benedek, in her discussion of mother-infant symbiosis (which has, she claims, hormonal as well as psychological origins for the mother), even notes that the infant's need for the mother is absolute, whereas the mother's for the infant is only relative: "The participation of primary drives in the symbiotic state has different meanings for mother and child."[32] Even Winnicott warns against thinking in terms of a "maternal instinct" and stresses that the changes brought about by pregnancy must be thought of in psychological terms, because they vary so much with the state of the mother:

Something would be missing, however, if a phrase such as "maternal instinct" were used in description. The fact is that in health women change in their orientation to themselves and the world, but however deeply rooted in physiology such changes may be, they can be distorted by mental ill-health in the woman. It is necessary to think of these changes in psychological terms.[33]

When we evaluate claims for the instinctual or biological basis for parenting, it turns out that evidence is hard to find.[34] There is little research on humans, and none of it is direct. There is little on animals. Moreover, it is not clear that we can use animal evidence anyway, since human culture and intentional activity have to so large an extent taken over from what is instinctual in other animals. We can rule out to begin with the claims based on assertion (as in the chapter epigraph taken from Jacobson), functionalist reasoning (Newton), and evidence searched for selectively (Kestenberg).

Chromosomes do not provide a basis either for the wish for a child or for capacities for nurturant parental behavior. Researchers on genetic and hormonal abnormalities find that androgen-insensitive chromosomal males (XY males who will not respond to androgens either prenatally or postnatally, who are born with female-looking genitalia and reared unambiguously as girls) are equally preoccupied with doll play and fantasies about having children, equally want children, and are equally nurturant toward the infants they adopt as chromosomally and hormonally normal females.[35] This is also true for females with XO chromosomal pattern (Turner's syndrome), who have no ovaries and therefore cannot bear children.

Hormonal differences may show a greater relation to maternal behavior, but ambiguously. In the case of humans, evidence comes indirectly from hormonal abnormalities. Androgen-insensitive genetic males reared as females, who are without female internal organs but who produce enough estrogen to bring about breast growth and feminization of body contours and bone structure at puberty, are in childhood as nurturant and preoccupied with children as normal females and, when they grow up, as good mothers to adopted children.*

Turner's syndrome females also develop an unambiguous female gender identity, and show no difference or slightly greater "femininity" in measures of maternalism and preoccupation with dolls, babies, and marriage than hormonally and chromosomally normal girls. XO females do not have gonadal hormones. They therefore do not develop a gender dimorphic central nervous system, and they do not have ovaries. But because all fetuses develop a female reproductive anatomy and genitalia in the absence of gonadal hormones, an XO baby looks like a girl; her lack of gonadal hormones is not noticeable until just before puberty. A Turner's syndrome baby is assigned and reared unambiguously as a girl, but she has at most trace elements of either sex's hormone. The maternal behavior and fantasies of marriage and babies in the case of Turner's syndrome girls cannot be a product of female hormones or a prenatally female differentiated brain.

Chromosomally female girls who have received abnormal quantities of androgens prenatally (either because of exogenously introduced progestin or because of endogenous hormonal malfunction that is only treated after birth) provide a final example of the possible relationship between hormones and maternalism. They tend to be less interested in dolls, more "tomboyish," and less interested in full-time motherhood than hormonally normal girls.** In the case of girls with endogenous hormonal malfunction, they also have fewer fan-

---

*They produce the same amount of estrogens (and androgens) as normal males, but because they cannot use the androgens they produce, their bodies develop in response to their much smaller level of estrogens.

**Measures of tomboyism in Money and Ehrhardt are highly culturally specific and stereotypic, and include factors like preference for athletics versus sedentary activity, self-assertion in a childhood dominance hierarchy and preference for playing with boys, as well as childhood disinterest in rehearsals of motherhood and putting marriage and romance second or equal to career achievement. Moreover, none of the girls studied in the controlled comparisons was over sixteen, so we do not know what their adult life outcomes were.

tasies and daydreams about marriage, pregnancy, and motherhood, though they do not exclude possibilities of marriage and children. They simply want other activities in addition. Similarly, adult women whose endogenous androgen production was not treated in childhood tended not to want full-time motherhood and did not fantasize or daydream about motherhood, although they often married and had children whom they breast-fed.

As all reports point out, these data on fetally androgenized females can be read as evidence either for hormonal or cultural determinism. Although they were reared as girls, the genitalia of fetally androgenized females are masculinized at birth. In the case of the adult women studied, their androgen production was never treated. In some of the childhood cases, sex was reassigned from boy to girl in infancy, or they had operations to create more feminized genitalia. In all cases, therefore, parents knew about their daughter's abnormalities. The evidence about them comes from self-report and mothers' reports. In some cases parents were explicitly warned not to discourage tomboyishness for fear of counterreaction on their daughters' part, and there is no information provided on what the girls themselves knew or were told about themselves. All these factors weaken the case for hormonal determinism, as does the fact that "tomboyism" was defined in culturally and historically specific ways. If fetal androgens are producing "unfeminine" preferences, these preferences are at variance with what would be considered unfeminine in a number of other societies.[36] Still, differences between fetally androgenized and normal females could be a product of hormonal difference or of difference in treatment and socialization.

We can draw no unambiguous conclusions about the relation of hormones to maternal instincts or maternalism in humans from these studies. All the girls were reared in a society that socializes particular personalities and preferences in girls and boys. Parents and doctors, and perhaps the girls themselves, knew about the abnormalities of many prenatally androgenized girls and androgen-insensitive males reared as females and may well have reacted to this knowledge in subtle or not-so-subtle ways. As Maccoby and Jacklin point out, however, even if we want to read these studies as supporting or even partially supporting a biological argument, the conclusions we can draw say nothing about the effects of *female* hormones on maternal behavior, feelings or preferences. They suggest only that *male* hormones may suppress maternalism.

For more direct experimental evidence for the effects of hormones on caretaking behavior, we are forced to turn from humans to rats:

Little is known concerning the possible hormonal basis of maternal behavior in species higher than rodents. To our knowledge, no work has been done relating maternal behavior in apes or humans to the amounts of hormones present in their bodies that are associated with pregnancy and childbirth.[37]

Hormones in rats do to some extent control parenting behavior. Studies have explored the effect of artificially introduced female and male hormones. They find that female hormones stimulate maternal behavior equally in virgin, nonparturient female rats and in male rats. This suggests that hormones connected to pregnancy, parturition, and lactation do contribute to caretaking behavior in female rats who have borne pups.*

However, caretaking behavior declines during the postparturition period, even if a parturient female is continually supplied with new infant litters. It is also, as the evidence from virgin females suggests, definitely connected to the experience of pregnancy and parturition themselves and not to a general "maternal instinct" which all female rats have. The behavior, finally, must be activated by contact with newborns. A mother rat separated from her litter for a few days will not effectively raise a substitute litter.

On the side of male hormones, fetally androgenized females (as male) rabbits and rats are less sensitive to the induction of nest-building hormones than are normal, nonparturient females. Researchers report that male rats are more likely to kill the first litter that is placed with them than are virgin females. However, if they are given subsequent litters, their aggressiveness is replaced by nurturance—licking, crouching over the infants, retrieving. Again, the implication here is that male hormones and aggressiveness may suppress caretaking behavior in rats.

Primate evidence provides no clear answer either. The amount of male participation in child care among different primate species varies widely.

We can conclude from these studies that synthetic female hormones prime newly parturient rats to care for their newborn. These hormones are not naturally present in other females, but if introduced artificially they can induce similar behavior in nonparturient virgin females and males. Even in rats, then, whatever hormones go to create mothering affect only those females who have themselves just borne a litter. This behavior decreases gradually after childbirth. Second, male androgens, or aggressiveness, may in some species of animals and may conceivably in humans—though here the evidence

---

*Studies of the effect of artificially introduced hormones always involve the use of synthetic hormones. Even if these produce similar effects to natural hormones, we have no way of knowing if their biological activity is identical.[38]

can be read in two ways—suppress some nurturant tendencies.

On the other side, all researchers on humans as well as on animals point out that infants activate maternal behavior in both nonparturient virgin females and in males, as well as in parturient females. Both virgin female and male rats show nurturant behavior to the young after several days of exposure to them, regardless of hormonal priming (by contrast, a female who has just given birth is responsive immediately). Similarly, many primate males routinely engage in some caretaking behavior. Even those primate males who do not routinely do caretaking often come to care for an infant if left alone with it in an experimental situation.

There have been almost no comparative studies of humans (again, I believe, because of most researchers' assumptions that women's maternal behavior is natural), though all writers assume that men can be nurturant and perform caretaking functions. One ongoing study reports that both men and women react similarly (as measured by pupil dilation) to infant sounds of pain and pleasure.[39] Money and Ehrhardt claim, though without supporting evidence, that both men and women respond to the stimulus of a small infant or child, though women may be quicker to do so than men. Both males and females, they insist, can engage in parenting behavior. This behavior is not gender-dimorphic, even if prenatal androgens may partially inhibit it in men. Ehrhardt argues that the most we can conclude is that among mammals it is usually the biological mother who is "most attentive" to her offspring.[40] This conclusion is guarded, and does not purport to explain the genesis of this greater attentiveness. Money and Ehrhardt are insistent about the postnatal malleability of dispositions and traits in men and women.

It may be that another basis for women's nurturance comes from exposure to newborns.[41] Mothers who have been separated from their premature infants for the first few weeks after birth tend to smile less at their infants, to hold them less closely, and to touch them affectionately less than mothers of normal infants or mothers of premature infants who were allowed to touch and hold these infants. Since fathers have not been studied in this context, we do not know if such contact would establish a similar bond with infants in men. Maccoby and Jacklin conclude,

Extrapolating from what is known about animals much lower than man, it would appear possible that the hormones associated with pregnancy, childbirth and lactation may contribute to a "readiness" to care for a young infant on the part of a woman who has just given birth. The animal studies also suggest, however, that contact with infants is a major factor in developing attachment and caretaking behavior in the juvenile and adult members of a species, and this is true for both individuals that have given birth and individuals (male or female) that have not.[42]

Whatever the hormonal input to human maternal behavior, it is clear that such hormones are neither necessary nor sufficient for it. Studies, and our daily experiences, show that nonparturient females and males can behave in nurturant ways toward infants and children, and can have nurturance called up in them. People who adopt children certainly want them as much as, and perhaps more than, some of those who have their own, and certainly behave in equally nurturant ways toward them. How a person parents, moreover, is to a large extent determined by childhood experiences and conflicts. No psychoanalyst, ethologist, or biologist would claim that instinct or biology *by themselves* generate women's nurturance. If we can extrapolate from Harlow's studies, we can conclude that mothering capacities and behavior in any *individual* higher primate presupposes particular developmental experiences.[43] Harlow studied mothering behavior in "unmothered" monkeys—monkeys who had been raised in a wire cage or with a cloth surrogate, but without their mother. He found them to range from extremely abusive to marginally adequate mothers of their first child. Those who were in the marginally adequate category had had some social experience, either at around one year or as a preadolescent and adolescent. We cannot infer definite conclusions about humans from Harlow's work. But Harlow's studies do imply that even if female hormones are called up during pregnancy and parturition, these are not enough to generate mothering capacities or cause mothering.

We can draw several conclusions concerning the biological basis of mothering. The cross-cultural evidence ties women to primary parenting because of their lactation and pregnancy functions, and not because of instinctual nurturance beyond these functions. This evidence also suggests that there can be a variety of other participants in child care. Children of both sexes, though more often girls, often perform caretaking functions in addition to women. The prehistoric reasons of species or group survival which tied women to children have not held for centuries and certainly no longer hold today. Women in contemporary society do not bear children throughout their childbearing years; there is almost no work incompatible with nursing (and bottle-feeding is available and widespread, either as a total source of food or for occasional feedings). Societies no longer need women's mothering for physical reproduction. The evolutionary-functional account does not explain why women mother today.

When we turn to the more directly biological evidence, we find no direct research on the hormonal basis of nurturance, as opposed to lactation, in humans. Indirect evidence, from persons with chromosomal and hormonal abnormalities, suggests that male hormones may partially inhibit maternal behavior, but the evidence can be read equally to suggest that they do not, whereas masculine socialization does. There is no evidence to show that female hormones or chromosomes make a difference in human maternalness, and there is substantial evidence that nonbiological mothers, children, and men can parent just as adequately as biological mothers and can feel just as nurturant.

The evidence from some animals (and it must be kept in mind that inference from animals to humans is highly problematic) shows that hormones directly connected to pregnancy, parturition, and lactation prime these animals for caretaking. It also shows that this priming lasts only for a certain period after parturition. This could be true in the case of humans as well. That is, there may be physiological processes in human females which in some sense "prepare" a woman for mothering her own newborn, but beyond lactation we have no evidence concerning what these might be. On the other side, the evidence from animals does not suggest that nonparturient females are any more nurturant than males, though they may be less aggressive.

Conclusions about the biological basis of parenting in humans can only be speculative. But the evidence from animals, plus observations of human parenting, allow us to conclude that the hormonal basis of nurturance in parturient females is limited. Even those who argue for physiological components to a woman's tie to her own newborn suggest that these last at most for the first few months of an infant's life. Benedek mentions the six-week period until the termination of the uterine involution, and the somewhat longer period until lactation ceases, and Winnicott suggests that the "projective identification" of the mother with her infant in the womb "lasts for a certain length of time after parturition, and then gradually loses significance."[44] This view accords with the animal evidence.

Even if androgens produce some sort of counterdisposition to parenting, fetally androgenized females become nurturant mothers just as do other females, and men can also be nurturant and respond to infants and children. There is, finally, no evidence to indicate that whatever disposition for parenting parturient women have prepares them for exclusive care of the infant. Nor is there anything to explain *biologically* why women mother toddlers and older children, though the early exclusive relationship probably produces some *psychological* basis for this later mothering.

Even these conclusions must be qualified. First, and most significant, both experimental research on primates and clinical evidence on humans make clear that individual psychological factors affect the expression of whatever hormonal preparation for caretaking exists. Women who have just borne a child can be completely inadequate mothers, just as adoptive mothers can be completely adequate. We do not know what the hormonal bases of caretaking in humans are, or whether there are any at all. We do know that whatever these are, they are not enough to create nurturance, at least not in all women who give birth.

Second, the evidence from animals suggests that there is no hormonal or instinctual basis for mothering in females other than those who have borne a child. Caretaking behavior can be called up both with hormones and without in both males and nonparturient females. Nor can we argue that biological aggressiveness in human males prevents nurturance, since boys in many societies, and men in our own and elsewhere, can provide anything from occasional to extensive care of young children. It does not seem, if we exclude wet-nursing, that any biological evidence will be forthcoming to support the assumption that women must be "substitute mothers" rather than men.

Arguments from nature, then, are unconvincing as explanations for women's mothering as a feature of a social structure. Beyond the possible hormonal components of a woman's early mothering of her own newborn (and even these do not operate independently), there is nothing in parturient women's physiology which makes them particularly suited to later child care, nor is there any instinctual reason why they should be able to perform it. Nor is there anything biological or hormonal to differentiate a male "substitute mother" from a female one. The biological argument for women's mothering is based on facts that derive, not from our biological knowledge, but from our definition of the natural situation as this grows out of our participation in certain social arrangements. That women have the extensive and nearly exclusive mothering role they have is a product of a social and cultural translation of their childbearing and lactation capacities. It is not guaranteed or entailed by these capacities themselves.

THE ROLE-TRAINING ARGUMENT

Nonfeminist theorists do not inquire about the reproduction of mothering or of the social relations of parenting, and seem to assume biological inevitability. This is true whether or not they recognize the sociological significance of the family and women's role in social reproduction. Feminist writers have alternate explanations, sometimes made explicit, sometimes assumed, each pointing to some elements in the process by which women come to mother. Moreover, they do so without relying on biological assumptions. At the same time, they are profoundly limited.*

One important tendency in the feminist literature looks (along with social psychologists) at role training or cognitive role learning. It suggests that women's mothering, like other aspects of gender activity, is a product of feminine role training and role identification. Girls are taught to be mothers, trained for nurturance, and told that they ought to mother. They are wrapped in pink blankets, given dolls and have their brothers' trucks taken away, learn that being a girl is not as good as being a boy, are not allowed to get dirty, are discouraged from achieving in school, and therefore become mothers. They are barraged from early childhood well into adult life with books, magazines, ads, school courses, and television programs which put forth pronatalist and promaternal sex-stereotypes. They "identify" with their own mothers as they grow up, and this identification produces the girl as a mother. Alternately, as those following cognitive-psychological trends would have it, girls choose to do "girl-things" and, I suppose, eventually "woman-things," like mothering, as a result of learning that they are girls. In this view, girls identify with their mothers as a result of learning that they are girls and wanting to be girl-like.[45]

Margaret Polatnick presents a different view, in specific disagreement with socialization theories. She asks not how women come to mother, but why men do not. Her explanation is in terms of power differences and social control. She takes men's power and women's powerlessness as a given, and suggests that men use their power to enforce the perpetuation of women's mothering: "Men don't rear children because they don't *want* to rear children. (This implies, of course, that they're in a position to enforce their preferences)."[46] Her account goes on to show why people in our society who have power over others would choose not to parent. Parenting, as an unpaid occupation outside the world of public power, entails lower status, less power, and less control of resources than paid work. Women's mothering reinforces and perpetuates women's relative powerlessness.

All of these views share the assumption that women's mothering is a product of behavioral conformity and individual intention. An

---

*My treatment of the role-learning argument in what follows is much briefer than my treatment of the biological argument, not because it is less important but because the rest of the book provides an alternate empirical account of female development.

investigation of what mothering consists in helps to explain how it is perpetuated, and indicates the limitations of traditional socialization and social control explanations for the reproduction of mothering.

To begin with, women's mothering does not exist in isolation. It is a fundamental constituting feature of the sexual division of labor. As part of the sexual division of labor, it is structurally and causally related to other institutional arrangements and to ideological formulations which justify the sexual division of labor. Mothering also contributes to the reproduction of sexual inequality through its effects on masculine personality.

Women's mothering is not an unchanging transcultural universal. Although women, and not men, have primary responsibility for children, many features of this responsibility change. Family organization, child-care and child-rearing practices, and the relations between women's child care and other responsibilities change in response particularly to changes in the organization of production. Women's role as we know it is an historical product. The development of industrial capitalism in the West entailed that women's role in the family become increasingly concerned with personal relations and psychological stability. Mothering is most eminently a psychologically based role. It consists in psychological and personal experience of self in relationship to child or children.

As culture and personality research has demonstrated, an important element in the reproduction of social relations and social structure is the socialization of people with psychological capacities and commitments appropriate to participation in these relations and structures. In an industrial late-capitalist society, "socialization" is a particularly psychological affair, since it must lead to the assimilation and internal organization of generalized capacities for participation in a hierarchical and differentiated social world, rather than to training for a specific role.[47] Production, for instance, is more efficient and profitable when workers develop a willing and docile personality. In the last analysis, however, it is possible to extract labor by coercion (and it is certainly the case that there is some coercive element in needing to enter work relations in the first place).

The use of coercion is not possible in the case of mothering. Clinical research shows that behavioral conformity to the apparent specific physical requirements of infants—keeping them fed and clean —is not enough to enable physiological, let alone psychological, growth in an infant.[48] Studies of infants in understaffed institutions where perfunctory care is given, and of infants whose caretakers do not hold them or interact with them, show that these infants may become mildly depressed, generally withdrawn, psychotically unable to relate, totally apathetic and, in extreme cases, may die. Infants need affective bonds and a diffuse, multifaceted, ongoing personal relationship to caretakers for physical and psychological growth.*

A concern with parenting, then, must direct attention beyond behavior. This is because parenting is not simply a set of behaviors, but participation in an interpersonal, diffuse, affective relationship. Parenting is an eminently psychological role in a way that many other roles and activities are not. "Good-enough mothering" ("good-enough" to socialize a nonpsychotic child) requires certain relational capacities which are embedded in personality and a sense of self-in-relationship.

Given these requirements, it is evident that the mothering that women do is not something that can be taught simply by giving a girl dolls or telling her that she ought to mother. It is not something that a girl can learn by behavioral imitation, or by deciding that she wants to do what girls do. Nor can men's power over women explain women's mothering. Whether or not men in particular or society at large—through media, income distribution, welfare policies, and schools—enforce women's mothering, and expect or require a woman to care for her child, they cannot require or force her to provide adequate parenting unless she, *to some degree* and *on some unconscious or conscious level,* has the capacity and sense of self as maternal to do so.**

Role training, identification, and enforcement certainly have to do with the acquisition of an appropriate gender role. But the conventional feminist view, drawn from social or cognitive psychology, which understands feminine development as explicit ideological instruction or formal coercion, cannot in the case of mothering be sufficient. In addition, explanations relying on behavioral conformity do not account for the tenacity of self-definition, self-concept, and psychological need to maintain aspects of traditional roles which continue even in the face of ideological shifts, counterinstruction, and the lessening

---

*I am not talking about "maternal deprivation," as it is conventionally labeled, which implies separation from or loss of the biological or social *mother*, or that *she herself* is not providing adequate care. What is at issue is the *quality of care*, and not who provides it: "The notion that the biological mother by virtue of being the biological mother is capable of caring for her child is without foundation";[49] "from the child's point of view, it matters little what sex mother is."[50]

**My argument here is extrapolated from clinical findings on the nature of mothering. A good empirical evaluation of the argument could be drawn from investigation of black slave women's mothering of slaveowners' children or from other situations of enforced parenting by slaves, serfs, or servants. (White) folk wisdom has it that slave nurses, although in every fundamental sense coerced, were excellent mothers, whose charges remembered them fondly. Kovel speaks to some outcomes for white men of this situation, but to oedipal-sexual issues rather than to issues concerning the development of self and general relational capacities in white children of both genders.[51]

of masculine coercion which the women's movement has produced.

A second deficiency of role-learning and social control explanations for the reproduction of mothering is that they rely on individual intention—on the part of socializers, of girls who want to do girl-things or be like their mothers, and on the part of men who control women. There is certainly an intentional component to gender role socialization in the family, in schools, in the media. However, social reproduction comes to be independent of individual intention and is not caused by it. There are several aspects to social reproduction, all of which apply in the case of the reproduction of mothering.

Practices become institutionalized in regularized, nonarbitrary ways. Aspects of society—social and economic relations, institutions, values and ideology—develop their own logic and autonomy and come to mutually interact with and maintain one another. Aspects of society are not newly created every day, although they do develop historically through the intended activity of people. The conditions people live in are given as the historical outcome of previous human social activity, which itself has exhibited some regularity and consistency.

In the case of a mother-child relationship, there is an interactive base of expectations of continuity of relationship. This interactive base develops once a woman begins to care for a particular child, and usually includes gratification as well as frustration for both the child and the mother. More generally, women's mothering as an organization of parenting is embedded in and fundamental to the social organization of gender. In any historical period, women's mothering and the sexual division of labor are also structurally linked to other institutions and other aspects of social organization. In industrial capitalist societies, women's mothering is central to the links between the organization of gender—in particular the family system—and economic organization.[52] Sexual inequality is itself embedded in and perpetuated by the organization of these institutions, and is not reproduced according to or solely because of the will of individual actors.

Intentional socialization theories, just as they are generally not sufficient to explain social reproduction, are insufficient to explain the reproduction of the social organization of gender and its major features. The social organization of gender, in its relation to an economic context, has depended on the continuation of the social relations of parenting. The reproduction of these social relations of parenting is not reducible to individual intention but depends on all the arrangements which go into the organization of gender and the organization of the economy.

These institutions create and embody conditions that require people to engage in them. People's participation further guarantees social
reproduction. Marx gives an example in the case of capitalism: "Capitalist production, therefore, of itself reproduces the separation between labour-power and the means of labour. It thereby perpetuates
the condition for exploiting the labourer. It incessantly forces him to
sell his labour-power in order to live, and enables the capitalist to
purchase labour-power in order that he may enrich himself. It is no
longer a mere accident, that capitalist and labourer confront each
other in the market as buyer and seller."[53] Or, for instance, Lévi-
Strauss describes a strongly enforced sexual division of labor as a condition for the reproduction of heterosexual marriage:

> Generally speaking it can be said that, among the so-called primitive tribes,
> there are no bachelors, simply for the reason that they could not survive. One
> of the strongest field recollections of this writer was his meeting, among the
> Bororo of central Brazil, a man about thirty years old: unclean, ill-fed, sad,
> and lonesome. When asked if the man were seriously ill, the natives' answer
> came as a shock: what was wrong with him?—nothing at all, he was just a
> bachelor. And true enough, in a society where labor is systematically shared
> between man and woman and where only the married status permits the man
> to benefit from the fruits of woman's work, including delousing, body paint-
> ing, and hair-plucking as well as vegetable food and cooked food (since the
> Bororo woman tills the soil and makes pots), a bachelor is really only half a
> human being. . . . [54]

> The sexual division of labor. . . . has been explained as a device to make the
> sexes mutually dependent on social and economic grounds, thus establishing
> clearly that marriage is better than celibacy. . . . The principle of sexual di-
> vision of labor establishes a mutual dependency between the sexes, compel-
> ling them thereby to perpetuate themselves and found a family.[55]

In the case of mothering, the economic system has depended for
its reproduction on women's reproduction of particular forms of labor power in the family. At the same time, income inequality between
men and women makes it more rational, and even necessary, in any
individual conjugal family for fathers, rather than mothers, to be primary wage-earners. Therefore, mothers, rather than fathers, are the
primary caretakers of children and the home.

Legitimating ideologies themselves, as well as institutions like
schools, the media, and families which perpetuate ideologies, contribute to social reproduction. They create expectations in people
about what is normal and appropriate and how they should act. Society's perpetuation requires that *someone* rear children, but our language, science, and popular culture all make it very difficult to separate the need for care from the question of who provides that

care. It is hard to separate out parenting activities, usually performed by women and particularly by biological mothers, from women
themselves.

Finally, people themselves need to be reproduced both daily and
generationally. Most theoretical accounts agree that women as wives
and mothers reproduce people—physically in their housework and
child care, psychologically in their emotional support of husbands
and their maternal relation to sons and daughters. If we accept this
view, we have to ask who reproduces wives and mothers. What is hidden in most accounts of the family is that women reproduce *themselves*
through their own daily housework. What is also often hidden, in
generalizations about the family as an emotional refuge, is that in the
family as it is currently constituted no one supports and reconstitutes
women affectively and emotionally—either women working in the
home or women working in the paid labor force. This was not always
the case. In a previous period, and still in some stable working-class
and ethnic communities, women did support themselves emotionally
by supporting and reconstituting *one another*.[56] However, in the current period of high mobility and familial isolation, this support is
largely removed, and there is little institutionalized daily emotional
reconstitution of mothers. What there is depends on the accidents of
a particular marriage, and not on the carrying out of an institutionalized support role.[57] There is a fundamental asymmetry in daily reproduction. Men are socially and psychologically reproduced by
women, but women are reproduced (or not) largely by themselves.

We also need to understand the intergenerational reproduction
of mothers. Parsons and theorists of the Frankfurt Institute have
added significantly to our total picture of social reproduction by providing a model of the reproduction of social relations across generations. They argue that in industrial capitalist society, generational
reproduction occurs through the creation in the family of men workers with particular personalities and orientations to authority. These
social theorists have attempted to integrate a theory of large-scale so-
cial-cultural structure and its institutional and ideological reproduction with a theory of the way this structure reproduces itself through
everyday interpersonal experiences and personality development in
its members. These theorists of social reproduction describe how
members of a society come to be (in Parsons's terminology) motivated
to comply with role expectations. They describe how the structural
organization of that institution in which people grow up, the family,
entails that people develop personalities which tend to guarantee that
they will get gratification or satisfaction from those activities which

are necessary to the reproduction of the larger social structure. In Max Horkheimer's terms, "In so far as the continuance of all social forms goes, the dominant force is not insight but human patterns of reaction which have become stabilized in interaction with a system of cultural formations on the basis of the social life process."[58] And Parsons reiterates his claim: "The integration of a set of common value patterns with the internalized need-disposition structure of the constituent personalities is the core phenomenon of the dynamics of social systems."[59]

Parsons and Frankfurt theorists have investigated the family, and especially the organization of parenting. Furthermore, in their concern to develop a theory of socialization that relies on institutional and structural mechanisms, rather than on individual intention, they have turned to psychoanalysis "as a 'psychology of family' pure and simple"[60] for their method of inquiry. They have begun to develop a psychoanalytic sociology of social reproduction.

The empirical efforts of Parsons and the Frankfurt theorists, however, have been directed toward the reproduction of relations of production, and to men as workers. They, as well as Freudian social theorists[61] and Marxist feminists[62] after them, have been concerned with the way the family and women socialize *men* into capitalist society.* They have developed an extensive and important analysis of the relation of masculine psychological development to capitalist achievement or properly submissive or bureaucratized work behavior, as well as to the relation of masculine attitudes to women and femininity.** But they have not discussed feminine development at all.

The account which follows takes these theories as methodological models and extends their psychoanalytic sociology. I do not mean to deny the basic differences between the theories of Parsons and critical theorists such as Horkheimer. These differences are both methodological and political—but it is their political differences which have often obscured the similarities of their descriptions and their similar use of psychoanalysis. Empirically, both accounts describe how the development of industrial capitalism has affected family structure and personality. This is phrased in critical theory in terms of the decline of paternal authority and the father's role in the home, in Parsons's case in terms of the overwhelming importance of the mother.

*Social psychological studies of the effect of "father absence" (and consequent maternal ambivalence, seductiveness, or overprotection) on development also focus almost entirely on male development.[63]

**They discuss in this context the oedipus complex, the importance and effects of maternal manipulation of masculine erotism, father absence and the decline of paternal authority, masculine repression and sublimation.

These changes have in turn affected masculine development: Men's orientation to authority and malleability as labor power have shifted.

Politically, Parsons is basically uncritical of the society he describes. Parsons focuses on the problem of order—so do critical theorists, but in Parsons's case, it always sounds as though he wants to understand order to contribute toward its maintenance. For the critical theorists, the problem of order is posed as the problem of understanding historically specific forms of domination. Parsons's theory, while treating culture, social organization, personality, and biology, tends to define society in terms of its value system, or culture. Critical theorists generally accord primary significance to the social organization of production, and relate values and particular forms of domination to this organization.

Finally, critical theorists like Horkheimer focus on disruptive elements which undermine the smooth reproduction of functional relationships. For Parsons, the family reproduces social and economic organization. For critical theorists, it both reproduces and undermines these forms. While Parsons makes a major contribution to our understanding of social reproduction, and especially to the part played by personality, it is evident that there are contradictions in the contemporary organization of gender and the family—ways in which expectations created in the family cannot be fulfilled, strains in women's and men's and parents' and children's roles and relationships, incompatible needs for women as child-rearers and workers in the labor force.

In the account which follows, I show how the structure of parenting reproduces itself. Like the psychoanalytic sociologists I discuss, I rely on psychoanalytic theory as an analysis of family structure and social reproduction. Psychoanalysis shows us how the family division of labor in which women mother gives socially and historically specific meaning to gender itself. This engendering of men and women with particular personalities, needs, defenses, and capacities creates the condition for and contributes to the reproduction of this same division of labor. The sexual division of labor both produces gender differences and is in turn reproduced by them.

The psychoanalytic account shows not only how men come to grow away from their families and to participate in the public sphere. It shows also how women grow up to have both the generalized relational capacities and needs and how women and men come to create the kinds of interpersonal relationships which make it likely that women will remain in the domestic sphere—in the sphere of reproduction—and will in turn mother the next generation. Women's mothering as an institutionalized feature of family life and of the sexual division of labor reproduces itself cyclically. In the process, it contributes to the reproduction of those aspects of the sexual sociology of adult life which grow out of and relate to the fact that women mother.

I suggested earlier that women's mothering was reproduced on a number of different levels. Because of the requirements of parenting, and particularly because of its contemporary largely psychological form, the genesis of psychological mothering capacities and orientations in women is fundamental and conditional to all of these. The capacities and orientations I describe must be built into personality; they are not behavioral acquisitions. Women's capacities for mothering and abilities to get gratification from it are strongly internalized and psychologically enforced, and are built developmentally into the feminine psychic structure. Women are prepared psychologically for mothering through the developmental situation in which they grow up, and in which women have mothered them.

Most conventional accounts of gender-role socialization rely on individual intention and behavioral criteria, which do not adequately explain women's mothering. Psychoanalysis, by contrast, provides a systemic, structural account of socialization and social reproduction. It suggests that major features of the social organization of gender are transmitted in and through those personalities produced by the structure of the institution—the family—in which children become gendered members of society.

3

Psychoanalysis and Sociological Inquiry

What is of concern here is not primarily Freud's speculation about archaic society but the insight into the family as a societally determined locus in which personality structure is formed, and which in turn is socially relevant.

FRANKFURT INSTITUTE FOR SOCIAL RESEARCH,
"The Family"

. . . when we are studying human beings as "persons" and not just as biological organisms, . . . what we do at each developmental stage with bodily organs such as the mouth, anus and genital is determined by the quality of our personality and personal relations at each stage, rather than vice-versa.

HARRY GUNTRIP,
Personality Structure and Human Interaction

Psychoanalysis provides an analysis and critique of the reproduction of sex and gender. Freud and his followers demonstrated how sexual repression in the family produces the potentially bisexual, polymorphous perverse infant as genitally heterosexual, monogamous adult, with boys appropriating their masculine prerogatives and girls acquiescing in their feminine subordination and passivity. They also demonstrated how closely psychic pain and disorganization (neurosis) were related to these "normal" outcomes. Freud's accounts of the psychological destructiveness of bourgeois marriage, gender differentiation, and child-rearing practices remain unsurpassed, and both psychoanalysts and feminists since Freud have deepened and extended his critique. The dynamics these accounts describe all result from a male-dominant but father-absent family where women mother. My account shows that psychoanalytic theory can also explain how this family produces women as mothers.

Psychoanalytic theory is unfamiliar to many people, and my own reading of it follows a tradition—that of object-relations theory—

without wide currency in the United States. This chapter provides an introduction to psychoanalytic theory in general and to object-relations theory as a basis for the sociological uses of psychoanalysis.

Psychoanalysis concentrates on unconscious mental processes, affects, and psychic structure. Psychoanalysts discuss the relationship between mental life and behavior, but psychoanalysis is not in the first instance a psychological theory about behavior. It is a theory developed through interpretation of a particular kind of behavior in the analytic situation—talk (play, in the analyses of children)—as an index of the content of unconscious processes and structure.* Psychoanalysis argues, unlike many other psychologies, that there is no one-to-one correspondence between unconscious processes or structure and the content of consciousness and intended activity. A particular unconscious process, affect (an idea, wish, preoccupation), or structural form can express itself in almost endless behavioral as well as conscious psychological modes.

The fundamental contribution of psychoanalysis lies in its demonstration of the existence and mode of operation of unconscious mental processes. Freud's first psychoanalytic discovery was that people engaged in mental activity which affected their physical activities and feelings but was not available to their conscious self.[2] This mental activity was not simply unconscious for the moment, or easily recalled. Rather, it was actively repressed from consciousness, because it was too threatening, painful, or frustrating. Moreover, this repression was itself usually not known. Freud's subsequent work investigated repression and other forms of unconscious mental activity. Freud originally postulated a "System Unconscious," a "System Preconscious" (those thoughts not currently conscious, but not repressed), and a "System Conscious."[3] He later rejected this formulation in favor of a formulation in terms of unconscious, preconscious, and conscious *processes*.[4]

Some unconscious mental activity, according to Freud, does not operate in the sequential, logical, reality-governed way that conscious thought and talk do.[5] It operates according to the laws of "primary process" that transform unconscious internal ideas and affects.** Pri-

*Psychoanalyst David Rapaport broadens the definition of behavior to include feelings and thought ("latent behavior"), and claims that the uniqueness of psychoanalytic theory is its stress on this "latent" behavior and the unconscious determinants of behavior. This terminological shift is part of an attempt throughout American psychoanalysis to argue for psychoanalysis as a science in positivist terms. For me, the strength of psychoanalysis is as an interpretative theory and not as a behavioral science.[1]

**The "id" operates according to the laws of primary process.

mary process activity (as in dreams) condenses several thoughts, perhaps by creating a metaphor for all of them. It symbolizes, letting one element or thought stand for another, or, by an association of opposites, letting a symbol stand for its opposite. It displaces, separating the affect invested in an idea from its content or several elements of an ideational complex one from the other. Thus the affect can be invested in a minor element of the total ideational complex; this defuses the intensity of the major idea.

It is not so much the recognition that all motives, purposes, and determinants of behavior are not available to an actor that makes psychoanalytic reasoning unique. As David Rapaport puts it,

All psychologies deal with conditions "unnoticed" by the subject, and with "unnoticed" or "unnoticeable" processes underlying his behavior. The psychoanalytic thesis of unconscious determination, however, differs from these . . . in several respects: (1) it explicitly conceptualizes that which is unnoticed or unnoticeable . . . ; (2) it asserts that the unnoticed or unnoticeable can be inferred from that which *is* noticed by the subject (and/or the observer), by means of the effects of the unnoticed and/or the unnoticeable upon that which is noticed . . . ; (3) it asserts that the rules governing the *noticed* are different from those governing the *unnoticed*, and that the unnoticed can be inferred by considering the deviations of the noticed from its usual patterns . . . ; (4) it makes a systematic distinction between the *unnoticed* and the *unnoticeable* (the *unnoticed* can become conscious, whereas the *unnoticeable*, by definition, cannot); it expresses this distinction by the terms "descriptive" vs. "dynamic" unconscious, and conceptualizes it as the distinction between the Systems *Pre*conscious and *Un*conscious . . . ; (5) while other psychologies treat the unnoticeable in nonpsychological terms (brain fields, neural connections, etc.), psychoanalysis consistently treats it in the psychological terms of motivations, affects, thoughts, etc.[6]

People use unnoticeable, unconscious operations in their psychological experience of others, as defenses—to cope with lack of control, ambivalence, anxiety, loss, feelings of dependence, helplessness, envy.* If they feel ambivalent about or out of control of a relationship, they may internalize, or introject, objects** in relation to themselves or in relation to a part of their self, experiencing external relationships as internal and their feelings in relation to someone else as an internal sense of self.[7] A very young child, for instance, may feel invulnerable and all-powerful because it has introjected, or taken as an internal object, a nourishing and protecting maternal image, which is now experienced continuously whether or not its mother is actually there. Alternately, it may feel rejected and alone whether or not its mother

---

*Defense operations are a major unconscious activity of the "ego," or incipient ego.
**In psychoanalytic parlance "objects" are people, aspects of people, or symbols of people.

is actually there, because it has taken as internal object an image of her as rejecting and denying gratification. Or, people may identify with others, modifying their self or their activity to resemble someone else who has abilities, attributes, or powers they want, fear, or admire.[8] In superego formation, for instance, the child does not simply act to avoid parental punishment (whether realistically expected or not), nor introject a representation of a punitive parent and feel itself admonished or punished by this parent. The child takes on this admonishing or regulating role itself, so that one aspect of its (unconsciously) experienced self punishes another. Introjection and identification are both forms of internalization: *"those processes by which the subject transforms real or imagined regulatory interactions with his environment and real or imagined characteristics of his environment, into inner regulations and characteristics."*[9]

People also engage in projection or externalization. They assume that others have qualities which are in fact their own, or that they have a relation to another which is in fact an internal relation of one part of the self to another (the highly self-judgmental person who thinks the whole world is judging).

Psychoanalysis describes other unconscious defenses in addition to internalizations and externalizations.[10] People may engage in reaction formation: convert a feeling or idea into its opposite; deny to themselves that an issue, or person, is important to them; displace feelings about someone onto someone or something else; or split objects into different parts or aspects. In splitting objects, they may, for instance, internalize an object, and then split the image of this person according to felt good and bad qualities. Or they may experience and represent the good and bad aspects of an object separately and introject only its bad aspects. This avoids anger at the person her- or himself, who can now be experienced as all good and gratifying. Internally, the actor, or self, experiences an all-bad, or frustrating, relationship, and possibly her or himself as bad, frustrated, or abandoned.

Psychoanalysis discusses psychic *structure* as well as psychological *processes*.* All schools of psychoanalytic theory argue that mental life is originally undifferentiated.** Psychic differentiation and structur-

---

*The concept of structure remains one of the murkiest in the psychoanalytic lexicon, but is at the same time important.

**In the original Freudian schema, the child is "all id"—all quasi-biological drives —and the ego arises out of the id. In that of the ego psychologists, the child is an "undifferentiated ego-id matrix"[11] or a "primal psychophysiological self."[12] In object-relations theory, the infant is originally "unitary ego"[13] or "ego-potential."[14]

alization arise (given physiological growth) out of a child's experiences of relationships. Freud holds that psychic structure assumes a tripartite division into id, ego, and superego.[15] This division makes metaphoric reference to "regions" of the mind (in psychoanalytic terminology, to the mind's "topography"). It makes functional reference to the way regular psychological functions seem to develop and operate in consistent modes (the "id" according to primary process laws, the "ego" according to the reality principle and secondary process activity, the "superego" as observer and evaluator). Psychic structure develops through experiences of anxiety and frustration. These experiences lead the infant to differentiate itself from the environment through the erection of particular defenses, to its permanent repression of certain relational orientations or internalized relational experiences, and to identifications and introjections that change its self or its experience of self in relationship.

The literature does not make either a theoretical or empirical argument for the exhaustiveness or inevitability of the tripartite division, though it proceeds as if such arguments had been made. Critics argue that the division has been unnecessarily and arbitrarily rigidified. For example, Freud considers the superego a single structural unit, but according to him it has three functions: conscience; "vehicle" of the person's ego ideal, what they would like to be; and observer of the ego. These develop from different kinds of frustration and anxiety during different periods.* All these experiences contribute to the creation of different aspects of psychic structure and to regularized interactions among these. There is no obvious reason for combining these functions into a single structural entity, nor for expecting that other experiences and psychic operations do not produce other differentiations within the psyche.[16] Since fundamental structural reorganization can emerge from analysis,[17] it is not possible to argue that structuralization happens only until a certain age, and that biological factors ensure closure with superego development at around age five.

Critics also argue that some characterizations of psychic structure have eliminated the acting subject as the central focus of psychoanalytic inquiry. They point out that Freud speaks of the separate aspects of the personality alternately as mental "regions," "structural

*Conscience develops through the family relationships of the oedipus complex and the way these are eventually given up in becoming and transforming the superego itself. The ego ideal develops throughout life, through identifications later with people and/or ideas as well as with parents in childhood. Freud does not explain how the superego as observer arises. It arises, presumably, beginning with the first experience of self as different from the other—of self as object as well as subject.

relations," and "agencies," each of which leads to a very different conception of psychological functioning. They remind us that the decision to translate *das Ich* ("the I") as the *ego* makes what was emphatically an agentic subject into an object.[18] They suggest that even the id (*das Es*, "the it") is part of a whole person and expresses agency in the form of (usually libidinal) want or wish, even if this agency is repressed or experienced as separate from the agent who is the "I."[19]

The interpretation of psychic structure that stresses the mental personality as object rather than subject is fundamental to the development of psychoanalytic ego psychology, the school that has come to dominate the American psychoanalytic tradition.[20] Ego psychology begins with an acceptance of Freud's drive theory, the notion that behavior and development are determined by inborn aggressive and libidinal drives seeking gratification. It adds a concern with another kind of inborn faculty—the "system ego"—a combination of functions or "apparatuses" (perception, memory, cognition) in the first instance independent of the drives and of psychological conflict. This faculty enables "adaptation" to the social and physical world and mediation between this world and the demands of other aspects of the psychic apparatus.

In focusing on these apparatuses, psychoanalysis further reduces the acting agent to a behaving organism. For the ego psychologists, not only is the "id" driven by quasi-biological uncontrolled drives. The ego—the "I"—also is now a system of apparatuses, of quasi-physiological functions that could be equally (and perhaps better) described by physiological and cognitive psychologists.* If our interest is in persons in their social (and inner social) world, these apparatuses provide at most a psychophysiological bedrock upon which the mental life of the person as subject can develop.

Psychoanalysts use terms in common to describe most psychological processes. But their conceptions of these processes and their explanations of their origins often differ. These differences are reflected in theories of personality and development that give varying weight to innate and social factors. Along with theories of psychic structure and process, these developmental theories form the core of psychoanalysis.

Freud, Melanie Klein, and ego psychologists stress the determin-

---

*These functions are *quasi*-physiological, according to Rapaport, because "the structural givens in question are not the muscular apparatuses of motility, nor the end organs of perceptions, etc., but rather their psychological regulations: for instance, those psychological structures through which the control and triggering of the motor apparatus is effected."[21]

ing importance of innate factors.* Freud argues that psychic development precedes and is determined by a biologically scheduled unfolding of stages of infantile sexuality. Sexuality, here, is expressed
by innate libidinal drives that seek gratification or tension release according to the "pleasure principle." In addition, sexuality is located
in particular "erotogenic zones." An erotogenic zone is the particular
arena (mouth, anus, genital) and practice (oral sucking, anal with-
holding or releasing, genital arousal or orgasm) which provides gratification. Aggressive drives also may seek gratification in these channels (oral biting, anal control, phallic narcissism).

Infants psychologically consist in unorganized, innate libidinal
drives that seek gratification. As they grow, the primary erotogenic
mode and zone in which they seek gratification change. Libido moves
from mouth to anus to genital; the infant is oriented at any time to
gratification of the libidinal demands in this area. The first few years
also organize sexuality, in terms of the kinds of gratifications, repressions, and fixations that will preoccupy unconsciously (and consciously) any individual.[23]

Klein's reformulation of psychoanalytic theory retains the primacy
and determining importance of drives, though her stress is on innate
aggressive urges and fantasies (of devouring and destroying parental
genitals or maternal breast, for instance) rather than on erotic
desires.[24] Ego psychology has also continued to emphasize quasi-
biological processes, adding to the assumption of an inbuilt unfolding
of libidinal stages an emphasis on the ego's adaptive apparatuses or
capacities. Social object-relations are important to these psychoanalytic schools, but these object-relations are determined by developmental libidinal level. That is, the infant's first relationship to the
social and physical world is "oral"; it then comes inevitably to make
anal issues primary, and so forth.

Both "cultural school" psychoanalysts and object-relations theorists have taken an alternate position emphasizing the importance of
society and culture. Cultural school psychoanalysts, like Erich Fromm,
Karen Horney, and Clara Thompson, oppose Freud's theory of the
instinctual determination of development and neuroses with an argument for the importance of culture in determining mental life,

*John Benjamin points out that Freud was not always an instinctual determinist.
He became one as a result of his mistake in attributing his hysterical women patients'
fantasies of being seduced by their fathers to actual seductions. Benjamin claims that
Freud even then continued to stress the determining importance of childhood experiences. But he stressed only universal experiences inherent in growing up as a human
being (a long childhood, for instance), and not experiences created by particular
families.[22]

personality, and development. They argue against Freud's claim that the developmental stages he describes are inevitable and universal. For example, Horney and Thompson argue that the cultural devaluation and social oppression of women are responsible for the clinical finding that women have low self-esteem, reject their femininity, and envy men their penises.[25]

The cultural school contribution is important, but is limited in fundamental ways. It borrows from anthropological culture and personality research an unanalyzed, holistic concept of culture, and a view that development consists in the direct internalization of the social and cultural world. Culture, in this conception, is a system of values and ways of doing things which are simply communicated to children. This view bypasses the specific implications of the actual social context in which the child learns. More important, it substitutes a simple unidirectional cultural determinism, a model of direct transmission of social reality to psychic reality, and total isomorphism between these, for the complex internal operations and emotions psychoanalysis has described. The person in this view is no longer an agent, has no way to work on or create that which is internalized. Cultural school psychoanalysts are right that the outside world affects the inside. But this influence is mediated through fantasy, introjection and projection, ambivalence, conflict, substitution, reversal, distortion, splitting, association, compromise, denial, and repression.

Object-relations theory has performed the task left by culture and personality anthropologists and cultural school psychoanalysts. It provides an alternative psychodynamic account of personality formation to the instinctual determinism of Freud, Klein, and the ego psychologists and to the direct environmental determinism of the cultural school. At the same time, it incorporates a view of the place of both drives and social relations in development. This theory has most influenced my approach to psychoanalytic theory.[26]

Object-relations theory shares with other psychoanalytic perspectives an emphasis on the basic importance of sexuality and agrees that sexuality is organized (distorted, repressed) during the early years. However, object-relations theory is distinguished from the instinctual determinists by its different conception of the role of drives with respect to the formation and expression of sexuality. Object-relations theorists argue that the child's social relational experience from earliest infancy is determining for psychological growth and personality formation. Balint, Fairbairn, and Guntrip, for example, all argue against the view that the biological requisites of the leading erotogenic zone (oral, anal, phallic, genital) determine the form of the child's object-relations. Rather, with the possible exception of an "oral" stage, the accession to experienced primacy or preoccupation with other "erotogenic zones" is a result of particular social interactions concerning these zones.* The quality of the whole relationship affects both the development of persons generally and the way they experience, manipulate, and fixate on bodily zones.

Zones, then, do not become eroticized through a maturational unfolding. They become libidinized because they become for the growing child vehicles for attaining personal contact. Fairbairn, for instance, argues that "erotogenic zones" arise in a process of hysterical conversion as a defense against unsatisfactory object-relationships. He speaks of the "erotogenic zone in which the dramas of disturbed personal relationships are localized."[28]

Similarly, innate drives do not naturally determine behavior and development. People do not operate according to the "pleasure principle" in its psychophysiological sense. People have innate erotic and aggressive energies. Infants, as psychoanalysis shows, are sexual. But people do not naturally seek release of tension from physiological drives or use their object-relations in the search for this release. Rather, they manipulate and transform drives in the course of attaining and retaining relationships.** When a person seeks drive release for its own sake, when insistent drives come to dominate life, this is to be explained in terms of that person's previous history.

These considerations do not mean that physiology, or psychophysiology, makes no contribution to development. Different people have greater or lesser physiological capacities for responding to the environment, for organizing stimuli, and so forth. These capacities shape any person's ability to participate in social relations in the first place. Nor are the "ego apparatuses," or "system ego," of the ego psychologists irrelevant to development. Perception, cognition, memory, planning, motor activity, are all necessary psychophysiological capacities, without which fantasy, defense operations, and symbolization would be impossible.

---

*Even in the "oral" stage, we might argue, with Jacobson, that orality—the orally gratified or deprived self and the breast—symbolize or stand for the whole early relationship to the primary caretaker.[27]

**Balint dissociates himself from Fairbairn's claim that libido is object-seeking and not pleasure-seeking. He appeals to the original German *lust*, which, he claims, is by definition pleasure-seeking, and claims that Fairbairn's theory is an artifact of the analytic situation rather than a description of development. He suggests a reformulation: For people in analysis, at least, object-seeking is at least as important as pleasure-seeking. Balint's theory stresses the primary object-directedness of the infant from birth, and tries to explain how particular orientations (for example, narcissism, autoerotism, or aggression) arise in the course of thwarted or disturbed object-relationships. These tendencies lead me to classify their theories together.[29]

Object-relations theorists advance their conception of the ego in personal terms rather than in terms of apparatus. They distinguish the "system ego" from what Guntrip calls the "person-ego" in the "personal psychology" of Winnicott and Fairbairn.[30] The "system ego" is an apparatus of control and adaptation, and the psychobiological substratum of the person. The "person-ego" is the person, self, subject in relationship, with conscious and unconscious motives and intentions. Guntrip refers to Hartmann's attempt to find the basis of ego apparatuses in brain physiology: "Had he found them, they would have had nothing to do with the reasons for the motivated actions of persons in real life."[31]

Ego psychologists argue against a behaviorist view of development in which the person passively receives environmental stimuli. They argue that the person has innate capacities to organize that which comes from the environment.[32] Their contribution here is extremely important, but it does not contribute to our understanding of the person as a motivated subject.*

My account of the reproduction of mothering focuses on those aspects of development which result in differing orientations to parenting. I am not concerned with all aspects of development, nor even all aspects of differential development between men and women. Differing orientations to parenting are located in the development of relational capacities and intrapsychic structure—in affective development. They are not located primarily in adaptive ego capacities. Relational capacities and intrapsychic structure emerge from processes of internalization.

I focus primarily on the ways that family structure and process, in particular the asymmetrical organization of parenting, affect unconscious psychic structure and process. Freud claimed, "The character of the ego is a precipitate of abandoned object-cathexes and . . . it contains the history of those object-choices."[34] But in Freud's clinical account, *all* elements of mental life are affected by relational experience. The defenses a child chooses are partially a product of innate tendency, but also of the defenses it experiences in those around it, and of finding out what works best. Conflict and ambivalence develop in situations where caretakers feel conflict and ambivalence,

*Psychoanalyst Roy Schafer points this out: "The ego, for example, is now generally said to be a system defined by its functions. This functional emphasis, which has its origins in Freud's writings, is eminently suitable for adaptational propositions concerning the ego system. But it has little or no value in dynamic propositions—those concerned with conflicting motivations."[33]

and not solely as a result of an innate anxiety threshold. A child also comes to channel libido and aggression in patterned ways as a result of its relational experiences and its interactions with caretakers, that is, the id becomes patterned and constructed. Thus, society constitutes itself psychologically in the individual not only in the moral strictures of the superego. All aspects of psychic structure, character, and emotional and erotic life are social, constituted through a "history of object-choices." This history, dependent on the individual personalities and behavior of those who happen to interact with a child, is also socially patterned according to the family structure and prevalent psychological modes of a society.*[35]

Elements of social structure, especially as transmitted through the organization of parenting as well as the features of individual families, are appropriated and transformed internally through unconscious processes and come to influence affective life and psychic structure. A child both takes into itself conflictual relationships as it experiences them, and organizes these experiences of self-in-relationship internally. What is internalized from an ongoing relationship becomes unconscious and persists more or less independent of that original relationship. It may be generalized as a feeling of self-in-relationship and set up as a permanent feature of psychic structure and the experience of self.

Internalization does not mean direct transmission of what is objectively in the child's social world into the unconscious experience of self-in-relationship. Social experiences take on varied psychological meanings depending on the child's feelings of ease, helplessness, dependence, overwhelming love, conflict, and fear. Internalization involves distortions, defenses, and transformations. It depends on the quality of affect in a relationship, on the setting of the relationship, on the physiological or erotic arena in which the relationship occurs, and on the child's maturational stage. The earliest internalizations are preverbal and experienced in a largely somatic manner. When these earliest self-representations and object-representations are recalled, they are recalled on a nonverbal level and psychosomatically.[36]

Internalization is mediated by fantasy and by conflict. A child may internalize a relationship to a physical part of a person (a breast, holding arms, feeding hand) or to psychological aspects of a person (the protecting mother or father, the mother or father who abandons

---

*Psychoanalysis by and large does not adequately deal with the social context of object-relations—their history and institutionalization. But we can use other forms of investigation to explain how the object-relations that become salient in the family have developed.

one). It may involve identification where the self or sense of self is modified, or may involve continuity of the same self or sense of self in relationship to a new or transformed object. Internalizations build upon one another; early internalizations inform and conflict with later ones, producing those internal conflicts and strains which are one foundation of psychic life.

Internalization takes place in and usually transforms an interpersonal situation in which at least two persons contribute to defining the (psychological) situation, and involves the definitions of self-in-relationship of each. A person lives in a multiple object world—in the internal, largely unconscious object world of their psyche which has laid its foundations in the past, in childhood, and in the external, largely conscious world of daily life.

Object worlds interact with and affect one another. Psychoanalysis shows how the unconscious inner world, or worlds, developed during childhood affect the external experiences of adulthood, and how different aspects of psychic life enter into conflict. These inner worlds and intrapsychic conflicts are imposed upon and give meaning to external situations. They affect the kinds of situations in which people put themselves, and their behavior and feelings within them. Adults unconsciously look to recreate, and are often unable to avoid recreating, aspects of their early relationships, especially to the extent that these relationships were unresolved, ambivalent, and repressed. All people are partly preoccupied with internal experience and mental life, partly live their past in the present. This preoccupation, moreover, can either enrich interpersonal relations (and work), or can distort and even destroy them.

The psychoanalytic view of the way intrapsychic structure, conflict, and sense of self affect social interaction holds as well on the social level. Culture and personality theory has shown that early experiences common to members of a particular society contribute to the formation of typical personalities organized around and preoccupied with certain relational issues. To the extent that females and males experience different interpersonal environments as they grow up, feminine and masculine personality will develop differently and be preoccupied with different issues. The structure of the family and family practices create certain differential relational needs and capacities in men and women that contribute to the reproduction of women as mothers.

Conscious aspects of development—the barrage of oughts about having babies and being a good mother from television, toys, storybooks, textbooks, magazines, schools, religion, laws, that Bernard and

Peck and Senderowitz describe so well—reinforce the less intended and unconscious development of orientations and relational capacities that the psychoanalytic account of feminine development describes.

CONSIDERATIONS ON "EVIDENCE"

The evidential basis of psychoanalysis is clinical. It is drawn mainly from the psychoanalysis of adults and children, and consists in interpretations made by analysts of what is said in the analytic situation. Psychoanalysis makes sense of symptoms, talk, behavior, and dreams which are described or arise in the analytic situation. Freud's clinical findings led him to his theories of psychic structure and process and his developmental theory.

Psychoanalytic clinical material (as well as the psychoanalytic "cure") develops in and through a patient's free associations in the constructed social situation of analyst and person being analyzed, in what is called the transference relationship. Ideal-typically, a patient in the analytic situation is presented with minimal social or environmental stimuli. They lie on a couch, cannot see the analyst, and the analyst talks only in response. Thoughts and feelings which come into the mind of the person being analyzed (their associations), their behavior in the analytic situation, and feelings about the analyst are treated as arising out of previous expectations and experiences of the patient (who does not, after all, know the analyst, and who therefore can only impute states, feelings, or actions to the analyst). These thoughts and feelings are "transferred" from those primary relationships that have affected a person's psychological development to the current relationship to their analyst. They express usually unconscious relational preoccupations and issues that help to determine the person's normal behavior and reactions. Psychoanalysis brings to consciousness, in the transference situation, these unconscious mental processes and structures, so that they can be reconnected with the original experiences and feelings that produced them, rather than unconsciously determining reactions and behavior in situations where they are no longer necessary (for psychic self-preservation) or appropriate.

Though psychoanalytic theory derives originally from clinical work, its claims often go well beyond this clinical basis. Thus, Freud has theories about social development, group behavior, and religion,[37] as well as psychobiological theories about drives, the brain, and erotogenic zones. But in contrast to these cultural and biological theories, and even in contrast to observations of children in nontherapeutic settings, psychoanalytic clinical material can be elicited only according to the methodology and mode of interpretation found in the analytic situation.* In my own work, I have found those aspects of the theory that remain closer to the clinical material more useful and persuasive. Thus, I have accepted psychoanalysis as a theory of psychological development, one that tells us how social forms and practices affect the individual, but not as a theory of the genesis of civilization and the nature of culture.

The sociological use of psychoanalytic theory requires consideration of the social setting of psychoanalytic claims. Psychoanalytic approaches to mental process, psychic structure, and development may be universally applicable (I think they are). Certain capacities may be innate to humans and may unfold according to a predetermined biological pattern, and operations like splitting, fantasy, repression, and so forth may be universal human reactions. Social experience may universally enable the development of an identity which comes to constitute the self, affect the nature of psychic structure formation, and organize sexuality.

The content of a description of development which proceeds according to these processes must be separated from its form and mode of operation, however. Psychoanalysts often claim universality for the content they have found, when this is in fact developed in the psychoanalysis of patient populations drawn almost entirely from people living in Western industrial capitalist societies. These people have grown up in one kind of family and one culture. Psychoanalysis assumes that "the family" is nuclear, and that an intense mother-child bond and parenting by the mother alone, possibly aided by one other woman, is natural and even necessary to proper development. There is little recognition of the historical specificity of this family form. Freud assumed a strongly patriarchal family with authority vested in the father, and the theory of the oedipus complex relies on a family of this description. But even since Freud's time, this authority has declined, and we have no evidence that the turn-of-the-century Viennese patriarchal family is universal.

In what follows, I reinterpret both the traditional psychoanalytic theory of feminine (and masculine) development and psychoanalytic clinical case studies in terms of the developing ego and the growth of relational potential and psychological capacities. The story I tell is for the most part not explicit in these accounts, but can be drawn

---

*As Michael Balint puts it, "It is an absolutely necessary condition for any reliable psychoanalytic theory to be based on facts that have been obtained in a setting in which transference is in existence. Transference is the basis of every analytical observation and, we may say, roughly although perhaps not quite exactly, that where there is no transference there is hardly any possibility of analytical theory."[38]

from them. I apply object-relations theory and the theory of the personal ego to our understanding of masculine and feminine development. This development is systemic, an outcome of family structures in which women mother.

The object-relations reformulation has not been brought to bear upon the question of gender. Object-relations theorists (like ego psychologists) have hardly begun to address questions concerning differences in female and male ego development, gender differences in object-relational experiences, and the effect these have on the differential constitution of mental structure and psychic life. Psychoanalysts continue to assume a biological and instinctual basis for the sexual division of labor, gender personality, and heterosexuality. Writing concerned with gender has continued to emphasize oedipal, libidinal issues and sexual orientation, has continued to see women as appendages of their libido, has continued to emphasize feminine sexuality, penis envy, masochism, genitality, frigidity, more than object-relations and ego development. My work here is a step away from that trend. By examining the psychodynamic considerations psychoanalysis introduces, it also can advance the sociological understanding of the organization of gender.

PART II:

The Psychoanalytic Story

4

Early Psychological Development

I once said: "There is no such thing as an infant," meaning, of course, that whenever one finds an infant one finds maternal care, and without maternal care there would be no infant.

D. W. WINNICOTT,
"The Theory of the Parent-Infant Relationship"

The reproduction of mothering begins from the earliest mother-infant relationship in the earliest period of infantile development. This early relationship is basic in three ways. Most important, the basic psychological stance for parenting is founded during this period. Second, people come out of it with the memory of a unique intimacy which they want to recreate. Finally, people's experience of their early relationship to their mother provides a foundation for expectations of women as mothers.

Psychoanalysts have long stressed the importance of the infant's early relationship to its caretaker or caretakers. They argue that the infant's mental as well as physical survival depends on this social environment and relationship. In Western industrial society, biological or adoptive mothers have tended to have nearly exclusive care for infants.* In Western society, also, households have tended to be nuclear, in that there is usually only one married couple with children in any household (and thus only one mother with young children), even though in large numbers of households until recently there were also grown children and nonfamily members like boarders, lodgers, and servants.[1] Caretaking typically has been synonymous with single

---

*In some classes during an earlier period, mothers may have shared or turned over this care to a nurse; in others, they may have been aided by a female relative. Recently, with the increase of labor force participation of mothers with very young children, they are probably aided during some hours by individual or group day-care arrangements.

mothering. The earliest relationship has been a relationship to a *mother*, and the mother-infant bond has been intense and relatively exclusive. Early development, then, consists in the building of a social and emotional relationship between mother and infant, both in the world and within the infantile psyche.

TOTAL DEPENDENCE AND THE NARCISSISTIC RELATION TO REALITY

A human newborn is not guided by instinct, nor does it yet have any of those adaptive ego capacities which enable older humans to act instrumentally.* The infant, "separated from the maternal body too early,"[2] is totally dependent on parental care until it can develop adaptive capacities. Parenting during this period must therefore include acting, in Margaret Mahler's term, as an infant's "external ego,"[3] serving to both mediate and provide its total environment.

The maturation of adaptive ego capacities that can take over from the parent, however, requires the development of an integrated ego, which controls and organizes these functions and behavior.** This maturation, although following innate biological potentialities, requires a particular kind of parental care from the time of the infant's birth, and varies according to the extent to which this care is consistent and free from arbitrariness. Anna Freud suggests that analysts have often attributed inadequate ego capacities to constitutional failing, when these are in fact the result of this early care: "At this early time of life the actions of the mother and her libidinal cathexis and involvement with the child exert a selective growth of some, and hold back, or fail to stimulate and libidinize, the growth of other potentialities. This determines certain basic trends in the child concerning his motility, the earliness or lateness of his verbalization, etc."[5]

The quality of care also conditions the growth of the self and the infant's basic emotional self-image (sense of goodness or badness, allrightness or wrongness). The absence of overwhelming anxiety and

---

*In what follows, my account assumes proper biological maturation. We are physiological creatures, and the development of any psychological stance, any capacity for intention, interpretation of meaning, communication—that is, any nonreflex behavior—requires the maturation of the physiological capacity which enables it.

**My usage here follows Sylvia Brody and Sidney Axelrad. They say, " 'Ego apparatuses' seems to us an unwieldy term because it suggests. . . that the ego is composed of a group of functions or that the functions are part of an ego equipment, whereas it is more precise and economical to say that the ego controls the functions. It also appears to us simpler to think of organic *structures* that allow for the maturation of behavior, and ego *functions* that serve to organize small units of behavior. . . . The term *apparatus* often dulls necessary distinctions between what is organic, what is behavioral, and what is functional."[4]

the presence of continuity—of holding, feeding, and a relatively consistent pattern of interaction—enable the infant to develop what Benedek calls "confidence"[6] and Erik Erikson "basic trust,"[7] constituting, reflexively, a core beginning of self or identity.

The infant's development is totally dependent on parental care, on the fit between its needs and wants and the care its caretaker provides. Fundamental aspects of the person's sense of self develop through this earliest relationship. Michael Balint claims that his or her earliest experience produces a basic stance in the individual "whose influence extends widely, probably over the whole psychobiological structure of the individual, involving in varying degrees both his mind and his body."[8] When there is some major discrepancy in the early phases between needs and (material and psychological) care,* including attention and affection, the person develops a "basic fault," an all-pervasive sense, sustained by enormous anxiety, that something is not right, is lacking in her or him. This sense, which may be covered over by later development and defenses, informs the person's fundamental nature and may be partly irreversible. The area of the basic fault is not conscious or easily talked about (and hence analyzed), because it originates in a preverbal period before the infant is self-consciously social.

Dependence, then, is central to infancy and central to the coming into being of the person. Fairbairn calls the early period "infantile dependence," and describes most infantile psychological activity as a reaction to this feeling of helplessness. As long as the infant cannot get along without its mother—because she acts as external ego, provides holding and nourishment, and is in fact not experienced by the infant as a separate person at all—it will employ techniques which attempt to prevent or deny its mother's departure or separateness. Orality and the oral attitude of incorporation (the fantasy of taking in the mother or her breast) as a primary infantile mode, for instance, is not an inevitable extrapolation from nursing. It is one defensive technique for retaining primary identification (a sense of oneness) when this is being eroded—when the mother is beginning to be experienced as a separate person. Or, for instance, the infant's internalization of aspects of its relationship to its mother which are experienced as bad often results in splitting off and repression of that

*I will use *care* and *caretaker* to refer to the whole primary relationship, and specify when I mean it to refer to the taking care of body needs. A primary relationship does not necessarily develop with anyone who sees to these needs, as we will see. Since I am trying to distinguish between quality of care and interaction and who provides it, I do not want always to use "mothering." Other terms which analysts use—attachment figure, mothering figure—seem too specific. What I mean is relating-one, or interacting-one.

part of the ego involved in this bad relationship. This internalization avoids reacting to these bad aspects in the outside world and possibly driving the infant's mother away. Separateness during this early period threatens not only anxiety at possible loss, but the infant's very sense of existence.

The development away from "absolute dependence" (the infant's original state) through relationship to its caretakers is, according to Winnicott, the same thing as the "coming into being" of the infant as a self.[9] The "ego support which maternal care provides"[10] protects the infant and gives the illusion that the infantile ego is stable and powerful when in fact it is weak. This protection of the infant is necessary for the development of a "true self" or "central self." Threats to the development of a self are a "major anxiety" of the early period (in fact, the "very nature of psychotic anxiety").[11] An infant who experiences this anxiety develops instead a "false self" based on reactions to intrusion.

The distinction between a "true" and "false" self here, although one of degree, is important. Winnicott's "true self" is the ability to experience oneself as an effective emotional and interpersonal agent. By contrast, a person who develops a "false self" develops reactively: "A false self emerges on the pattern of conformity or adaptation to, or else rebellion against, the unsatisfactory environment. Its aim is survival in minimum discomfort, not full vigorous spontaneous creative selfhood. The result is either tame goodness or criminality."*[12]

Physiology and psyche are thus indistinguishable in the newborn. The very continued existence and development of both depends on parental care. Winnicott's and Fairbairn's perceptions are supported by studies of institutionalized children provided with the apparent physical requirements for growth but not provided with emotional relationships.[16] These children may grow up without ego capacities sufficient to establish relationships, may not develop basic motor and verbal skills, may be psychotic, and, in extreme cases, die.

The care that is provided in any society is not randomly assigned or performed. When individual women—mothers—provide parenting, total dependence is on the mother. It is aspects of the relationship

---

*R. D. Laing has worked extensively with this distinction in his early studies, as has Sullivan in his work on the self-system.[13] As many critics of ego psychology have pointed out, Hartmann, in extolling the adaptive ego,[14] and Anna Freud, Edith Jacobson, and others, in claiming that defenses are the basis of ego formation,[15] verge on making a necessary virtue out of what object-relations theorists (Laing, Guntrip, Fairbairn, Winnicott) and nonpsychoanalytic critics of the contemporary family consider a product of specific modes of child care and family organization.

to *her* that are internalized defensively; it is *her* care that must be consistent and reliable; it is *her* absence that produces anxiety. The infant's earliest experience and development is in the context of, and proceeds out of, an interpersonal relationship to its mother.

This relationship, however, is not symmetrical. Mother and child participate in it in radically different ways, though they may be equally involved. At birth, the infant is not only totally dependent but does not differentiate itself cognitively from its environment. It does not differentiate between subject/self and object/other. This means that it does not differentiate the gratifications of its needs and wants. The infant experiences itself as merged or continuous with the world generally, and with its mother or caretakers in particular. Its demands and expectations (not expressed as conscious wants but unconscious and preverbal) flow from this feeling of merging. Analysts call this aspect of the earliest period of life primary identification, aptly emphasizing the infant's object cathexis of someone it does not yet differentiate from its self. Freud claims that primary identification is "not in the first instance the consequence or outcome of an object cathexis; it is a direct and immediate identification and takes place earlier than any object cathexis."[17]

In this period the infant is cognitively narcissistic; its experience of self is an experience of everything else in its world: "What is 'not-I' is libidinally and cognitively perceived as part of 'I.' "[18] Originally, the infant's lack of reality principle—its narcissistic relation to reality—is total. Mahler emphasizes this totality, and calls the first few weeks of life the period of "normal autism,"* "a stage of *absolute* primary narcissism, which is marked by the infant's lack of awareness of a mothering agent."[21] From this state of undifferentiation—between the "I" and the "not-I," and between inside and outside—the infant first begins to differentiate the quality of experience ("pleasurable and good" from "painful and bad"). From this develops a "dim awareness" of the object helping to produce this experience.

After this, the infant reaches a "symbiotic" stage of "mother-child dual unity," a stage reaching its height during the fourth or fifth month, and lasting approximately through the infant's first year.

---

*Psychoanalysts first studied the earliest period of development through adult psychotics—through the "narcissistic neuroses"—and their language concerning this period often retains the imprint of these origins. Mahler has developed her account of normal development from her work with psychotic children. Her use of the label *autism* derives from her observation of "a most striking inability, on the part of the psychotic child, even to see the human object in the outside world, let alone to interact with him as with a separate human entity."[19] She speaks of the normal infant's "state of primitive hallucinatory disorientation."[20]

During this stage, the infant oscillates between perceptions of its mother as separate and as not separate. For the most part, in spite of cognitive perception of separateness, it experiences itself as within a common boundary and fused, physically and psychologically, with its mother. Accordingly, it does not experience gratifications and protections as coming from her.

Thus the infant's cognitive narcissistic relation to objects has conventionally "narcissistic" consequences. Mahler, following Freud, who pointed to the baby's seeming self-sufficiency and lack of attention to the world by referring to " 'His majesty the baby,' "[22] refers to "infantile omnipotence." This omnipotence, she suggests, stems from the sense of the mother's continual presence and hence power in relation to the world for the child. The mother functions, and is experienced, as the child's "external ego." The child maintains this sense of omnipotence by projecting any unpleasurable sensation or perception, of whatever origin, beyond the boundary of its symbiotic unity with its mother. The child behaves as if it were still a unit with its mother; it does not yet knowingly initiate protection, care, or contact.

Alice Balint describes this situation in more forceful terms. The infant's behavior, she says, is functionally egoistic, in that it ignores the interests of the mother: "We come nearest to it with the conception of egoism. It is in fact an *archaic, egoistic* way of loving, originally directed exclusively to the mother; its main characteristic is the complete lack of reality sense in regard to the interests [both libidinal and ego-interests] of the love-object."[23] However, this behavior is not egoistic in our adult sense—conscious ignoring of its mother's interests. It is, rather, "naive egoism," an unintended consequence of the infant's lack of reality sense and perception of its mother as separate.

Thus the early period of total dependence is dual.[24] The infant is totally dependent. When separateness is not a threat, and the mother is feeling totally dependable, total dependence transforms itself into an unproblematic feeling on the part of the infant that this is of course how things should be. Yet the infant is not aware of the other as separate, so experiences dependence only when such separation comes to its attention, through frustration, for instance, or the mother's departure. At this point, it is not only helplessness and object loss which threaten, but also loss of (incipient) self—disintegration.

PRIMARY LOVE

The infant can be emotionally related to an object, even as its self and object representations are merged. Cognitive narcissism does not entail the infant's loving only itself. Several theorists, best represented by Michael and Alice Balint and John Bowlby, have pointed to an emotional cathexis highly charged by its embeddedness in total dependence and in the infant's experience of fusion with its mother and unreflective expectation of everything from her. They argue for a primary and fundamental sociality in the infant.[25] They imply, further, that the infant experiences this primary sociality in our society in relation to its mother. Their theory, like those of other object-relations theorists, has been developed in opposition to an alternate psychoanalytic position derived from Freud and followed by ego psychologists. This Freudian position hypothesizes primary narcissism and primary autoerotism on the part of the infant, and it holds that the earliest object-relation derives from the infant's need for food.

Freud asserts that the infant originally cathects both itself *and* its caretaker: "The human being has originally two sexual objects: himself and the woman who tends him—and in doing so we are postulating a primary narcissism in everyone."[26] The most straightforward reading of this claim is that the infant's libidinal cathexes are shared among all important objects including its incipient self, that "a primary narcissism" is not the same thing as "total primary narcissism." The libido directed toward itself would be the forerunner of later necessary self-esteem and self-love.

However, Freud, in his other writings, and his ego psychology followers have instead taken the position that the infant originally has no cathexis of its environment or of others, but concentrates all its libido on its self (or on its predifferentiated psyche). The infant is generally libidinally narcissistic; hence, the hypothesis of primary narcissism. (Freud and others occasionally speak instead of primary autoerotism, since narcissism in the true sense—libido turned toward the ego—is possible only after an ego has developed.) This Freudian position also holds that the infant seeks only the release of tension from physiologically based drives—operates according to the "pleasure principle." The source of this gratification, whether it is self-induced (burping, elimination) or from a caretaker, is irrelevant to the infant. Accordingly, the child is first drawn from its primary libidinally narcissistic stage because of its need for food. Freud suggests that the infant's ego (self-preservative) instincts direct it to the source of nurturance—the mother's breast—and then to the mother. Thus, in this formulation (in the same essay where he speaks of *two* original sexual objects), the original relation to the mother is for self-preservation and a libidinal attachment develops out of this. The child comes to cathect the mother only because she nourishes and cares for it.*

From this theory Freud derives the notion of an "anaclitic" or "attachment"-type object-relationship—literally "leaning-on." In this case, sexual instincts "lean on" (or depend on) self-preservative instincts.[28] The attachment here is not that of child to mother, but of sexual instincts to ego instincts. More generally, people who choose an "anaclitic object," or love in an anaclitic manner, choose an object modeled on the mother, more broadly as an opposite to the self. Those who choose a "narcissistic" object, or who love narcissistically, choose someone modeled on the self. Freud does not note the contradiction here. He considers anaclitic love—loving someone like the mother—as "complete object love," but expects women to take men for sexual objects.

Michael Balint and Alice Balint, in contrast to Freud and the ego psychologists, have developed a theory of primary love which explains the early cathexis as the (still nonverbal) infant experiences it.[29] According to them, the infant, even while not differentiating itself from its environment or among the objects in its environment, brings from its antenatal state a strong cathexis of this environment. This generalized cathexis very quickly becomes focused on those primary people, or that person, who have been particularly salient in providing gratification and a holding relationship. These people are the objects of primary love, which is object-directed and libidinal, and which exists in rudimentary form from birth.

The hypothesis of primary love holds that infants have a primary need for human contact for itself. Attempts to fulfill this need play a fundamental role in any person's development and eventual psychic makeup. Balint and Fairbairn support this position from logical argument and clinical finding: All extreme narcissism can be explained as a withdrawal from object relations; psychotics are defended against object relationships and not returned to an earlier state; infants need holding and contact from a person who is emotionally there, not simply food and cleaning; how and by whom a want is fulfilled is as important to all their patients as that it is fulfilled.

Alice and Michael Balint propose that primary love is observable only in its breach. If satisfied, it brings forth a quiet sense of well-

*Freud's position, and that followed, according to Bowlby, by Anna Freud, Spitz, and to some extent by Klein, is what Bowlby usefully characterizes as a "secondary drive theory" about the nature of the child's original tie to the mother: "In so far as a baby becomes interested in and attached to a human figure, especially mother, this is the result of the mother's meeting the baby's physiological needs and the baby's learning in due course that she is the source of his gratification."[27]

being and perfect tranquillity in the infant. If not satisfied, it calls forth vehement demands—crying and a violent display of energy. This form of love is totalistic and characterized by naive egoism. The infant's ultimate aim is to *"be loved and satisfied, without being under any obligation to give anything in return."*[*30]

Michael Balint suggests that the character of primary love accounts for both Freud's conception that the infant is originally passive and Klein's that it is driven primarily by innate aggressive drives. Freud did not notice that the tranquillity he noted had a cause, that it resulted from satisfied primary object love. Klein did not notice the tranquillity itself, because such tranquillity is not noticeable in the way that crying and screaming are.

Bowlby argues the same position from his research on the development of attachment behavior in infants and from the evidence of ethology. This evidence, he claims, supports the hypothesis that animals show many responses which are from the first comparatively independent of physiological requirements and which promote social interaction between species members.[**] Bowlby argues for a "primary object clinging" theory: "There is in infants an in-built propensity to be in touch with and to cling to a human being. In this sense there is a 'need' for an object independent of food which is as primary as the 'need' for food and warmth."[32]

I am persuaded by Bowlby's evidence and by Alice and Michael Balint's and Fairbairn's clinical arguments (and by my own informal observations). Freud and many other psychoanalysts incorrectly based their theory of psychological origin on a physiological foundation. This error stemmed from not noticing that much touching and clinging happens in the routine case during feeding, and from observing that the social relations of feeding are important, and that orality and the oral mode can become a focus of severe conflict and a symbol for the whole experience of infancy.[†]

---

*Here, as in much of the theory of the primary relationship, the imputation of such advanced causative and relational thinking to the newborn is not demonstrated. Balint is trying to render in words a behavioral manifestation and nonverbal (to use Fairbairn's term) "libidinal attitude" in the infant.

**Harlow's famous finding that the infant monkeys prefer artificial mothers made of warm soft terrycloth, but without a bottle, to wire mothers with a bottle, is a good example of this.[31]

†As Jacobson puts it, "The memory traces left by any kind of libidinal stimulation and gratification in the past are apt to cluster around this primitive, first, visual mother-image. . . . The images of the orally gratified or deprived self will tend to absorb the engrams of all kinds of physical and emotional stimuli, satisfactions or derivations experienced in any area of the whole self."[33]

Another psychoanalytic claim apparently at odds with Alice and Michael Balint's account derives from the traditional psychoanalytic tendency to understand object-relations as deriving from specific libidinal modes and zones. Benedek, Fairbairn, and to a certain extent Freud and Klein stress the infant's oral relationship to the mother and her breast.* Benedek, for example, suggests that the early mother-infant symbiosis is "oral" and "alimentary" (but that it also concerns more generalized issues of giving and succoring on the part of the mother).[35] Fairbairn claims that in addition to primary identification, infantile dependence consists in an oral-incorporative libidinal attitude.[36] Following Klein he revises Freudian theory to suggest that all neurotic patterns—formerly thought to derive from the stages of development of the component instincts—are at bottom "techniques" for dealing with conflicts in object-relations modeled on early oral conflicts and deriving from the way that objects have been internalized during the oral stage.

Fairbairn in this context does not free analytic theory from libidinal determinism. He simply offers the statement that between infancy and a "mature" object-relationship (which includes a genital and giving libidinal attitude), all object-relationships, both internal and external, are primarily based on the oral incorporative, "taking" mode (concerned with taking and giving, emptying and filling). Infantile dependence here is the same thing as oral dependence, although it is not simply the need for food, but rather the need for relationship to the orally providing mother which is at issue. Fairbairn's grounding in Kleinian theory here is apparent, and probably accounts for his zonal emphasis, in spite of his denial of zonal determinism.**

Alice and Michael Balint argue that their observations of primary love, and their analytic finding that all forms of narcissism have their root in originally disturbed object-relations, replace the hypothesis of primary narcissism and go beyond the subsumption of the primary relationship under the need for food and oral contact:

The oral tendency to incorporate appeared as only one special form of expression of this kind of love which could be present in a more or less clearly

---

*Bowlby characterizes the theories of Benedek and Fairbairn as "primary object seeking" theories[34] in that they hold that there is an inbuilt propensity to relate to the human breast for its own sake and not only as a channel for milk, and that relationship to the mother comes when the infant learns that the mother is related to (or comes with) her breast.

**For Klein also, the early period is defined in terms of the oral relation to the mother's breast and the handling of innate sadistic and aggressive impulses toward it. Klein describes the primary psychological modes of relating also in oral terms—of projection and introjection, of taking and giving, of greed.

marked form. The conception of narcissism did not do justice to the fact that this kind of love was always firmly directed towards an object; the concept of passive object-love (the wish to be loved) was least satisfactory, especially because of the essentially active quality of this kind of love.[37]

It is possible to bring clinical and observational support to either position in these debates. To my mind the support for the object-relations position is stronger. However, each position reflects a fundamentally different conception of human nature—whether human connection and sociality or human isolation and self-centeredness are more in need of psychological and social explanation. Each affects arguments about the basis for human selfishness and human cooperation. For our immediate purposes, these positions imply different starting points from which to describe human development.

THE BEGINNINGS OF SELF AND THE
GROWTH OF OBJECT LOVE

Neither the primary narcissism position nor that of primary orality is typically advanced in an extreme form, however. For Freud, primary narcissism gives way to some object relation in the normal course of development. And for those who stress the primacy of orality or the need for food, the relation to the mother eventually broadens to include nonoral components and an emotional, nonphysiological component. All psychoanalysts agree with Alice Balint that, finally, the infant's active libidinal and emotional "love for the mother" comes to be uniquely important in its own right.

During the early months, the child comes gradually to perceive the mother as separate and as "not-me." This occurs both through physiological maturation and through repeated experiences of the mother's departure. At the same time, it begins to distinguish aspects of maternal care and interaction with its mother, and to be "able to wait for and confidently expect satisfaction."[38] This beginning perception of its mother as separate, in conjunction with the infant's inner experience of continuity in the midst of changing instances and events, forms the basis for its experience of a self.

Thus a person's self, or identity, has a twofold origin and twofold orientation, both of which derive from its early relational experiences. One origin is an inner physical experience of body integrity and a more internal "*core* of the self." This core derives from the infant's inner sensations and emotions, and remains the "central, the crystallization point of the 'feeling of self,' around which a 'sense of identity' will become established."[39] Its development is not inevitable, but depends on the provision of a continuity of experience. As Winnicott puts it, the "inherited potential which is experiencing a continuity of being, and acquiring in its own way and at its own speed a personal psychic reality and a personal body scheme"[40] comes to constitute the infant as a person.[41]

The second origin of the self is through demarcation from the object world. Both ego boundaries (a sense of personal psychological division from the rest of the world) and a bounded body ego (a sense of the permanence of physical separateness and of the predictable boundedness of the body) emerge through this process. The development of the self is relational. Winnicott suggests that a good relationship between infant and caretaker allows the infant to develop a sense of separate self—a self whose existence does not depend on the presence of another—at the same time as it develops a sense of basic relatedness.[42]

Along with the growth of the self and of differentiation from the mother goes the lessening of dependence. At first, the infant is absolutely dependent and, because it does not experience itself as separate, has no way of knowing about maternal care and can do nothing about it. It "is only in a position to gain profit or to suffer disturbance."[43] As absolute dependence lessens, the infant becomes aware of its need for particular aspects of maternal care and relationship, and can relate them to personal impulse. Gradually thereafter, the infant no longer experiences this environment entirely as acting upon it. It develops capacities that enable it to influence and not simply react to the environment.

The mother is no longer interchangeable with any other provider of care once absolute dependence is mitigated. The developing self of the infant comes to cathect its particular mother, with all the intensity and absoluteness of primary love and infantile dependence. While it has attained perceptual and cognitive recognition of the separateness and permanence of objects, it does not yet have an emotional certainty of the mother's permanent being, nor the emotional certainty of being an individuated whole self.* Separation from her during this period, then, brings anxiety that she will not return, and with it a fundamental threat to the infant's still precarious sense of self. Felt dependence increases as real dependence declines.

Unfortunately (from the point of view of the naively egoistic infant) its mother has (and always has had) things to do and interests which take her away from it. Even those analysts who argue that the emotional-libidinal mutuality, or complementarity, in the mother-

---

*What Mahler calls "libidinal object constancy."

infant relationship derives from an instinctual bond between them, recognize that there is an asymmetry in this mutuality. As Benedek puts it, "The infant's need for the mother is absolute, while the mother's for the infant is relative. Accordingly, the participation of primary drives in the symbiotic state has different 'meanings' for mother and child."[44]

Alice Balint discusses the implications for the child of the fact that "maternal love is the *almost* perfect counterpart to love for the mother."[45] According to her, the child experiences from early in life an "instinctual rejection by the mother," which disturbs its naive egoism. This disturbance requires it to face the essential difference between love for the mother and mother-love: Its mother is unique and irreplaceable, whereas it is replaceable—by another infant, by other people, and by other activities.

The reality principle, then, intrudes on an emotional level as well as on the cognitive level. The child comes to recognize that its mother is a separate being with separate interests and activities. The reality principle is in the first instance this separateness: "It is at this point that the rule of the reality sense starts in the emotional life of man."[46] The fact that the infant still needs maternal love is of course crucial. One possible solution—turning the naive egoism to hatred in retaliation for the mother's "rejection"—would simply preserve the same (lack of reality-based) attachment and perpetuate the infant's feeling of vulnerability.[47] This is the reaction that Fairbairn describes: The infant does not simply reject early bad objects but internalizes them in order to both hate and control them.[48] They are internalized, Fairbairn says, because they seem indispensable, and then repressed because they seem intolerable.

This change in its situation is not wholly to the infant's disadvantage. From the point of view of adult life, and from the point of view of that side of the infant that wants independence, total merging and dependence are not so desirable. Merging brings the threat of loss of self or of being devoured as well as the benefit of omnipotence. Discomfort and the loss of merging result both in the further development of the infantile ego and in the growth of a different kind of object love.

As I have indicated, the infant achieves a differentiation of self only insofar as its expectations of primary love are frustrated. If the infant were not frustrated, it would not begin to perceive the other as separate. Frustration and ambivalence generate anxiety. Freud first argued that anxiety triggers the development of ego capacities which can deal with and help to ward off anxiety.[49] Thus, anxiety spurs the development of ego capacities as well as the creation of ego boundaries.*

For my purposes, what is important is that much of this anxiety, conflict, and ambivalence is not generated endogenously through infantile development, but is an infantile reaction to disruptions and discomforts in its relation with its mother. Once again, this primary object-relation has fundamental consequences for infantile experience. For instance, as a defense against ambivalence toward its mother and feelings of helplessness, the infant may split its perception of her and internalize only the negative aspect of their relationship. Or, it may internalize the whole relationship and split and repress only its negative aspect.

Early defenses lead to psychic structure formation. Internalization and repression of negatively experienced aspects of relationships often lead to a splitting off of those aspects of the self that participate in and are committed to these relationships. They are one major early ploy which structures the ego and its object-relationships. They help to demarcate that which will be experienced as external from that which will be experienced as internal. They help to constitute and organize the internal in ways which, once repressed, continue well beyond the period in which they were experienced as necessary.[52] Another defense emerging from frustration which structures the ego is the development of identifications. The child moves from primary identification to identification with aspects of its mother as a differentiated person, as one who frustrates or (seemingly) aggresses. Or it takes over controls previously exercised from without in order to prevent such control.

An important element in the child's introduction to "reality" is its mother's involvement with other people—with its father and possibly with siblings.[53] These people are especially important in the development of a sense of self and in the child's identifications. The sense of boundary, for instance, develops not only in relation to the mother, but also through comparison with others. Father and siblings—or other important people in the caretaker's life who are perceived as coming between caretaker and infant, but do not do primary caretaking themselves—are in some ways more easily differentiated from

*Anna Freud and Brody and Axelrad have made this insight the basis for major analyses of these processes.[50] Bypassing Hartmann's analysis of the development of autonomous ego functions, they argue that the ego as a control apparatus (Brody and Axelrad) and as the seat of character defenses (Anna Freud) is entirely a product of conflict and ambivalence, and of attempts to deal with anxiety. As Brody and Axelrad put it, "The emergence of the affect of anxiety and the beginning of ego formation take place in conjunction with one another, and . . . the two events flow out of a joint process."[51]

the self, because the infant's first association with them involves envy and a perception of self in opposition.

In a nuclear family, a father plays a central role in differentiation for the child. Because he is so involved with the child's mother, his role in the child's later defensive identifications—identification with his power or closeness to the child's mother, for instance—is also crucial. The ego develops partly as a system of defenses against such early experiences.

The child uses its father not only in its differentiation of self. The father also enables more firm differentiation of objects. The infant, as it struggles out of primary identification, is less able to compare itself and its mother, than to compare mother and father, or mother and other important people she relates to. This comparison indicates the mother's boundedness and existence as a separate person. The comparison also reveals the mother's special qualities—finding out that the whole world does not provide care increases her uniqueness in the child's eyes.

Father and other people are important as major constituting elements of the "reality principle" and as people enabling differentiation of self and differentiation among objects. Yet it is the relation to the mother, if she is primary caretaker, which provides the continuity and core of self, and it is primarily the relation to her which must be worked out and transformed during the child's earliest years. This is because the development of a libidinal relationship to the father and oppositional identifications with him are well in advance of his becoming an internal object. The construction of a mental image of him and internalization of aspects of relationship to him lag well behind those of the mother. Therefore, the relation to the father does not become as early involved in the internal organization of psychic structure and the development of fundamental representations of self.[54]

The infant's object-relationships, in addition to the nature of its self, change with its growing recognition of its mother's separateness. The infant uses its developing physical and mental capacities to adapt to her interests and her modes of behavior and thus attempts to retain connection to her.

John Bowlby describes one major form this reaction takes in his account of attachment.[55] Attachment behavior is behavior directed toward binding the mother to the child, especially through the maintenance of physical closeness to her. Children preoccupied with attachment are concerned to keep near their mother and demand a large amount of body contact. Attachment behavior, which begins to develop around six months and reaches its peak around a year to eighteen months, requires experienced separateness, and the ability to perceive and differentiate objects. It is directed toward and grows in relation to a particular person or persons who have provided the most intensive and strong relationship to the infant.

In a conventional nuclear family, the primary attachment figure is almost always the mother, but Bowlby and others are careful to distinguish attachment from dependence. A child is dependent on whoever is providing care at any moment, whereas attachment develops in response to the quality of interaction, and not to having primary physiological needs met. Attachment develops in relation to a particular person who is often, but does not need to be, the child's primary caretaker. This person is the child's primary affectional object, however, and interacts in some intense and strong way with it.

Children may develop attachments to more than one person, to the degree that they have played an important emotional part in the child's life. Thus, kibbutz children are more "attached" to their natural parents than to their nurses, who provide most of their care but do not interact as intensively or exclusively with any single child. Children whose mothers are available all day but are not responsive or sociable with them may become more "attached" to their fathers, who are not frequently available but interact intensively and strongly with these infants when they are around. Moreover, children may be equally attached to mother and father in comparison with strangers.*[56]

Learning to crawl and walk allows the child progressively to control proximity. To separate and return physically to its mother permits it to gain feelings of independence through mastery of its environment and greater equality in relationship.

Emotionally, the child's primary love for its mother, characterized by naive egoism, must usually give way to a different kind of love, which recognizes her as a separate person with separate interests. This attachment to the mother, and the growing ability to take her interests into account, is a prototype for later attachment to other objects experienced as separate. For many analysts, this is the most important aspect of relational development.**

---

*These findings are crucial for those of us who think there are enormous benefits to be gained by everyone—men, women, children—if men and women parent equally and who support researchers arguing for the developmental importance of attachment and the constancy of object relations.

**They use a variety of concepts to describe the same transition. For Winnicott, the transition is "from a relationship to a subjectively conceived object to an object objectively perceived."[57] For Fairbairn, it is a shift from "infantile dependence," characterized by a taking attitude, to "mature dependence," characterized by giving or by mutual cooperation in which the object is seen as a separate person with her or his own in-

This change on the part of the infant is gradual. The infant's experience is a cycle of fusion, separation, and refusion with its mother. It progressively differentiates itself through maturation of its perceptual and cognitive capacities and through the variety of its experiences of relationship.[61] Boundaries grow weak and strong, are sometimes between whole self and whole mother (or other object), sometimes include parts of the mother within the self boundaries or exclude parts of the self as outside. Qualities of the mother are introjected and become part of the self-image and qualities of the self are projected outward. Along with these shifts go equally varied emotional changes, as the child goes from contented oneness, fulfilled primary love, and feelings of trust and omnipotence to feelings of helplessness and ambivalence at the mother's power and her control of satisfactions and proximity; from assertions of separateness, rejection, and distancing of the mother to despair at her distance and fleeing to the mother's arms.

By the end of the first few years, a sense of identity and wholeness, a sense of self in relationship, has emerged. Many of the vicissitudes of these shifts have resolved themselves or disappeared. Others have become permanent elements of the psyche.

A NOTE ON EXCLUSIVE MOTHERING

My account here concerns the person who provides primary care in a particular family structure at a particular time, and not, inevitably, the mother.* It is important to stress this point, because psychoanalytic theory (and accounts influenced by it) assumes an inevitable and necessary *single* mother-infant relationship. Such an assumption implies major limits to changing the social organization of gender. The reason for this psychoanalytic assumption is that psychoanalytic writers, who focus on primary relationships themselves, by and large do not analyze, or even notice, these relationships in the context of a particular historical period and particular social arrangements. They tend rather to reify arrangements that in our society ensure that

---

terests.[58] For Jacobson, the infant develops "true object relationships"—relationships based on a sense of totality of self in relation to totality of separate other.[59] For Alice Balint, the infant must replace egoistic love with "altruistic love"—a "social-reality-based form of love" which takes into account the mother's (or later loved object's) interests. She suggests that "archaic love without reality sense is the form of love of the id," and that "the social-reality-based form of love represents the manner of loving of the ego."[60]

*Whether or not, as I have argued, women have hitherto always been primary caretakers, and whether or not this was once (close to) necessary for species survival.

women who are at least social, and usually biological, mothers do provide almost exclusive care.

Because the mother-infant relationship is so largely nonlinguistic, and because caretaking does include some minimal physiological and psychological requirements, it is easy to assume exclusive parenting by the biological mother. And it is easy to accept such a position, to see this relationship as a less socially constructed relationship than other relationships we engage in or study. There has, moreover, been confusion concerning whose interests exclusive mothering serves. As I argue here, the psychoanalytic theory of the mother-infant relationship confounds an implicit claim for the inevitability and necessity of exclusive mothering by the biological mother with an argument for the necessity of constancy of care and a certain quality of care by some*one* or some few *persons*.

A certain constancy and quality of care are most certainly necessary to achieve basic requirements of being a person (the ability to relate, protection against psychosis, and so on). Psychoanalysts, though, assume and even argue that any dilution of primary care militates against basic ego development.[62] This claim results partly from the kinds of situations of multiple parenting and maternal deprivation that psychoanalysts have chosen to discuss.[63] They have studied infants who have suddenly lost their mother after becoming attached to her; infants in situations when any early change in the parenting person has gone along with great family turmoil and crisis (a maternal death, or sudden breakdown or hospitalization); infants in understaffed foundling homes, war nurseries, and child-care centers for the children of women prisoners; and infants in institutions where there was no attempt to provide constancy of care in any infant's life. The psychoanalytic claim for the necessity of primary care is made in spite of the fact that an astonishing proportion of clinical cases reported by psychoanalysts mention that a nurse cared for the person under discussion in childhood, without noting this as abnormal, as controverting evidence, as an exception to the rule, or as worthy of investigation.[64]

The psychoanalytic claim is also made in spite of the fact that those few studies which do compare children who have been singly and multiply parented, provided other factors are kept constant, do not support their conclusions. Bowlby recognizes in his recent work that household structure makes a difference in the number and nature of attachment figures. He even suggests that attachment may be more secure and intense in an infant who has a few attachment figures rather than only one.[65] Bettye Caldwell reports only slight differences among infants and among mother-infant relationships in cases of rearing by a single mother and cases where the "caretaking role was shared with another female."[66] In a later study, she reports no differences in child-mother and mother-child attachment between infants who spent time in day-care centers and those cared for at home exclusively by their mothers.[67] She points out, moreover, that good day care—several adults and several children together—may be closer to the historical and cross-cultural norm for child-rearing than that which we have come to think natural.*

Child psychiatrist Michael Rutter and psychologist Rudolph Schaffer both summarize studies which evaluate variations in parenting.[68] When one major mothering person shares her duties with a small but stable number of mother-surrogates (when she goes out to work, for instance),[69] when there is shared responsibility for infants with a high degree of continuity (as in the Israeli kibbutzim),[70] when societies have extended households and share child care,[71] there is no evidence that children suffer from such arrangements. Where children do suffer is in multiple parenting situations associated with sudden separation from their primary caretaker, major family crisis or disruption in their life, inadequate interaction with those caretakers they do have, or with so many caretakers that the child cannot form a growing and ongoing bond with a small number of people. In fact, these are the settings in which the psychoanalytic argument was formed. Schaffer affirms, "There is, we must conclude, nothing to indicate any biological need for an exclusive primary bond; nothing to suggest that mothering cannot be shared by several people."[72]

There does not seem to be evidence to demonstrate that exclusive mothering is necessarily better for infants. However, such mothering is "good for society." Exclusive and intensive mothering, as it has been practiced in Western society, does seem to have produced more achievement-oriented men and people with psychologically monogamic tendencies. This form of parenting, along with other reduc-

---

*Although I am obviously more sympathetic to this position than to the traditional psychoanalytic one, I think it only fair to point out that it, like the other, is probably a historical product. Bowlby, Spitz, and others who argued for the importance of the mother were reacting to a variety of makeshift arrangements that had not given children sufficient emotional care during the war and against traditional practices in many child-care institutions. At the same time, I think, they were probably also riding the tide of the feminine mystique and the attempt to return Rosie the Riveter to her home. Currently the economy needs women in the paid labor force, and the women's movement has raised questions about parenting. In this context, today's researchers find that the quality of care is what is important, not that it be provided by a biological mother. Psychoanalysis shifts from emphasizing the breast (which only a biological mother can provide) to the total holding and caring relationship (which can be provided by anyone with appropriate emotional capacities).

tions in the role of kinship and size of household, also contributes to the interchangeability and mobility of families.* It has facilitated several other tendencies in the modern family such as nuclearization and isolation of the household, and the belief that the polity, or the society, has no responsibility for young children.

Another problem with the psychoanalytic account's false universality is its assumption that the type of exclusive care mothers in this society give is, like the fact of exclusivity, natural and inevitable. The account thus reifies the quality of care as well as the gender and number of people who provide it. Psychoanalysts do not often notice** the extensive differences within single mothering that are possible. Infants may be carried on the hip, back, or chest, in a loose sling which molds to the mother's body or directly against her body, or they may be swaddled, left in a cradleboard, or left in a crib except for brief nursing periods. They may sleep alone, with their mother, or with their mother and father. They may be weaned at six months, when they can just begin to experience the cognitive difference between themselves and the outside world, or at two, three, or five, when they can walk and talk. These differences obviously have effects, which, again, have not been treated sufficiently in the psychoanalytic literature.[74] The typical Western industrial arrangement, in which infants are left in cribs except for brief periods of time when they are held and nursed, and in which they are weaned during the first year, provides relatively little contact with caretakers in the world societal spectrum. In a comparative framework, it is not the extreme constancy of care which psychoanalysts assume.

These objections do not invalidate the psychoanalytic account, but they show how to read it. And they indicate its real subject: a socially and historically specific mother-child relationship of a particular intensity and exclusivity and a particular infantile development that this relationship produces. Psychoanalysis does not describe those parenting arrangements that have to be for infants to become people. The account is certainly adequate and accurate for the situation it describes and interprets. It should not be read, however, as prescription or inevitable destiny. An account of the early mother-infant relationship in contemporary Western society reveals the overwhelming importance of the mother in everyone's psychological development, in their sense of self, and in their basic relational stance. It reveals that becoming a person is the same thing as becoming a person in relationship and in social context.

*Whose usefulness Parsons and Goode have described.[73]
**With the exception of periodic generalization about primitive society and longer nursing periods.

5

The Relation to the Mother and the Mothering Relation

The ideal mother has no interests of her own. . . . For all of us it remains self-evident that the interests of mother and child are identical, and it is the generally acknowledged measure of the goodness or badness of the mother how far she really feels this identity of interests.

ALICE BALINT,
"Love for the Mother and Mother Love"

I can give you no idea of the important bearing of this first object upon the choice of every later object, of the profound effects it has, in its transformations and substitutions, in even the remotest regions of our sexual life.

FREUD,
Introductory Lectures

I have argued that the most important feature of early infantile development is that this development occurs *in relation to* another person or persons—in the account I am giving, to a mother. A description of early development, then, is a description of a social and interpersonal relationship, not only of individual psychological or physiological growth. We can now isolate and investigate each side of this relationship: the mother's experience of her child and the child's experience of its mother. An investigation of the child's experience of being mothered shows that fundamental expectations of women as mothers emerge during this period. An investigation of the requirements of mothering and the mothering experience shows that the foundations of parenting capacities emerge during the early period as well.

THE EFFECTS OF EARLY MOTHERING

The character of the infant's early relation to its mother profoundly affects its sense of self, its later object-relationships, and its feelings about its mother and about women in general. The continuity of care enables the infant to develop a self—a sense that "I am." The quality of any particular relationship, however, affects the infant's personality and self-identity. The experience of self concerns *who* "I am" and not simply *that* "I am."

In a society where mothers provide nearly exclusive care and certainly the most meaningful relationship to the infant, the infant develops its sense of self mainly in relation to her. Insofar as the relationship with its mother has continuity, the infant comes to define aspects of its self (affectively and structurally) in relation to internalized representations of aspects of its mother and the perceived quality of her care.[1] (As I have indicated, to call this quality "perceived" brackets the variety of fantasies and transformations the infant may engage in to deal with its anxiety and ambivalence.) For instance, the experience of satisfactory feeding and holding enables the child to develop a sense of loved self in relation to a loving and caring mother. Insofar as aspects of the maternal relationship are unsatisfactory, or such that the infant feels rejected or unloved, it is likely to define itself as rejected, or as someone who drives love away. In this situation, part of infantile attention, and then the infantile ego, remains preoccupied with this negatively experienced internal relationship. Because this situation is unresolvable, and interferes with the ongoing need for love, the infant represses its preoccupation. Part of its definition of self and its affective energy thus splits off experientially from its central self, drawing to an internal object energy and commitment which would otherwise be available for ongoing external relationships. The growing child's psychic structure and sense of self thus comes to consist of unconscious, quasi-independent, divided experiences of self in affective (libidinal-attached, aggressive, angry, ambivalent, helpless-dependent) relation with an inner object world, made up originally of aspects of its relation to its mother.

The infant's mental and physical existence depends on its mother, and the infant comes to feel that it does. It experiences a sense of oneness with her and develops a self only by convincing itself that it is in fact a separate being from her. She is the person whom it loves with egoistic primary love and to whom it becomes attached. She is the person who first imposes on it the demands of reality. Internally she is also important. The infant comes to define itself as a person through its relationship to her, by internalizing the most important aspects of their relationship. Its stance toward itself and the world—its emotions, its quality of self-love (narcissism), or self-hate (depression)—all derive in the first instance from this earliest relationship.

In later life, a person's early relation to her or his mother leads to a preoccupation with issues of primary intimacy and merging. On one psychological level, all people who have experienced primary love and primary identification have some aspect of self that wants to re-create these experiences, and most people try to do so. Freud talks about the turn to religion as an attempt to recreate the lost feeling of oneness.[2] Michael Balint suggests that adult love relationships are an attempt to recreate primary intimacy and merging, and that the "tranquil sense of well-being" is their ultimate goal: "This primary tendency, I shall be loved always, everywhere, in every way, my whole body, my whole being—without any criticism, without the slightest effort on my part—is the final aim of all erotic striving."[3]

The preoccupation with issues of intimacy and merging, however, can also lead to avoidance. Fear of fusion may overwhelm the attraction to it, and fear of loss of a love object may make the experience of love too risky. When a person's early experience tells him or her that only one unique person can provide emotional gratifications— a realistic expectation when they have been intensely and exclusively mothered—the desire to recreate that experience has to be ambivalent.[4]

The earliest relationship and its affective quality inform and interact with all other relationships during development. As Benedek puts it, "It is characteristic of the spiral of human development that the representations of the primary object relationship with the mother are in continual transaction with the representations of all later object relationships according to the age and maturity of the child and the significance of the particular object."[5] In later years as well, the relation to the mother informs a person's internal and external relational stance. Fairbairn considers the child's relationship with its mother as "the foundation upon which all his future relationships with love objects are based."[6] His theory of personality and the clinical evidence he discusses elaborate and support this claim. Even Freud, whose clinical work and theory provide more insight into later relationships, emphasizes the way the mother, through her influence on all subsequent relationships, remains as an important inner object throughout her growing infant's life.[7]

The actual relationship to the mother, and the infant's feelings about her, also remain important. Alice Balint argues that the essence of "love for the mother" is that it is not under the sway of the reality principle.[8] The child does not originally recognize that the mother has or could have any separate interests from it. Therefore, when it finds out that its mother has separate interests, it cannot understand it.

This contrasts to love for the father. The child knows its father from the beginning as a separate being, unless the father provides the same kind of primary relationship and care as the mother.* Thus, it is very much in the nature of things when the father expresses his own interests.** Balint concludes that *"love for the mother is originally a love without a sense of reality, while love and hate for the father—including the Oedipus situation—is under the sway of reality."*

This dichotomy has several consequences. First, the child can develop true hate and true ambivalence more easily in relation to a father whose wants differ from those of his child. The child's reaction to its mother in such a situation is not true hate, but confusion that is part of the failure to recognize the mother's separateness. That children are more obedient to their father results not primarily from any greater strictness on his part, nor from the fact that he represents "society" or "authority" (as Freud and others would have it). Instead, Balint claims, "the child behaves towards the father more in accordance with reality because the archaic foundations of an original, natural identity of interests has never existed in its relation to the father."†[10]

Although the father represents reality to the child, he is at the same time a fantasy figure whose contours, because they are less tied to real object-relational experiences for the child, must be imagined and are often therefore idealized.[12] As a special person who is not consistently present but is clearly important to the mother, he may become an object of attraction, one whose arrival—as a break from the daily routine—is greeted joyously, with particular attention. If the mother has been present during his absence, there is no need for the ambivalence growing from anxiety and remembered loss—classic attachment behavior—which the child often reserves for its mother when she reappears.‡

*Recall, also, Jacobson's claim that comparison of self to father provides major impetus to the original establishment of separateness in the child.

**Folk tales, Balint claims, reflect this dichotomy: "The wicked mother is always the stepmother, while the wicked father is not necessarily the stepfather, and this is true for both son and daughter."[9]

†In another part of her essay, Balint stresses the mother's absolute control over her child's existence, and suggests that society, to defend against this, has transferred rights over children's lives to the father. She concludes, "It argues for the primordiality of the maternal right that it is an informal and private affair of the woman. The paternal right, however, is a social institution."[11] Balint here uncritically appropriates the prevailing opposition between public and domestic life, and even assigns this opposition a "primordial" status. She points correctly, however, to the structural basis of the opposition. We can infer that on the level of fantasy and ideology there has been a trade-off between women's right to exclusivity of primary connection to children and men's to primary access to society.

‡He can also be, as a more familiar person than a stranger, an attachment figure in the traditional sense. His goings and comings, when they leave his child with a

This dual orientation is not just a product of the mother-infant bond, but is created by the typical father's relationship to his infant as well. Dorothy Burlingham has found that fathers see babies not as babies but as potentially grown-up—that they are more likely than mothers to transform their perception of their newborn into fantasies about the adult it will become, and about the things they (father and child) will be able to do together when the infant is much older.[14] She also points to the ways that paternal treatment (which does not start at birth) enforces the infant's separateness, and to the contrast between the father's treating his infant as an object or toy (stimulating and exciting it, lifting and tossing it) and the mother's holding and cuddling it.

Juliet Mitchell, in *Psychoanalysis and Feminism*, speaks to the sociological dynamics of this asymmetry.[15] Drawing on a psychoanalytic model of development, she points out that the early mother-infant relationship, though socially constructed, is experienced by the child as presocial, or nonsocial. It is the person who intervenes in this relationship—the father—who represents culture and society to the child. Hitherto, the social organization of parenting has meant that it is women who represent the nonsocial—or the confusion of biological and social—and men who unambiguously represent society. Mitchell argues that the child's becoming social and enculturated is the same thing as becoming social and enculturated in patriarchal society.

These contrasts between the relation to the mother and the relation to the father are not unique to infancy. Alice Balint argues that people continue not to recognize their mother's interests while developing capacities for "altruistic love" in the process of growing up. They support their egoism, moreover, by idealizing mothers and by the creation of social ideology:

Most men (and women)—even when otherwise quite normal and capable of an "adult," altruistic form of love which acknowledges the interests of the partner—retain towards their own mothers this naive egoistic attitude throughout their lives. For all of us it remains self-evident that the interests of mother and child are identical, and it is the generally acknowledged measure of the goodness or badness of the mother how far she really feels this identity of interests.[16]

---

stranger or relieve it from her or him, can bring traditional attachment reactions—crying, following, and stopping of play when the father leaves, touching, creating proximity, and clinging when he returns.[13] Kotelchuck shows, however, that attachment behavior was stronger toward mothers than fathers, though mothers and fathers were closer to each other than either was to the stranger.

This statement does not mean that mothers have no interests apart from their children—we all know that this kind of overinvestment is "bad" for children. But social commentators, legislators, and most clinicians expect women's interests to enhance their mothering and expect women to want only interests that do so. Psychoanalytic theory is paradigmatic here, as Balint's use of "all of us" suggests.

Psychoanalytic accounts assume that good and desirable maternal care will indeed arise from the mother's "empathy" with her infant and her treatment of it as an extension of herself—as someone whose interests she knows through total regressive identification, or as someone whose interests are absolutely identical with her own. It seems to me* that one explanation for the assumption that the baby's interest is really the maternal interest and for the lack of analytic recognition (in theory, though not in clinical accounts) of possible conflicting interests is that these theories reproduce those infantile expectations of mothers which they describe so well. Anna Freud, as Alice Balint, understands this tendency:

The mother is merely the representation and symbol of inevitable frustration in the oral phase, just as the father in the oedipal phase is the representative of inevitable phallic frustration which gives him his symbolic role of castrator. The new concept of the rejecting mother has to be understood in the same sense as the familiar older concept of the castrating father. . . . Even a most devoted mother finds it a difficult task to fulfill her infant's needs.[17]

Children wish to remain one with their mother, and expect that she will never have different interests from them; yet they define development in terms of growing away from her. In the face of their dependence, lack of certainty of her emotional permanence, fear of merging, and overwhelming love and attachment, a mother looms large and powerful. Several analytic formulations speak to this, and to the way growing children come to experience their mothers. Mothers, they suggest, come to symbolize dependence, regression, passivity, and the lack of adaptation to reality.[17] Turning from mother (and father) represents independence and individuation, progress, activity, and participation in the real world: "It is by turning away from our mother that we finally become, by our different paths, grown men and women."[18]

These attitudes, and the different relations to mother and father, are generalized as people grow up. During most of the early period, gender is not salient to the child (nor does it know gender categories).

*With due recognition of the riskiness of sociology of knowledge evaluations of validity, and especially of the way psychoanalytic "insights" have been used within the field of psychoanalysis itself to discredit opposing theories.

However, the fact that the child's earliest relationship is with a woman becomes exceedingly important for the object-relations of subsequent developmental periods; that women mother and men do not is projected back by the child *after* gender comes to count. Women's early mothering, then, creates specific conscious and unconscious attitudes or expectations in children. Girls and boys expect and assume women's unique capacities for sacrifice, caring, and mothering, and associate women with their own fears of regression and powerlessness. They fantasize more about men, and associate them with idealized virtues and growth.

THE MATERNAL ROLE

Psychoanalysts agree on a clinical conception of what constitutes "good mothering." Because of the infant's absolute physiological and psychological dependence, and the total lack of development of its adaptive ego faculties, the mother must initially make "total environmental provision" for her infant. This provision includes more than simple fulfillment of physiological needs and relief of drives. Maternal care is crucial for the infant's eventual ability to deal with anxiety and to master drives and environment.[19]

If the mother fails to serve as her infant's external ego, and requires the infant to develop adaptive ego capacities before it is ready, or if she controls the environment and serves as an adaptive ego for too long, the infant is prevented from developing capacities to deal with anxiety. Those relational capacities and that sense of being which form the core of the integrative "central ego" do not emerge. The mother must know when and how to begin to allow the child to differentiate from her—to allow some of the functions which she provides to be taken over by the infant's budding adaptive ego capacities.[20] Thus, she must guide her child's separation from her. In the process, she often awakens her child's ambivalence toward her, and unintentionally brings on its rejection of her and of the care which she has provided.

These processes take place on a physical level as well. The infant develops the physical capacity to go away from the mother before it has an operative conception of a psychologically "safe" distance from its mother. Therefore, the mother begins with almost total responsibility for what Bowlby describes as the "maintenance of proximity." Through the child's early years, however, responsibility for the maintenance of proximity shifts, and must shift, to the child. By the end of the child's third year, it maintains proximity as much as does its mother; thereafter the maintenance of proximity is increasingly left to the child.

At every stage of this changeover, the mother must be sensitive to what the child can take and needs. She needs to know both when her child is ready to distance itself and to initiate demands for care, and when it is feeling unable to be distant or separate. This transition can be very difficult because children at this early stage may one minute sense themselves merged with the mother (and require complete anticipatory understanding of their needs), and the next, experience themselves as separate and her as dangerous (if she knows their needs in advance). The mother is caught between engaging in "maternal overprotection" (maintaining primary identification and total dependence too long)[21] and engaging in "maternal deprivation" (making premature demands on her infant's instrumentality).[22] Winnicott describes the magic mother: "If now [when the child begins to be capable of giving signals] she knows too well what the infant needs, this is magic and forms no basis for an object relationship."[23]

The ability to know when and how to relinquish control of her infant, then, is just as important as a mother's initial ability to provide total care. I have described Winnicott's claim that a failure in this latter task leads the infant to develop only reactively. But a mother may fulfill her initial responsibilities to her infant, and then not be able to give up this total control. Winnicott suggests that in such a case, an infant has two options. Either it must remain permanently regressed and merged with its mother, or it must totally reject its mother, even though this mother has, until now, been a "good mother" from the infant's point of view.

The accounts of these theorists suggest that good maternal behavior requires both a constant delicate assessment of infantile needs and wants and an extreme selflessness. Winnicott, for instance, points out that the infant is aware only of the failure of maternal care—of the overwhelming disruptions which result from too little care, and the lack of autonomy and sense of effectiveness which result from too much—and otherwise takes this care for granted. The infant is unaware of satisfactory care from the mother, because it is "almost a continuity of the physiological provisions of the prenatal state."[24] In similar terms, Michael Balint, in his description of primary love, has pointed out that the satisfactions of this love bring well-being and tranquillity and fulfill infantile expectations, whereas the failure to satisfy it brings a violent and intense reaction.*

*Bowlby provides a telling example of the taken-for-grantedness which psychoanalytic theorists expect of and attribute to mothers, in the form of a sentimental chapter epigraph:

Analysts do not consider their prescriptions difficult for most "normal" mothers to fulfill. This is because of their view of the special nature of mothers, mothering, and mother-infant relationships. (Mothering, effuses Winnicott, is an "extraordinary condition which is almost like an illness, though it is very much a sign of health."[26]) They suggest that women get gratification from and fulfill maternal role expectations at a fundamentally different level of experience from that of any other human relationship. Mothering requires and elicits relational capacities which are unique. Analysts emphasize that the mother-infant relationship provides gratification to mother as well as infant, and that good-enough mothering is done through empathy, primary identification, and experiencing the infant as continuous with the self and not separate.

Analysts stress different aspects of mutuality in the mother-infant relationship. Benedek, for instance, claims that the relationship centers on oral and alimentary psychological issues, fantasies, modes of relating—for *both* mother and infant.[27] Alice Balint makes the more general claim that the infant's lack of reality principle and its primary love toward its mother is reciprocated by the mother. Mother and infant are instinctually interdependent: "The two parties in this relation are libidinously equal. Libidinally the mother is receiver and giver to the same extent as her child."[28] This *"interdependence of the reciprocal instinctual aims"*[29] enables the infant's primary love based on naive egoism to work. It can afford to ignore possible opposing interests on the part of the mother because, according to Balint, mother's and baby's interests are completely complementary. For the mother, also, the interests of her baby are the same as her own, and gratification is always mutual: "What is good for one is right for the other also."[30] Furthermore, both love for the mother and mother love are remote from reality: "Just as the child does not recognize the separate identity of the mother, so the mother looks upon her child as a part of herself whose interests are identical with her own."[31]

Women get gratification from caring for an infant, analysts generally suggest, because they experience either oneness with their infant or because they experience it as an extension of themselves. The basis for "good-enough" early mothering is "maternal empathy" with her infant, coming from total identification with it rather than (more intellectual) "understanding of what is or could be verbally expressed" about infantile needs:

They must go free/Like fishes in the sea
Or starlings in the skies/Whilst you remain
The Shore where casually they come again.[25]

The important thing, in my view, is that the mother through identification of herself with the infant knows what the infant feels like and so is able to provide almost exactly what the infant needs in the way of holding and in the provision of an environment generally. Without such identification I consider that she is not able to provide what the infant needs at the beginning, which is a *live adaptation to the infant's needs*.[32]

Christine Olden claims that the mother, during her infant's first few weeks, "gives herself up and becomes one with him."[33] The mother feels "a new kind of love for the child who is at once her own self and yet separate and outside, [and] concentrates entirely on the infant."[34] For these theorists, gratification of the infant serves the same psychological purpose as self-gratification, because the infant is one with the self of the mother and their interests are therefore identical.

Many mothers and infants are mutually gratified through their relationship, and many mothers enjoy taking care of their infants. Still, when we say that the mother-infant relationship has been exclusive, mutual, and special, this means different things from the child's point of view than from its mother's.

For the child, the relation to its mother *is* its social experience and guarantees its psychological and physical development. The infant relates to its mother, in reality and in fantasy, or it does not relate. For the mother, the relationship has a *quality* of exclusivity and mutuality, in that it does not include other people and because it is different from relationships to adults. However, a mother also participates in her family and in the rest of the community and society. She experiences herself as a socialized adult member of this society and knows the meanings of family, child-rearing, and mothering within it. She usually participates in a marriage with a deep sexual division of labor, in which she is financially dependent,* and she expects her husband to be dominant. Her mothering, then, is informed by her relationship to her husband, her experience of financial dependence, her expectations of marital inequality, and her expectations about gender roles.

For sociologists Parsons and Bales, the asymmetry in this situation is crucial.[35] It typifies the asymmetry which founds their theory of development. For them, the mother represents a "superordinate" social system as well as participating in the mother-child social system. As a representative of this larger system, and with encouragement from it, she socializes the child into it, by denying reciprocity. The child's integration into larger social units as it grows up proceeds ac-

---

*This is almost inevitable in contemporary marriage, given the income and earnings inequality of men and women.

cording to the same principle, in which the socializing agent plays a part in two systems and uses this dual participation to move the child from one to the other.

The analytic account, by contrast, tends to see only the psychological level of the maternal role. Even at this level, only Benedek and Alice Balint at least mention a potential psychological asymmetry in the mother-infant mutuality and suggest that this lack of symmetry requires the infant to emerge from its naive egoism. It is not surprising that only women analysts mention this.* Male theorists (Bowlby and Winnicott are cases in point) ignore the mother's involvements outside of her relationship to her infant and her possible interest in mitigating its intensity. Instead, they contrast the infant's moves toward differentiation and separation to the mother's attempts to retain symbiosis.**

Though the analytic formulation is extreme in its lack of recognition of the differences in commitment, the analysts nevertheless point to important characteristics of the mother-infant relationship and to necessary maternal (or parental) capacities. The particular characteristics they point to, moreover, indicate when, in human development, parental capacities first arise. Empathy, the sense of the infant as an extension of the self, reciprocated primary love, primary identification and sense of oneness, orality, mutual mother-infant attachment, are part of both contemporary mother-infant relationships and, as my account of early development makes clear, relational states of the incipient infantile ego.

Analysts explain how some adults—that is, mothers—come to reexperience these originally infantile states. They imply that empathy, or experiencing the child as continuous with the self, may grow partially out of the experience of pregnancy and nursing (though nonbiological mothers can be fine parents). However, their major argument is that (with or without pregnancy and nursing) the ability to parent an infant derives from having experienced this kind of relationship oneself as a child and being able to regress—while remaining adult—to the psychological state of that experience.

On a theoretical level, then, *anyone*—boy or girl—who has participated in a "good-enough" mother-infant relationship has the rela-

---

*Nor that a woman sociologist chose to make Benedek's insight the take-off point for an insightful article on parenthood.[36]

**It is hard to tell whether Parsons and Bales fit this masculine pattern. They see personality in terms of social roles and not enough in terms of psychological conceptions of personality. Thus, the theory does not indicate *how* mothers *experience* their participation in the two levels of social system which they describe.

tional basis of the capacity for parenting. Benedek equates the total early infantile experience with preparedness for parenting:

When the infant integrates the memory traces of gratified needs with his developing confidence in his mother, he implants the confidence in his well-being, in his thriving good self. In contrast, with the memory traces of frus-trating experiences he introjects the frustrating mother as "bad mother" and himself as crying and frustrated, as "bad self." Thus he inculcates into his psychic structure the core of ambivalence. These primary ego structures, con-fidence and the core of ambivalence, originating in the rudimentary emo-tional experiences of early infancy, are significant for the infant of either sex. They determine the child's further relationships with his mother and through it, to a great extent, his personality. A generation later these primary ego structures can be recognized as motivating factors in the parental attitudes of the individual.[37]

This early experience does not differentiate by gender:

The primary drive organization of the oral phase, the prerequisite and con-sequence of the metabolic needs which sustain growth, maturation, and lead to the differentiation of the reproductive function, is the origin of parental tendencies, of motherliness and fatherliness. It should then be emphasized, as is evident, that the primary drive organization of the oral phase has no sex differentiation; it is asexual.[38]

Empirically, however, analysts assume that women will parent, and that the parenting capacities laid down in people of *both* genders will be called up in *women only*. In some places, for instance, Benedek assumes women's mothering and claims that the *mother's* experiencing of her relationship to her infant as oral and alimentary originates in the oral relationship which she had with her own mother.[39] Winnicott in the same vein bypasses the issue of gender and emphasizes that regression to infantile feelings and the experience of oneness enables a *mother* to empathize with her infant.[40]

There is a contradiction here. All people have the relational basis for parenting if they themselves are parented. Yet in spite of this, women—and not men—continue to provide parental (we call it "ma-ternal") care. What happens to potential parenting capacities in males?

Because most analysts assume that physiology explains women's child-care responsibilities ("It is women's biological destiny to bear and deliver, to nurse and to rear children"), they do not generally ask this question. Those that do provide inadequate answers. Some who argue that the foundations for parenting are laid down in both boys and girls in the earliest relation to the mother assume subsequent physiological differentiation. Benedek, for instance, speaks of "innate maleness" and "innate femaleness," though she never explains what these consist in.[41] Others hypothesize physiological bases for the *wish for a child*—Kestenberg's vaginal sensations[42] or Freud's symbolic penis-baby equation (when a girl cannot get a penis, she substitutes the wish for a child)[43]—but do not relate these to *maternal capacities*. As I have argued here, physiology is not a sufficient explanation for women's current mothering role and capacities.

Another prevalent assumption is that girls naturally identify with their mother as they grow up, and that this makes them into mothers.[44] How and why this identification happens are left vague and unanalyzed. But as cognitive psychologists have shown, children identify with a parent of a particular gender because they have already learned that this is how to be appropriately feminine or masculine.[45] Identification is a product of conscious teaching about gender differences, that is, a learning phenomenon. Psychoanalytic clinical studies illustrate particularly vividly how parents teach children about what biological gender differences are supposed to mean, and what their biology is supposed to entail for their adult role. The identification they describe takes place in a socially constructed, heavily value-laden context. Identification and learning clearly goes on, and helps to make women into mothers, but these processes are not sufficient.

Finally, analysts describe in persuasive clinical detail how the "wish for a child"[46] or "the need to be pregnant"[47] develops in *specific* women out of their early relationship to their own mother, and especially out of the particular contradictions and conflicts within this. Their accounts by implication claim to show how *women in general* come to wish for a child, or need to be pregnant. Being a parent, they argue, calls up a *woman's* early experience and relationship to *her* own mother.

Both the form (primary identification, primary love, and so forth) and the content of a mother's mutual relation with her infant grow out of her early experience. Her mothering experience and expectations are informed (for the most part unconsciously) by her own childhood history, and her current and past relationships, both external and internal, to her own natal family. This history and these relationships have over the course of her development come to have their own independent psychological reality. A mother's regression to early relational stances in the course of mothering activates these early constituted internal object-relationships, defenses, and conflicts. Thus, a complex object world affects and gives character to even the most seemingly psychologically private and exclusive mother-infant relationship.

Klein discusses the dynamics of maternal regression and the identifications and interactions it entails.[48] She speaks of the mother's multiple identifications and the variety of internal object-relationships which go into her mothering. A mother identifies with her own mother (or with the mother she wishes she had) and tries to provide nurturant care for the child. At the same time, she reexperiences herself as a cared-for child, thus sharing with her child the possession of a good mother.

Both her identification with her mother and her reexperience of self as child may lead to conflict over those particular issues from a mother's own childhood which remain unresolved.[49] One mother, for instance, may delight in the earliest mothering experience, when she can attend to her infant's early needs, and then withdraw and be rejecting when the child becomes more independent. Another may behave in exactly the reverse manner. Both alternatives depend on the associations and (unconscious) memories and feelings related to these issues in each's own infancy. Motherhood may be a (fantasied) attempt to make reparation to a mother's own mother for the injuries she did (also in fantasy) to her mother's children (her siblings). Alternatively, it may be a way to get back at her mother for (fantasied) injuries done by her mother to her.

The contradiction remains. The experiences these accounts describe are experiences that children of both genders have. Yet none of them explains why the wishes and conflicts which contribute to the sense of self as parent, the desire to be a parent, and parenting capacities and practices become activated in women and not in men. They do not examine the dynamic or outcome of these same experiences, wishes, and conflicts in boys.*

CONCLUSIONS

Psychoanalytic theory describes a mother-infant relationship of particular quality, and argues that the foundation for the mother's participation in such a relationship is laid in her early relationship to her own mother. But the foundation for parenting is laid in a *boy's* early relationship to *his* mother as well. The early relationship generates a basic relational stance and creates potential parenting capacities in everyone who has been mothered, and a desire to recreate such a relationship as well. My account of the early mother-infant relation-

---

*Jacobson discusses the development of a "wish for a child" in boys, but in this case treats it as the product of special complications and conflicts. In her clinical case study of the development of the wish for a child in a girl, the complications and conflicts she describes are equally severe, and she describes an enormous amount of explicit teaching about sex differences which obviously influenced the way they got resolved, that is, in the wish for a child. Yet she treats this outcome as entirely unproblematic.[50]

ship in Western industrial society reveals the conscious and unconscious attitudes and expectations that all people—male and female —have of their mothers in particular, and of women in general. These expectations build into the reproduction of mothering, but expectations are not enough to explain or assure it.

Because neither the theory nor the clinical accounts directly ask why women, and not men, parent, they cannot provide a complete answer. The clinical focus on specific relational issues and unconscious conflicts, however, and specific elements in a mother's early relationship to her own mother, points us in the right direction, beyond vague appeals to identification and unsubstantiated biological assumptions.

In what follows, I argue that the relationship to the mother differs in systematic ways for boys and girls, beginning in the earliest period. The development of mothering in girls—and not in boys—results from differential object-relational experiences, and the ways these are internalized and organized. Development in the infantile period and particularly the emergence and resolution of the oedipus complex entail different psychological reactions, needs, and experiences, which cut off or curtail relational possibilities for parenting in boys, and keep them open and extend them in girls.

6

Gender Differences in the Preoedipal Period

We knew, of course, that there had been a preliminary stage of attachment to the mother, but we did not know that it could be so rich in content and so long-lasting, and could leave behind so many opportunities or fixations and dispositions. During this time the girl's father is only a troublesome rival; in some cases the attachment to her mother lasts beyond the fourth year of life. Almost everything that we find later in her relation to her father was already present in this earlier attachment and has been transferred subsequently on to her father. In short, we get an impression that we cannot understand women unless we appreciate this phase of their pre-Oedipus attachment to their mother. FREUD,
"Femininity"

Our insight into this early pre-Oedipus phase in girls comes to us as a surprise, like the discovery, in another field, of the Minoan-Mycenaen civilization behind the civilization of Greece. FREUD,
"Female Sexuality"

Family structure produces crucial differentiating experiences between the sexes in oedipal object-relations and in the way these are psychologically appropriated, internalized, and transformed. Mothers are and have been the child's primary caretaker, socializer, and inner object; fathers are secondary objects for boys and girls. My interpretation of the oedipus complex, from a perspective centered on object-relations, shows that these basic features of family structure entail varied modes of differentiation for the ego and its internalized object-relations and lead to the development of different relational capacities for girls and boys.

The feminine oedipus complex is not simply a transfer of affection from mother to father and a giving up of mother. Rather, psychoanalytic research demonstrates the continued importance of a girl's external and internal relation to her mother, and the way her relation to her father is added to this. This process entails a relational complexity in feminine self-definition and personality which is not characteristic of masculine self-definition or personality. Relational capacities that are curtailed in boys as a result of the masculine oedipus complex are sustained in girls.

Because of their mothering by women, girls come to experience themselves as less separate than boys, as having more permeable ego boundaries. Girls come to define themselves more in relation to others. Their internalized object-relational structure becomes more complex, with more ongoing issues. These personality features are reflected in superego development.

My investigation, then, does not focus on issues at the center of the traditional psychoanalytic account of the oedipus complex—superego formation, gender identity, the attainment of gender role expectations, differential valuations of the sexes, and the genesis of sexual orientation. It takes other issues as equally central. I will be concerned with traditional issues only insofar as my analysis of oedipal object-relations of boys and girls sheds new insight on the different nature of male and female heterosexual object-relations.

My interpretation of the feminine oedipus complex relies for the most part on the early psychoanalytic account of female development. Aspects of this account of female psychology, sexuality, and development have been criticized and shown to be inaccurate or limited.[1] However, those elements of it which I emphasize—the clinically derived description and interpretation of experienced female object-relations in a nuclear family in which women mother and fathers are more remote figures to the children—have not been subjected to substantial revision within the psychoanalytic tradition nor criticism from without, and remain valid.*

EARLY PSYCHOANALYTIC FORMULATIONS

Freud's account of the boy's oedipus complex is relatively simple and straightforward.[2] In response to, or in collaboration with, his heterosexual mother, a boy's preoedipal attachment to her becomes charged with phallic/sexual overtones. He comes to see his father as a rival for his mother's love and wishes to replace him. He fantasizes taking his father's penis, murdering or castrating him. He fears retaliation, and specifically castration, by his father for these wishes; thus he experiences a conflict between his self-love (narcissistic interest in his penis

---

*My reading of this account, however, as a description and interpretation of family structure and its effects in male-dominant industrial capitalist society would not be accepted by all psychoanalysts.

and body integrity) and his love for his mother (libidinal cathexis). As a result, he gives up his heterosexual attachment to his mother, radically repressing and denying his feelings toward her. (These feelings are not only repressed, but also are partly expressed in "aim-inhibited" modes, in affectionate feelings and sublimated activities.) At the same time, a "successful" resolution of his oedipus complex requires that he remain heterosexual. Therefore, he is supposed to detach his heterosexual orientation from his mother, so that when he grows up he can reattach it to some other woman.

He receives a reward for his self-sacrifice, in addition to his avoidance of punishment. The carrot of the masculine oedipus complex is identification with his father, and the superiority of masculine identification and prerogatives over feminine (if the threat of castration is the stick). A new psychic integration appears in place of the oedipus complex, as the boy's ego is modified and transformed through the incorporation of paternal prohibitions to form his superego, and as he substitutes a general sexual orientation for the specific attachment to his mother (this attachment is composed of both the remainders of his infantile love and his newer sexualized and genitalized attachment).

Freud originally believed that the object-relational configurations of the feminine and masculine oedipus complexes were completely symmetrical. According to this view, little girls at around age three, and as genital component drives become important, discover that they do not have a penis.[3] They automatically think they are castrated and inferior, and experience their lack as a wound to their self-esteem (a narcissistic wound). As Freud says, they "fall a victim to envy for the penis."[4] They also develop contempt for others, like their mother, who do not have penises and at the same time blame her for their own atrophied state. This contempt, plus their anger at her, leads them to turn away in anger and hostility from their mother, who has been their first love object. They turn to their father, who has a penis and might provide them with this much desired appendage. They give up a previously active sexuality for passive sexuality in relation to him. Finally, they change from wanting a penis from their father to wanting a child from him, through an unconscious symbolic equation of penis and child.

At the same time, their mother becomes a rival because she has sexual access to and possession of their father. The female oedipus complex appears only when the mother has become a rival and the father a desired object. It consists in love for the father and rivalry with the mother, and is symmetrically opposed to the male oedipus complex. Heterosexual orientation is thus an oedipal outcome for girls as well as for boys. (Freud also speaks to differences in oedipal outcome—the girl does not need to give up her oedipus stance in the same manner as the boy, since she no longer has castration to fear.*)

THE DISCOVERY OF THE
PREOEDIPAL MOTHER-DAUGHTER RELATIONSHIP

Jeanne Lampl-de Groot described two clinical examples of a "negative oedipus complex" in girls, in which they cathected their mothers and saw their fathers as rivals.[5] This fundamentally disrupted Freud's original postulation of oedipal symmetry. Analysts continued to hold to much of Freud's original account, but Lampl-de Groot's discovery also substantially modified views of feminine oedipal object-relations, and turned attention to the unique qualities of the preoedipal mother-daughter relationship.

In Freud's original view, a daughter sees her mother only as someone who deprives her first of milk, then of sexual gratification, finally of a penis. A mother is seen as initiating only rivalry and hostility. In the light of Lampl-de Groot's finding, Freud reviewed his own clinical experience. He came to agree with her that the preoedipal phase was central in feminine development, that daughters, just as sons, begin life attached exclusively to their mothers.[6] Children were not originally bisexual, though they were potentially so. They were, rather, gynesexual, or matrisexual.

The discovery of the preoedipal mother-daughter relationship required a general reformulation of psychoanalytic theory and its understanding of the development of object-relations. Freud had claimed that the oedipus complex was the nucleus of neurosis and the basis of personality formation, and he was now led to revise radically this claim.** Freud compares his new insight into the preoedipal phase of feminine development to a similarly layered historical discovery. Just as the Minoan-Mycenaean civilization underlies and explains the origins and form of classical Greece, so the preoedipal phase in girls underlies and explains the origins and form of the feminine oedipus complex.

Freud points to three major features of a girl's preoedipal phase and her relationship to her mother during this phase. First, her

---

*Freud is especially interested in the implication of this difference for feminine superego formation, but his account is not directly relevant here. Further on I examine the biases inherent in his formulation and some of its logical and clinical contradictions.

**Since that time, major contributions to the theory of development have been concerned much more with the preoedipal years—the early mother-infant relationship and early infantile development. Few analysts now hold that the oedipus complex is the *nucleus* of neurosis, though they might say it contributes to its final *form*.

preoedipal attachment to her mother lasts through all three periods of infantile sexuality, often well into her fourth or fifth year. Second, this attachment is dramatically intense and ambivalent. Finally, Freud reports a surprising finding from his analysis of women with a strong attachment to their father: This strong attachment has been preceded by an equally strong and passionate attachment to their mother. More generally, he finds that a woman's preoedipal attachment to her mother largely determines both her subsequent oedipal attachment to her father and her later relationship to men in general.

A girl's preoedipal relationship to her mother and her entrance into the oedipus situation contrast to those of a boy. Freud and Brunswick claim that a boy's phase of preoedipal mother-attachment is much shorter than a girl's, that he moves earlier into an oedipal attachment.[7] What this means is not immediately apparent. If a girl retains a long preoedipal attachment to her mother, and if a boy's oedipal attachment is to his mother, then both boy and girl remain attached to their mother throughout the period of childhood sexuality. Brunswick suggests further that both boy and girl pass from a period of "passive" attachment to their mother to one of "active" attachment to her. On one level, then, it looks as though both boy and girl maintain similar attachments to their mother, their first love object, throughout most of their early years.

On another level, however, these attachments to the mother are very different—the retention of dichotomous formulations is necessary. On the basis of Freud's account and a later more extended discussion by Helene Deutsch in the *Psychology of Women*,[8] one can argue that the *nature* of the attachment is different. A boy's relation to his mother soon becomes focused on competitive issues of possession and phallic-sexual oppositeness (or complementarity) to her. The relation becomes embedded in triangular conflict as a boy becomes preoccupied with his father as a rival. A girl, by contrast, remains preoccupied for a long time with her mother alone. She experiences a continuation of the two-person relationship of infancy. Playing with dolls during this period, for instance, not only expresses "the *active* side of [the girl's] femininity" but also "is probably evidence of the exclusiveness of her attachment to her mother, with complete neglect of her father-object."[9]

The issue here is the father as an internal object, or object of conflict and ambivalence. As we saw in the previous chapters, fathers often become external attachment figures for children of both genders during their preoedipal years. But the intensity and exclusivity of the relationship is much less than with a mother, and fathers are from the outset separate people and "special." As a result, representations of the father relationship do not become so internalized and subject to ambivalence, repression, and splitting of good and bad aspects, nor so determining of the person's identity and sense of self, as do representations of the relationship to a mother. As a boy moves into oedipal attachment and phallic-possessive competition, and as he tries to consolidate his masculine identity, his father does become an object of his ambivalence. At this time, the girl's intense ambivalent attachment remains with her mother.

The content of a girl's attachment to her mother differs from a boy's precisely in that it is not at this time oedipal (sexualized, focused on possession, which means focused on someone clearly different and opposite). The preoedipal attachment of daughter to mother continues to be concerned with early mother-infant relational issues. It sustains the mother-infant exclusivity and the intensity, ambivalence, and boundary confusion of the child still preoccupied with issues of dependence and individuation. By contrast, the boy's "active attachment" to his mother expresses his sense of difference from and masculine oppositeness to her, in addition to being embedded in the oedipal triangle. It helps him to differentiate himself from his mother, and his mother from his father.

The use of two different concepts for the early relationship between mother and daughter (mother-infant relationship, with reference to issues of development; preoedipal, with reference to the girl's relation to her mother) obscures the convergence of the two processes. The terminological distinction is an artifact of the emergence of different aspects of psychoanalytic theory at different times ("preoedipal" emerged early in investigating the feminine oedipus complex; "mother-infant relationship" emerged later, as research focused on the early developmental stage as a distinct period).

There is analytic agreement that the preoedipal period is of different length in girls and boys. There is also an agreed on, if undeveloped, formulation concerning those gender differences in the nature and quality of the preoedipal mother-child relationship I have been discussing. This claim stands as an empirical finding with substantial descriptive and interpretive clinical support. The implications of these early developmental tendencies for psychological gender differences also stand on their own (Freud's claim that the early attachment to her mother affects a girl's attachment to her father and men, for instance). But Freud and his colleagues do not explain how such differences come about.

The different length and quality of the preoedipal period in boys and girls are rooted in women's mothering, specifically in the fact that a mother is of the same gender as her daughter and of a different gender from her son. This leads to her experiencing and treating them differently. I do not mean this as a biological claim. I am using *gender* here to stand for the mother's particular psychic structure and relational sense, for her (probable) heterosexuality, and for her conscious and unconscious acceptance of the ideology, meanings, and expectations that go into being a gendered member of our society and understanding what gender means. Being a grown woman and mother also means having been the daughter of a mother, which affects the nature of her motherliness and quality of her mothering.

It is not easy to prove that mothers treat and experience differently preoedipal boys and girls. Maccoby and Jacklin, in the currently definitive review of the observational and experimental literature of psychology on sex differences, claim that the behavioral evidence— based on interviews of parents and observations of social science researchers—indicates little differential treatment.*[10] They report that most studies of children in the first four or five years concerning parent-child interaction, parental warmth, reaction to dependence or independence, and amount of praise and positive feedback show no difference according to the gender of the child.** They also report no gender difference in proximity-seeking, touching, and resistance to separation from parents or caretakers in young children.† These studies measure observable behaviors, which can be coded, counted and replicated, and they take for proof of gender difference only statistically significant findings.

Yet a report summarizing the proceedings of a panel on the psychology of women at the annual meeting of the American Psychoan-

---

*Rather, the studies they report produce such inconsistent findings that one could support almost any hypothesis about gender differences in treatment by selective references.

**On many measures, however, they find that where studies do report a gender difference, it tends to be in the same direction. For instance, where mothers do talk more to children of one gender, it turns out to be to girls; where they touch, hold, or spend more time feeding, it tends to be boys.

†The arousal of gross motor behavior, punishment, and pressure against what is thought to be gender-inappropriate behavior all tend to happen more to boys. I am wary of this seemingly scientific investigation. The message of Maccoby and Jacklin's book is that one cannot find any consistent gender differences anywhere if one looks at the "hard scientific facts." As support against biological arguments for gender differences, these findings may do the trick. But I was left feeling a little as if a magic disappearing trick had been performed. All the experiences of being manipulated, channeled, and restricted which women and men have been commenting on, and which they have felt deeply and continuously, were suddenly figments of our imagination.

alytic Association in 1976 claims that "there is increasing evidence of distinction between the mother's basic attitudes and handling of her boy and girl children starting from the earliest days and continuing thereafter."[11] This surprising contradiction suggests that academic psychologists and psychoanalysts must be looking at quite different things. The kinds of differences I am postulating (and that psychoanalysts are beginning to find) are differences of nuance, tone, quality. These differences are revealed in a small range of analytic clinical case material as well as in some cultural research. These cases give us insight into the subtleties of mothers' differential treatment and experiencing of sons and daughters and of the differential development that results.*

PREOEDIPAL MOTHER-DAUGHTER RELATIONSHIPS: THE CLINICAL PICTURE

Many psychoanalysts report cases of particular kinds of mother-infant relationships which throw light on differences in the preoedipal mother-daughter and mother-son relationship.**[13] Fliess presents the psychopathological extreme and also the most numerous examples, unintentionally showing the way a certain sort of psychotic mother inflicts her pathology predominantly on daughters.[14] The mothers of his patients carried to an extreme that which is considered to be, or is described as, "normal" in the preoedipal mother-infant relationship. His account is significant because, having chosen to focus on a certain kind of neurotic patient and accompanying early patient-mother relationship, it turns out that an overwhelmingly large percentage (almost eight times as many) of his case illustrations are women. His explanation for this disproportion is that "the picture is more easily recognized in the female because of the naturally longer duration of the preoedipal phase."[15] This explanation is tautological, because he is talking about precisely those features of maternal be-

---

*Not to give up on the academic psychology findings completely, we know that some forms of similar maternal behavior may produce different effects on sons and daughters. For instance, Kagan and Freeman and Crandall report that maternal criticism and lack of nurturance correlate with intellectual achievement in girls but the opposite behavior does in boys. Maternal overprotection and affection predict later conformity in boys, whereas conformity in girls is predicted by excessive severity of discipline and restrictiveness.[12] Therefore, the similarity in maternal behavior which Maccoby and Jacklin report may not have similar effects on feminine and masculine development.

**In what follows, I rely on extensive accounting and quoting. This is necessary because a simple assertion of the distinctions that I wish to demonstrate would not be persuasive without the clinical illustrations.

havior which in a less extreme but similar form create and maintain a preoedipal relationship in the normal case.

The mothers that Fliess describes were "asymbiotic" during the period when their child needed symbiosis and experienced oneness with them. They were unable to participate empathetically in a relationship to their child. However, from the time that these daughters began to differentiate themselves mentally from their mothers and to practice physical separation, these mothers became "hypersymbiotic." Having denied their daughters the stability and security of a confident early symbiosis, they turned around and refused to allow them any leeway for separateness or individuation. Instead, they now treated their daughters and cathected them as narcissistic physical and mental extensions of themselves, attributing their own body feelings to them. The mothers took control over their daughters' sexuality and used their daughters for their own autoerotic gratification. As Fliess puts it, "The mother employs the 'transitivism' of the psychotic"—"I am you and you are me"[16]—in her experiencing and treatment of her daughter. The result, in Fliess's patients, was that these daughters, as neurotics, duplicated many features of their mothers' psychotic symptoms, and retained severe ego and body-ego distortions. Their ego and body-ego retained an undifferentiated connection to their mother. Their relation to reality was, like an infant's, mediated by their mother as external ego.

Thus, these mothers maintained their daughters in a nonindividuated state through behavior which grew out of their own ego and body-ego boundary blurring and their perception of their daughters as one with, and interchangeable with, themselves. If we are to believe Fliess's account, this particular pathology—the psychotic distortion and prolongation of the normal preoedipal relationship—is predominantly a mother-daughter phenomenon.[17]

Olden, Enid Balint, and Angel provide further examples of the tendencies Fliess describes. Balint describes a state she calls "being empty of oneself"—a feeling of lack of self, or emptiness.[18] This happens especially when a person who has this feeling is with others who read the social and emotional setting differently but do not recognize this, nor recognize that the person herself is in a different world.

Balint claims that women are more likely to experience themselves this way. Women who feel empty of themselves feel that they are not being accorded a separate reality nor the agency to interpret the world in their own way. This feeling has its origins in the early mother-daughter relationship. Balint provides a case example to illustrate. She claims that the "empathy" of the patient's mother was

a false empathy, that from the outset it was probably a distorted projection of what the mother thought her infant daughter's needs
should be. As her daughter grew, and was able to express wants and
needs, the mother systematically ignored these expressions and gave
feedback not to her actual behavior but rather to what she had in the
first place projected onto her child. Balint describes the results of this
false empathy: "Because of this lack of feed-back, Sarah felt that she
was unrecognized, that she was empty of herself, that she had to live
in a void."[19] This mother-infant interaction began in earliest infancy,
but certainly continued throughout the patient's childhood. It is useful to quote Balint at length to indicate the quality of this mother-
daughter interaction:

(*i*) [Although she] on the surface developed satisfactorily, there was apparently a vitally important area where there was no reliable understanding between mother and daughter.
(*ii*) Although the mother tried her best, she responded more to her own pre-
conceived ideas as to what a baby ought to feel than to what her baby actually
felt. . . . Probably Sarah's mother could not bear unhappiness or violence or
fear in her child, did not respond to it, and tried to manipulate her so that
everything wrong was either put right at once or denied.
(*iii*) What was missing, therefore, was the acceptance that there might be bad
things, or even good ones, which must be recognized; that it is not sufficient
merely to put things right; moreover, that the child was neither identical with
her mother, nor with what the mother wanted her to be. . . .
    Sarah's mother was impervious to any communication which was differ-
ent from the picture she had of her daughter, and, in consequence, Sarah
could not understand her mother's communications and felt that her mother
never saw her as she was; neither found an echo in the other; and consequently only a spurious interaction between the growing child and the environment could develop.[20]

Olden describes a disruption in mother-child empathy that occurs
when mothers who had originally formed (or seem to have formed)
an appropriate unity with their infant were then unable to give it
up.[21] She is describing "a specific psychic immaturity that will keep
a mother from sensing her child's needs, from following his pace and
understanding his infantile world; and in turn keep the child from
developing ego capacities."[22] Olden does not note that both cases she
recounts are mother-daughter cases (one in which the daughter—a
child—was in analysis, the other from an analysis of the mother).
Both mothers felt unreal and were depressed. Olden described characteristics that both Balint and Fliess describe. The mothers lacked
real empathy but had pseudo-empathy which kept the daughters
from forming their own identity, either through identifying and feeling like someone or through contrasting themselves to someone (this

was more true for the daughter who had less relationship to her father). The mothers attained instinctual gratification through their daughters, not through directly using their daughters for autoerotic gratification, but by identifying vicariously with their sexuality and sex lives.

The Olden cases move even further from pathology than Balint, and further toward the norm that the direction of pathology implies. These mothers felt real closeness to their daughters, unlike the Balint and Fliess examples.* Olden describes

two very immature mothers who shared and, as it were, acted out the children's wishes yet were unable to perceive their children's real needs. These mothers and their children were extremely attached to each other; some of their friends characterized the relationship as "overidentification." Despite this emotional closeness, or perhaps on account of it, the mothers were unable to empathize with their children; the goal and function of this "closeness" was exclusively narcissistic.[23]

These mothers had maintained the primitive narcissistic mother-infant fusion with their children. This enabled them vicariously to gratify their own frustrated instinctual needs by virtue of projecting themselves onto the child.[24]

Angel provides further examples, this time by contrasting adult patients rather than by discussing the mother-infant relationship itself.[25] He is contrasting "symbiosis and pseudosymbiosis"—two versions of fantasies and wishes of merging in adult patients.

In (real) symbiosis, according to Angel, there is an extreme fear of merging as well as a wish to merge, because there is no firm sense of individuation in the first place. In pseudosymbiosis, there need not be and is not such fear, because the distinction between self and object is firm, and the wish to (re)merge is only a defensive one, usually against feelings of aggression toward the object:

1. In symbiosis, merging fantasies are a true reflection of the state of the ego; the self and object representations are merged.
2. In pseudosymbiosis, merging fantasies are defensive formations, and the self and object representations are more or less distinct.
3. In adults with true symbiotic object relations, the scale is weighted heavily on the side of fixation to the infantile symbiotic phase. In pseudosymbiosis, the element of fixation is minimal or absent, and the scale is weighted heavily on the side of defensive regression.[26]

Between symbiosis and pseudosymbiosis is a middle syndrome, which arises through fixation to the period when separateness is being es-

*The mothers were, in Fliess's terms, hypersymbiotic but not asymbiotic.

tablished but still fluctuates and is in doubt. Like Olden, Angel does not tie his distinction to gender differences. His case examples of true symbiosis and in-between syndrome are women, however, and his case example of pseudosymbiosis is a man. This points again to gender differences in issues of separateness and sense of self.

The choices of examples by Fliess, Olden, Angel, and Balint are not accidental. The patterns of fusion, projection, narcissistic extension, and denial of separateness they describe are more likely to happen in early mother-daughter relationships than in those of mothers and sons. The same personality characteristics in mothers certainly produce problematic mother-son relationships, but of a different kind. In all these cases, the mother does not recognize or denies the existence of the daughter as a separate person, and the daughter herself then comes not to recognize, or to have difficulty recognizing, herself as a separate person. She experiences herself, rather, as a continuation or extension of (or, in the Balint case, a subsumption within) her mother in particular, and later of the world in general.

In the next two examples, my interpretation is less secure. Both authors give examples of mothers and daughters and mothers and sons to demonstrate a larger issue—as Burlingham phrases it, "empathy between infant and mother,"[27] and as Sperling puts it, "children's interpretations and reaction to the unconscious of their mother."[28] It is my impression that although there was certainly understanding or empathy between mothers and children of both genders, and ways in which children of both genders lived out their mother's preoccupations or fantasies, the quality of the child's empathy and its reaction to the mother's unconscious differed according to gender. * With one possible exception,** Burlingham and Sperling describe girls who act *as extensions of* their mothers, who act out the aggression which their mothers feel but do not allow themselves to recognize or act on. They describe boys, by contrast, who equally intuitively *react to* their mothers' feelings and wishes as if they were the *objects* of their mothers' fantasies rather than the subjects.† Girls, then, seem to become and experience themselves as the self of the mother's fantasy, whereas boys become the other.

---

*It is hard to substantiate this impression without repeating all of the cases involved. I report them, however, because there are few such cases in the literature. I encourage the most committed (or skeptical) to read them.

**Ann, described by Sperling.

†In one case, for instance, a son (Paul, described by Sperling) has become a substitute for the mother's brother, toward whom she had and continues to have very complicated feelings.

Neither Burlingham nor Sperling links her insights to gender differences. However, Burlingham mentions that when she and her children were in analysis at the same time, and an issue preoccupying her would arise in the analysis of her children, appearing "out of context...as if it were a foreign body,"[29] these links were more obvious with sons than daughters. Burlingham does not have an explanation. If my interpretation is right, then the explanation is that her daughter's preoccupations, as continuations of her, might appear more ego syntonic—seeming to emerge out of her daughter's ego—and thus be less identifiable than issues which emphasized her sons as acted-on objects.

These accounts indicate the significance of gender differences, despite the lack of attention paid to these differences. With the exception of Balint, who says that being empty of oneself is found more often in women, the authors claim simply to focus on a certain kind of person and certain kind of early mother-infant relationship, and then either use predominantly mother-*daughter* examples or mother-daughter and mother-son examples which reflect gender-linked variations in the processes they discuss, as in the cases of Angel, Burlingham, and Sperling. All these accounts indicate, in different ways, that prolonged symbiosis and narcissistic overidentification are particularly characteristic of early relationships between mothers and daughters.

PREOEDIPAL MOTHER-SON RELATIONSHIPS: THE CLINICAL PICTURE

Both the absence of mother-son examples in some discussions, and their character in others, indicate how early mother-daughter relationships contrast to those between a mother and son. In Burlingham and Sperling, sons are objects for their mothers, even while they maintain symbiotic bonds of empathy and oneness of identification. In the Angel case, a man pretends symbiosis when boundaries are in fact established.

Psychoanalytic and anthropological clinical accounts further illuminate specific tendencies in early mother-son relationships.[30] Bibring argues that the decline of the husband's presence in the home has resulted in a wife "as much in need of a husband as the son is of a father."[31] This wife is likely to turn her affection and interest to the next obvious male—her son—and to become particularly seductive toward him. Just as the father is often not enough present to prevent or break up the mother-daughter boundary confusion, he is also not available to prevent either his wife's seductiveness or his son's growing reciprocated incestuous impulses. A mother, here, is again experiencing her son as a definite other—an opposite-gendered and -sexed other. Her emotional investments and conflicts, given her socialization around issues of gender and sex and membership in a sexist society, make this experience of him particularly strong. The son's solution, moreover, emphasizes differentiation buttressed by heavy emotional investment. He projects his own fears and desires onto his mother, whose behavior he then gives that much more significance and weight.

Slater's account of Greek mother-son relationships in the Classical period, read into his later work on contemporary American society, gives us further insight into the dynamics Bibring discusses.*[32] Greek marriages, Slater suggests, were characterized by a weak marital bond, and the society was ridden with sex antagonism and masculine fear and devaluation of mature women. Wives were isolated in their marital homes with children. In reaction, mothers reproduced in their own sons the same masculine fears and behaviors that their husbands and the men in their society had. They produced in these sons a precarious and vulnerable masculinity and sense of differentiation by alternating sexual praise and seductive behavior with hostile deflation, ridicule, and intrusive definitions of their sons' intrapsychic situation. Like the maternal treatment Bibring discusses, this treatment kept sons dependent on their mothers for a sense of self-sufficiency and self-esteem. At the same time, it emphasized these sons' sexuality and sexual difference, and encouraged participation in a heavily sexualized relationship in boys who had not resolved early issues of individuation and the establishment of ego boundaries.**

---

*Slater discusses the psychic outcome of structural features of the family and the organization and ideology of gender not unique to Greek society but very much present in our own. His later works do not present his analysis in such full detail, though they assume that it is very much applicable to American society. Therefore, I rely in what follows on the analysis of Greece to shed light on our contemporary situation.

**This combination of the blurring of generational boundaries between mother and son, and the elevation of the son to a role as masculine partner, or opposite, to the mother, replicates Lidz's description of schizophrenogenic family structure and practice for boys.[33] Slater in fact suggests that maternal treatment of sons in Greece was schizophrenogenic. He points out that we have no record of the actual incidence of madness in ancient Greek society, but that Greek culture was dominated by maternally caused madness: "No other mythology with which I am familiar contains so many explicitly designated instances of madness. . . . The most striking fact is that of all the clear instances of madness deliberately produced in one being by another, none can be said to be caused by a truly masculine or paternal agent. Most are afflicted by goddesses, and the remainder by the effeminate Dionysus, himself a previous victim at the hands of Hera. . . . Nor is the relationship between the sex of an agent and the sex of a victim a random one: in the overwhelming majority of cases madness is induced in persons of the opposite sex."[34]

Bibring's and Slater's work implies that in societies like ours, which are male-dominated but have relatively father-absent families and little paternal participation in family life and child care, masculinity and sexual difference ("oedipal" issues) become intertwined with separation-individuation ("preoedipal") issues almost from the beginning of a boy's life.* This conclusion receives confirmation from Whiting's cross-cultural analyses of patrilocal societies with sleeping arrangements in which children sleep exclusively with their mothers during their first two years (and husband/fathers sleep elsewhere) and postpartum sex taboos.[35] Such societies are usually characterized by a general pattern of sex segregation and sex antagonism—again, a (perhaps) extreme form of the sex-gender arrangements in modern society.

Such arrangements create difficulties for the development of a sense of masculinity in boys. Although their account is allegedly about feminine role identification, Whiting and his colleagues are in fact talking about the period of early infancy. In some formulations of the problem, it is clear that they are concerned with fundamental feelings of dependence, overwhelming attachment, and merging with the mother, developed by a son during the intense and exclusive early years, that he feels he must overcome in order to attain independence and a masculine self-identification.[36] They suggest further that an explicitly sexual relationship between mother and son may exist. Citing "clinical evidence from women in our own society suggesting that nursing is sexually gratifying to some women at least,"[37] and informant reports in one society with postpartum sex taboo and mother-infant sleeping arrangements that mothers had no desire for sex as long as they were nursing, they suggest that "it is possible that the mother obtains some substitute sexual gratification from nursing and caring for her infant."[38]

Cross-cultural accounts of father-absence and mother-infant sleeping arrangements do not mention the effects of extreme father-absence and antagonism between the sexes on mother-daughter relationships or on female development.** It may well be that the kind of mother-daughter boundary confusion and overidentification I have discussed here is the answer. Slater suggests that it is not simply sleeping arrangements but maternal ambivalence and inconsistent

---

*Slater does not restrict his discussion to the period of the early mother-son relationship. But all the relational and ego problems he discusses, and his use of the label "oral-narcissistic dilemma" to summarize these, point to early mother-infant issues: myths concerned with birth, with maternal attacks on the infant in the womb or on the neonate, with oral reincorporation by the mother; or with the maternal lack of reality principle vis-à-vis her son.

**In fact, their omission provided the original impetus for my study here.

behavior toward sons which lead to the results Whiting describes. Without this ambivalence and seductiveness, mother-infant sleeping arrangements may not produce conflict and dependency. Alternatively, it may be that dependency in girls is not, in the patriarchal cultural case, an obstacle to the successful attainment of femininity.

I conclude, from the evidence in Bibring's, Slater's and Whiting's accounts, that a mother, of a different gender from her son and deprived of adult emotional, social, and physical contact with men (and often without any supportive adult contact at all), may push her son out of his preoedipal relationship to her into an oedipally toned relationship defined by its sexuality and gender distinction. Her son's maleness and oppositeness as a sexual other become important, even while his being an infant remains important as well. Because of this, sons (men) come to have different kinds of preoedipally engendered problems than daughters (women). Greenacre points to these in her discussion of the genesis of "perversions" and especially of fetishism, which, according to psychoanalysts, are predominantly masculine phenomena.[39]

Greenacre suggests that fetishes, and other perversions as well, serve to deny (on an unconscious level usually) that women do not have penises: "The phallic woman [is a] ubiquitous fantasy in perversions."*[40] The reason the fetishist needs to deny the existence of different genitalia than his own is that his sense of his own genital body identity is not firm. Being presented with different genitalia, therefore, he feels threatened and potentially castrated himself. Greenacre argues that fetishism is a result of conflict centering on issues of separation and individuation in the early years. It results from boundary confusion and a lack of sense of self firmly distinguished from his mother, leading him to experience (again, all this is probably not conscious) as his own what he takes to be the castration of first his mother and then women in general.

Greenacre's account points to gender differences surrounding early issues of differentiation and individuation. Even while primary separateness is being established in boys, issues of masculinity and conflicts around genital differences are important. Her account also leads me to conclude that the early period is sexualized for boys in a way that it is not for girls, that phallic-masculine issues become intertwined with supposedly nongender-differentiated object-relational and ego issues concerning the creation of a sense of separate self.

*I realize that this kind of claim verges on the incredible to those unpersuaded by psychoanalytic theory. It is certainly the area in psychoanalytic theory in which I feel least comfortable, but in this case Greenacre's account is persuasive and illuminating.

According to Greenacre and Herman Roiphe, children of both genders go through a phase during their second year when their genitals become important as part of their developing body self and their developing gender identity.[41] Conflictual object-relations concerning these issues can lead a child to focus anxiety and emotion on genital difference—to develop castration anxiety or penis envy. Greenacre's account indicates, however, that this aspect of individuation is more important and conflictual for men. That the early mother-son relationship is likely to emphasize phallic oedipal issues along with preoedipal individuation issues explains this difference. It is another instance in which a supposedly nongender-differentiated process has different meanings for boys and girls.*

In a society like ours, in which mothers have exclusive care for infants and are isolated from other adults, in which there is physical and social separation of men/fathers from women/mothers and children, and institutionalized male dominance, a mother may impose her reactions to this situation on her son, and confuse her relationship to him as an infant with a sexualized relationship to him as a male.** It is precisely such a situation which accounts for the early entrance into the oedipus situation on the part of boys in our society.

CONCLUSIONS

The clinical and cultural examples I have discussed all point to the conclusion that preoedipal experiences of girls and boys differ. The girl's preoedipal mother-love and preoccupation with preoedipal issues are prolonged in a way that they are not for the boy. With the exception of Whiting's cross-cultural analysis, all the examples I cite are cases which their authors have taken to be noteworthy for their "abnormality" or "pathology." However, the extent of such pathology varies (from preoccupation to mild neurosis to psychosis). More important, there is systematic variation in the form it takes depending on whether a person is female or male—on whether we are talking

---

*As noted previously, children of both genders go through a symbiotic phase of unity, primary identification, and mutual empathy with their mother, and then go through a period of differentiation from her—but these issues remain more central for women.

**Barbara Deck (personal communication) suggests that whether the boy is a child or an adult makes a big difference to his mother. As a little man with a penis, he excites her; however, in order for her fondling and sexualized treatment not to produce conscious guilt, he must remain a neuter baby. This ambivalence does not arise in the case of a girl baby, who is "just a baby" or at most a "baby mother/self." She is not an *other*, like a "baby husband" or a "baby father."

about mother-daughter or mother-son relationships. In all cases the pathology reflects, in exaggerated form, differences in what are in fact normal tendencies. The cases give us, as Freud suggests about neurosis in general, insight into what we would otherwise miss just because it is subtle, typical, and familiar. These cases, then, point to typical gender differences in the preoedipal period, differences that are a product of the asymmetrical organization of parenting which founds our family structure.

Because they are the same gender as their daughters and have been girls, mothers of daughters tend not to experience these infant daughters as separate from them in the same way as do mothers of infant sons. In both cases, a mother is likely to experience a sense of oneness and continuity with her infant. However, this sense is stronger, and lasts longer, vis-à-vis daughters. Primary identification and symbiosis with daughters tend to be stronger and cathexis of daughters is more likely to retain and emphasize narcissistic elements, that is, to be based on experiencing a daughter as an extension or double of a mother herself, with cathexis of the daughter as a sexual other usually remaining a weaker, less significant theme.

Other accounts also suggest that mothers normally identify more with daughters and experience them as less separate. Signe Hammer's book, *Daughters and Mothers: Mothers and Daughters*, based on interviews with over seventy-five mothers, daughters, and grandmothers, describes how issues of primary identification, oneness, and separateness follow mother-daughter pairs from a daughter's earliest infancy until she is well into being a mother or even grandmother herself:

Most of the daughters in this book have received enough support from their mothers to emerge from the stage of complete symbiosis in early infancy. But for the vast majority of mothers and daughters, this emergence remains only partial. At some level mothers and daughters tend to remain emotionally bound up with each other in what might be called a semisymbiotic relationship, in which neither ever quite sees herself or the other as a separate person.[42]

Hammer's study is certainly confirmed by my own discussions with a number of mothers of daughters and sons, first in a women's group devoted to the discussion and analysis of mother-daughter relationships in particular and family relationships in general, and later with individual acquaintances. Finally, the resurfacing and prevalence of preoedipal mother-daughter issues in adolescence (anxiety, intense and exclusive attachment, orality and food, maternal control of a daughter's body, primary identification) provide clinical verification of the claim that elements of the preoedipal mother-daughter relationship are maintained and prolonged in both maternal and filial psyche.[43]

Because they are of different gender than their sons, by contrast, mothers experience their sons as a male opposite. Their cathexis of sons is more likely to consist from early on in an object cathexis of a sexual other, perhaps in addition to narcissistic components. Sons tend to be experienced as differentiated from their mothers, and mothers push this differentiation (even while retaining, in some cases, a kind of intrusive controlling power over their sons). Maternal behavior, at the same time, tends to help propel sons into a sexualized, genitally toned relationship, which in its turn draws the son into triangular conflicts.

Early psychoanalytic findings about the special importance of the preoedipal mother-daughter relationship describe the first stage of a general process in which separation and individuation remain particularly female developmental issues. The cases I describe suggest that there is a tendency in women toward boundary confusion and a lack of sense of separateness from the world. Most women do develop ego boundaries and a sense of separate self. However, women's ego and object-relational issues are concerned with this tendency on one level (of potential conflict, of experience of object-relations), even as on another level (in the formation of ego boundaries and the development of a separate identity) the issues are resolved.

That these issues become more important for girls than for boys is a product of children of both genders growing up in families where women, who have a greater sense of sameness with daughters than sons, perform primary parenting functions.* As long as women mother, we can expect that a girl's preoedipal period will be longer than that of a boy and that women, more than men, will be more open to and preoccupied with those very relational issues that go into mothering—feelings of primary identification, lack of separateness or differentiation, ego and body-ego boundary issues and primary love not under the sway of the reality principle. A girl does not simply identify with her mother or want to be like her mother. Rather, mother and daughter maintain elements of their primary relationship which means they will feel alike in fundamental ways. Object-relations and conflicts in the oedipal period build upon this preoedipal base.

---

*I must admit to fudging here about the contributory effect in all of this of a mother's sexual orientation—whether she is heterosexual or lesbian. Given a female gender identity, she is "the same as" her daughter and "different from" her son, but part of what I am talking about also presumes a different kind of cathexis of daughter and son deriving from her heterosexuality.

7

Object-Relations and the Female Oedipal Configuration

It is only in male children that we find the fateful combination of love for the one parent and simultaneous hatred for the other as a rival.

FREUD,
"Female Sexuality"

A girl's family setting creates a different endopsychic situation for her than for a boy. This second major difference between feminine and masculine oedipal experiences both results from and gives further meaning to the first, to the greater length and intensity of the preoedipal mother-daughter relationship, and it contributes to further differentiation in relational capacities and needs.

FEMININITY: WOMEN'S OEDIPAL GOAL

Freud and the early analysts were attuned to oedipal gender differences. For them, the major oedipal task was preparation for heterosexual adult relationships. Given this, a girl's major task is to become oriented to men. In the traditional paradigm, a girl must change her love object from mother to father, her libidinal mode from active to passive, and finally her libidinal organ and erotism from clitoris to vagina. A boy has to make no such parallel changes.[1]

"Orientation to men" has taken on definite meaning in psychoanalytic conceptions. Feminine heterosexuality (for psychoanalysts, femininity *means* genital heterosexuality) in this model has Victorian characteristics that include women's passivity and the subordination of sex to procreation. (Psychoanalyst Roy Schafer reminds us, in a perceptive article on Freud's psychology of women, of the "Victorian precept that in sexual relations 'a lady doesn't move.' "[2])

I will not evaluate all the debates about female sexuality that have taken place within psychoanalysis here.* It is enough to reiterate that there seems to be only one kind of female orgasm,[5] and that psychoanalysts have foundered in all attempts to define activity and passivity unambiguously or without resort to normative conceptions. (The lady engages in "a desperate form of activity"[6] in playing her required inactive part; people who experience themselves repeatedly as victims—the "accident-prone"—certainly create and affect these situations as much as being affected by them; the vagina can be—and often is, in fantasy, myth, symbol, and conscious and unconscious experience—equally grasping, taking, demanding as receptive and awaiting; women, as men, can be sexually aroused and initiating.) Once we deny the biological, instinctual component of the clitoral-vaginal shift and of the activity-passivity distinction, then the way these phenomena are experienced, or enter as psychological fantasy elements into relationships, can be investigated. These phenomena derive from specific social relationships, and from normative definitions of the sexual situation imposed on and learned by members of particular societies. In the psychoanalytic case at hand, the normative definition of the situation is an assumption that heterosexual genitality is a major desired developmental goal, and the oedipus complex is the first arena in which that goal is negotiated.

There is no question that heterosexual orientation is a major outcome of the oedipal period for most girls, and that the traditional psychoanalytic account of the development of female sexuality and the growth of the girl's relationship to her father describes this. There is some question, however, about how we should read this outcome. Freud and his colleagues put us in a peculiar position here. On the one hand, they assume that heterosexual orientation and genital (vaginal) primacy is biologically normal and is women's biological destiny. This assumption, as Schafer points out, is based on an unstated but strong evolutionary value system in which "nature has its procreative plan," "individuals are destined to be links in the chain of survival," and "it is better for people to be 'natural' and not defy 'the natural order.' "[7] Only from this evaluative viewpoint can psychoanalysis take all other forms of sexuality to be arrests in development, illness, inversion, perversion: "We are operating in the realm of societal value systems concerning taken-for-granted evolutionary obligations; we are not operating in any realm of biological necessity, psycho-biological disorder, or value-free empiricism."[8]

---

*For example, debates over whether little girls experience vaginal sensations and awareness and why this matters;[3] debates over Sherfey's attempt to integrate Masters and Johnson's research into psychoanalytic theory;[4] and so forth.

On the other hand, psychoanalytic clinical findings indicate that there is nothing inevitable, natural, or preestablished in the development of human sexuality. Moreover, a reading of cases, and the theory derived from them, suggests that sexual orientation and definition is enforced and constructed by parents. Parents are usually heterosexual and sexualize their relationship to children of either gender accordingly, employing socially sanctioned child-rearing practices (including, with few exceptions, the sanction of psychoanalysts).[9] We can, then, take the psychoanalytic account to describe the genesis of heterosexual orientation in women. But we must reject any assumption that what this account describes is natural, self-evident, and unintended. To the contrary, it seems to be both consciously and unconsciously intended, socially, psychologically, and ideologically constructed. And, as I will discuss further here, it is not inevitable.

The attainment of heterosexual orientation as the psychoanalytic account describes it involves an identification on the part of children with parents of their own gender—a boy with his father, a girl with her mother. The processes in this identification are not necessarily conscious (superego formation, for instance), but the choice of parent to identify with clearly is. A boy gives up his mother in order to avoid punishment, but identifies with his father because he can then gain the benefits of being the one who gives punishment, of being masculine and superior. (He develops "what we have come to consider the normal male contempt for women."[10]) A girl identifies with her mother in their common feminine inferiority and in her heterosexual stance.* According to the account, she also prepares through this identification for her future mothering role. Both in clinical examples and in theoretical formulations this identification is clearly a learning phenomenon: Children learn their gender and then identify and are encouraged to identify with the appropriate parent.**

My analysis here is not so concerned with this traditional psychoanalytic account—with feminine heterosexuality, genital symbolization, sexual fantasy, conscious masculine or feminine identification —as with the kind of social and intrapsychic relational situation in which that heterosexuality and these identifications get constituted.

---

*Psychoanalytic accounts do not discuss a girl's oedipal identification with her mother with the *kind* of attention to process and outcome that they direct to a boy's identification with his father. Most simply assert the identification, if they mention it at all, and do not tell us why or how it happens. Lampl-de Groot is on the more explicit side, as is Brunswick.[11]

**This order of events is implicit in the psychoanalytic account, but is explicit in cognitive-developmental models of gender-role identification.[12]

Psychoanalysts, by contrast, in their emphasis on the difficult libidinal path to heterosexuality, have passed over the relational aspects of the situation. What I will be concerned with is the way conflictual object-relations during the oedipal period become defensively appropriated and internalized by growing girls so that they transform their intra-psychic object-world—their inner fantasized and unconsciously experienced self in relation to others. These object-relations grow out of contemporary family structure and are mutually created by parents and children. The traditional account, concerned with hetero-sexual orientation, focuses on a girl's cathexis of her father. My account, again taking this as already shown, demonstrates the continuing significance of a girl's relation to her mother throughout the oedipal period. Sexual orientation is in the background here. My account does give a fuller understanding of women's heterosexuality in our society, but as part of a more general understanding of women's internal and external relational position.

Similarly, I argue that the way gender personality is constituted in the oedipus complex does not have to do only with identification processes—a child becoming like, or modifying its ego to be like, its parent. Rather, the ego in its internal object-relational situation changes, and changes differently for boys and girls. Boys and girls experience and internalize different kinds of relationships; they work through the conflicts, develop defenses, and appropriate and trans-form the affects associated with these relationships differently. These object-relational differences, and their effect on defenses, splits, and repressions in the ego, better explain the important differences in masculine and feminine personality and the important aspects of feminine personality that emerge from the oedipus complex than does the more conscious and intended identification with the same gender parent.

THE RELATION TO THE MOTHER AND THE
FEMININE "CHANGE OF OBJECT"

In the classical account of the feminine oedipus complex, a girl totally rejects her mother when she discovers that her mother cannot give her a penis: "Whereas in boys the Oedipus complex is destroyed by the castration complex [a boy gives up his love for his mother out of fear of castration by his father], in girls it is made possible and led up to by the castration complex."[13] Penis envy—the feminine form of the castration complex—leads a girl to turn to her father exclusively, and thenceforth to see her mother only as a sexual rival. This account stresses the completeness of the girl's turn to her father and rejection of her mother, and the depth of her hostility: "The girl abandons the mother as a love object with far more embitterment and finality than the boy."[14]

Such a view, while theoretically useful in its retention of views of the feminine and masculine oedipus complex as mirror opposites, was too simple to encompass even Freud's own work.[15] To begin with, the girl enters the triangular oedipus situation later, and in a different relational context than the boy. Even when she does so, the continuity of preoedipal issues in women's lives suggests that a girl does not give up this preoedipal relationship completely, but rather builds whatever happens later upon this preoedipal base. Freud's characterization, unusual for him, of the girl's preoedipal connection to her mother as "attachment" rather than as cathexis, or love, emphasizes this persistence. His characterization points to the dual nature of attachment: A girl actively attaches herself, and chooses her attachment, to her mother, and at the same time is passively, and not as a matter of choice, attached—an appendage or extension. Freud's usual term *cathexis* implies, by contrast, activity and direction. In the first instance then, a girl retains a sense of self and relation to her mother which has preoedipal, or early developmental, characteristics. She is preoccupied with issues of symbiosis and primary love without sense of the other person's separateness.

Girls do not simply remain "preoedipal" longer, however. As psychoanalysts describe it, the relational experience of the oedipus complex itself is not symmetrical with that of boys. According to Freud and other analysts, a girl usually turns from the exclusive relationship with her mother to her father as an object of primary libidinal interest. When we look at the kinds of explanations put forth for this turning, however, we find that they testify to the strength of a girl's ongoing relationship to her mother as much as to the importance of her relationship to her father. These explanations are partial accounts of a complex process in which different elements may be more or less primary for different girls.[16] They all pay tribute to Freud's original clinical contention that an oedipal girl turns to her father because she is looking for a penis, but they provide different accounts of the nature and causes of her search.*

Horney, Jones, and Klein, followed by Janine Chasseguet-Smirgel and Béla Grunberger, give us one polar view of the turn to the father.[17] They argue that a girl originally wants a penis (man) *libidi-*

---

*They do *not* claim, like Freud, that penis envy has a crucial effect on the rest of a woman's life, however, but only that it is part of a girl's oedipal search.

nally—for sexual gratification—and not *narcissistically*—for her own sexual organ. Their argument is that no *explanation* for a girl's turning to her father is needed—that this is simply the expression of an innate heterosexuality which develops spontaneously in a girl. Horney, for instance, suggests that Freud's penis envy hypothesis and penis-baby equation is a rather complicated explanation for "the manifestation of so elementary a principle of nature as that of the mutual attraction of the sexes." "The causal connection," she suggests, "may be the exact converse . . . it is just the attraction to the opposite sex, operating from a very early period, which draws the libidinal interest of the little girl to the penis."[18] Klein and Jones also conceptualize the development of heterosexuality as a natural development. In their terms it grows out of a girl's primary awareness of her vagina, and out of transition from frustrated oral cathexis of the breast and mother, to oral cathexis of the paternal penis, to genital cathexis of the penis and oedipal desires for the father. In all these accounts, a girl comes to the oedipus complex primarily through innate feminine heterosexual drives and through the belief that her father will satisfy impulses aroused by maternal oral frustration. Narcissistic penis envy comes after, and is a defensive flight from, these libidinal oedipal desires and her fear of their consequences (if she had a penis herself, the girl would not desire her father sexually, and therefore would not have to fear the consequences of this desire—maternal retaliation,* the extinction of her sexuality,** or internal rupture from the penetration†).

This account points us in useful directions. We can sympathize with Horney's despair at the contortions of Freud's account and the logical leaps (a girl's masculinity as the only basis for her femininity) he makes to get a girl to where most people have always been anyway. And Horney's approach does address some problems which Freud's account passes over. In Freud's account, a girl/woman really never does come to be heterosexual, that is, to want heterosexual intercourse for itself. She first wants a penis narcissistically (as her own body organ), turns to her father (develops a heterosexual orientation) because he will give her one, and then comes to want a baby from him as an alternate narcissistic extension (a substitute for the penis she can never have). Nowhere in this account does she want sex for anything except reproduction and the restitution of her narcissistic wound. In the Horney-Jones-Klein account, at least, a woman does want (hetero) sex for its own sexual sake.

*In Klein's formulation.
**In Jones's formulation.
†In Horney's formulation.

There are problems in the account, however, precisely in areas where it does not follow more general psychoanalytic principles and methodology. "The ultimate question," Jones asks, "is whether a woman is born or made."[19] Given the terms in which Freud had set the debate—that all children until the oedipal period are "little men" —it seems eminently reasonable to answer, as he and Horney did, that woman was born:* "I do not see a woman—in the way feminists do [in the way Freud does, would be more appropriate here]—as *un homme manqué*."[21] The clinical findings of psychoanalysis, however, in contrast to Freud's implication, demonstrate extensive variations in psychosexual developmental processes and outcomes: final sexual orientation for both sexes is definitely a developmental process influenced by many environmental factors. Moreover, the Horney-Jones-Klein account does not follow what I take to be a fundamental rule of psychoanalytic evidence, that it come out of clinical experience. It relies on a biological hypothesis of natural heterosexual drives which psychoanalysts have no way of testing or supporting with clinical or observational methods, and it has no explanation for how or why these drives should come to the fore when they are claimed to do so.

The contribution of the Horney-Jones-Klein account, however, is that it treats sex and reproduction—even if in too directly biological a manner—as not inextricably linked. It therefore treats heterosexual attraction as a thing in itself and as intrinsically gratifying. (Horney, in answer to Freud, also argues that the experience of childbirth and suckling must be seen as a woman's experience in itself and not as a poor substitute for a penis.)

Since the Horney-Jones-Klein explanation for heterosexual attraction—primary innate heterosexuality—cannot be supported with their methodology and is undercut by the whole of psychoanalytic clinical experience and interpretation, we need to look elsewhere for how women's heterosexual orientation comes about. Psychoanalytic clinical findings suggest that there are two components to this. One is that a girl's relation to her mother motivates her to look elsewhere for other kinds of relationships, and for the powers which a penis might bring her. Second, she is likely to be encouraged to look elsewhere to fulfill these generalized needs by her father, who also lends

*I disagree here with Mitchell's argument that Freud correctly understands that femininity is made.[20] If he had asserted that gender and sexual orientation for both sexes is a social product, that children were originally ungendered, her argument would make more sense. But Freud holds the inconsistent and sexist position that man is born whereas woman is made. Nevertheless, it is ironic that feminists should turn to Horney as a major founder of the "cultural school" for support for claims about the social origins of femininity, penis envy, and so forth, when her position is so biologically based.

them a sexualized tone. Psychoanalysts accord normative significance to such behavior: A father is supposed to make himself available (while not making himself available) to his daughter. Social psychologists find that fathers in fact do so.

Marjorie Leonard makes the most explicit psychoanalytic argument for the importance of fathers to the development of feminine, heterosexual orientation.[22] Leonard argues that the father's role is crucial to his daughter's development during her oedipal period and during preadolescence and early adolescence (another period when heterosexual orientation is being negotiated). She gives clinical examples of ways a father can be not there enough, which leads a girl to idealize her father and men, or to endow them with immensely sadistic or punitive characteristics—or can be there too much (be too possessive, seductive, or identified with their daughter), requiring her to develop defensive measures against involvement with him and with men. Fathers, Leonard argues, must be able to make themselves available as a heterosexual love object and to offer affection without being seduced by their daughters' fantasies or seducing them with their own. Otherwise, she implies, a girl will not develop proper heterosexuality.

Whatever we make of this claim about proper heterosexuality, it seems, from both psychoanalytic clinical reports and from social psychological research, that fathers generally sex-type their children more consciously than mothers along traditional gender-role lines, and that they do encourage feminine heterosexual behavior in their young daughters.[23] Maccoby and Jacklin cite comments by fathers reported by Goodenough, when asked to describe daughters two to three years old and to give examples of ways these children are more feminine or masculine:

A bit of a flirt, arch and playful with people, a pretended coyness.

Soft and cuddly and loving. She cuddles and flatters in subtle ways.

I notice her coyness and flirting, "come up and see me sometime" approach. She loves to cuddle. She's going to be sexy—I get my wife annoyed when I say this.[24]

They point out that it is irrelevant whether or not these descriptions are accurate. What is of interest "is that the fathers appeared to enjoy being flirted with by their daughters" and encouraged this feminine behavior:

The mothers in the Goodenough study reported instances in which their husbands had put pressure on them to dress their daughters in dresses rather than pants, to keep their hair long, etc., when the mother would not have considered it especially important for their daughters to look dainty and feminine at this young age.[25]

Maccoby and Jacklin conclude,

Fathers appear to want their daughters to fit their image of a sexually attractive female person, within the limits of what is appropriate for a child, and they play the masculine role vis-à-vis their daughters as well as their wives. This may or may not generate rivalry between mother and daughter, but there can be little doubt that it is a potent force in the girl's development of whatever behavior is defined as "feminine" by her father.[26]

This sort of account explains the observations of Horney, Jones and Klein concerning the seemingly spontaneous generation of a girl's feminine behavior in relation to her father. This behavior is one side of an interaction. A daughter looks for a primary person in her life other than her mother, and a father involves himself with his children in ways which encourage stereotypic gender-role behavior.

We can understand better both why a girl is open to her father's encouragement of their relationship in the first place, and how she helps to initiate it, by examining other psychoanalytic accounts of the girl's turn to her father. These suggest, not surprisingly, that the roots of her availability and effort to find a new involvement can be found in her previous relation to her mother. All psychoanalytic accounts of the feminine change of object indicate that this change both results from, and finds its meaning in, this early relationship. This relationship, as we have seen, is an ambivalent one, and the girl's turn to her father comes out of both sides of her ambivalence.

In Freud's original account, a girl's accumulated hostility to her mother makes her turn to her father. Freud explains this hostility sometimes by stressing deprivation by the mother and sometimes by stressing ambivalence and anger about powerlessness itself (these, of course, are not unrelated). In the former (better known) view, children of both genders blame their mother for not fulfilling (insatiable) oral needs, for transferring her care and breast to a younger sibling, and for arousing and then forbidding sexual desires.[27] Lampl-de Groot expresses this view: "As long as the children of both sexes have the same love object—the mother, the possibility of satisfying passive as well as active libidinal strivings exists to the same extent (in the oral, anal and phallic phases), and both sexes are subject to the same disappointments in love and the same narcissistic blows."[28]

Freud and his colleagues must, however, also account for why a *girl* turns to her father as a result of this when her brother does not. Yet their other positions prevent them from creating a satisfactory explanation. First, they do not hold the Horney theory of innate heterosexuality, nor are they willing to accord recognition in their theory to the possible part played by a father in wooing a girl, but not a boy, into libidinal cathexis of him.* Second, while recognizing gender differences in the quality and length of the preoedipal period, they have no *theoretical* notion that these differences might themselves make a girl more likely to turn away from her mother.

Instead, Freud develops an explanation in terms of "penis envy": Her mother has deprived only the girl in a special way, by arranging matters so that her daughter does not have a penis. In an experience contemporaneous with the accumulation of hostility toward her mother, a girl learns of the existence of penises and of the fact that she does not have one. She is outraged and upset, blames her mother for her lack, discovers that her mother has no penis either, rejects her mother out of anger at her own deprivation and contempt for the mother's "castrated" state, and turns to her father to give her a penis.

There are several problems in this account. One again brings us back to Freud's original dilemma—how can similar experiences in boys and girls produce different results? Freud tends to stress contempt even more than anger in a girl's rejection of her mother. Contempt enables a girl to act on her hostility: "With the discovery that her mother is castrated it becomes possible to drop her as an object, so that the motives for hostility, which have long been accumulating, gain the upper hand. . . . As a result of the discovery of women's lack of a penis they are debased in value for girls."[29] A girl, in this view, loved her "phallic," active mother; this mother she can simply "drop." If we follow this logic, a boy, who also has reasons for hostility, who, according to Freud and Brunswick, comes to debase and disparage his mother for not having a penis, should give up women as love objects as well. Brunswick suggests that his contempt may lead a boy at this time to give up his *mother* as a love object and turn his attention to superego formation and sublimations, but she never implies that this abandonment has implications for his more general sexual orientation.

What we need to understand is why a girl, but not a boy, seems to be looking for an excuse to "drop" her mother. We also have to understand why the discovery that she does not have a penis is such a trauma to a girl in the first place. As Schafer reminds us, again pointing to Freud's inconsistencies, "Freud was remarkably incurious about the background of these reactions."[30] This lack of curiosity must be more than accidental, more than a simple oversight:

*I will discuss some reasons for this blind spot (see Chapter 9).

Insofar as it is the hallmark of psychoanalytic investigation, and particularly of Freud's thinking, that it always presses its questions further and further in the interest of establishing the fullest understanding possible of the particularity of response on the part of individuals in specific circumstances, especially when these reactions are intense, disturbing, profoundly formative, and enduringly influential, it is all the more remarkable that at this point there are virtually no questions forthcoming. . . . We cannot have a simple, self-evident *shock theory* of the girl's extreme mortification and consequent penis envy. . . . It was [Freud], after all, who taught us how to establish through psychoanalysis the historical background and determination of psychological traumata.[31]

To answer these questions, we have to look at what came before —to the preoedipal period and to parts of the traditional account which Freud and his colleagues do not emphasize. As we have seen, Freud, Brunswick, and Lampl-de Groot stress the intensity and ambivalence of the girl's early relationship to her mother. They also argue, in a more object-relational vein than the deprivation hypothesis, that any first love relation is "doomed to dissolution"[32] just because of its ambivalence and intensity, and because of the restrictions and compulsions which the child must undergo to maintain it: "The mother-child relationship is doomed to extinction. Many factors militate against it, the most potent perhaps its primitive, archaic nature. Ambivalence and passivity characterize every primitive relation and ultimately destroy it."[33] This latter claim points to that feature of a girl's situation which accounts for her anger and rejection of her mother. The special nature of the preoedipal mother-daughter relationship—its intensity, length, and ambivalence—creates the psychological basis for a girl's turn to her father.

When an omnipotent mother perpetuates primary love and primary identification in relation to her daughter, and creates boundaries and a differentiated, anaclitic love relation to her son,* a girl's father is likely to become a symbol of freedom from this dependence and merging. A girl is likely to turn to him, regardless of his gender or sexual orientation, as the most available person who can help her to get away from her mother. The turn to the father then, whatever its sexual meaning, also concerns emotional issues of self and other. These issues tend to be resolved by persons in roles that are systematically gender-linked, not because of qualities inherent in persons of either gender but because of family organization.

This interpretation is supported by Chasseguet-Smirgel's reformulation of female development, which stresses both the common-

---

*She also allows him greater independence, which is not dealt with in the psychoanalytic tradition.

alities in the relationship of children of either gender to their mother, and the unsatisfactory nature of the girl's early relationship to her mother.[34] Chasseguet-Smirgel expands on the suggestions of Freud, Brunswick, and Lampl-de Groot that the preoedipal mother, simply as a result of her omnipotence and activity, causes a "narcissistic wound" (the threats to ego and body-ego integrity, the sense of powerlessness and dependence that Winnicott discusses) in children of both sexes.* This narcissistic wound creates hostility to the mother in a child. Children of both sexes, even with kind mothers, will maintain a fearsome unconscious maternal image as a result of projecting upon it the hostility derived from their own feelings of impotence. (They may simultaneously have an image of an omnipotent protective mother—thus the witch and the fairy godmother.) A preoedipal girl already feels "painfully incomplete" then, but "the cause of this feeling of incompleteness is to be found in the primary relation with the mother and will therefore be found in children of both sexes."[35]

All children, according to Chasseguet-Smirgel, must free themselves from their mother's omnipotence and gain a sense of completeness. Insofar as a boy achieves this liberation, he does so through his masculinity and possession of a penis. As I have suggested earlier and as Chasseguet-Smirgel reiterates, a boy's mother, living in a male-dominant society and in a family where her husband is not present as much as her son, cathects him heterosexually precisely on account of his maleness. (This, as I have pointed out, also has costs for the boy.) His penis and masculinity both compensate for his early narcissistic wound and symbolize his independence and separateness from his mother.

A girl's experience is likely to be different on two counts. A daughter does not have something differen and desirable with which to oppose maternal omnipotence, as does a son. Equally important, however, is that "the mother does not cathect her daughter in the same way that she cathects her son"[36] in the first place—she does not cathect her as a sexual other but, as I have discussed, as part of a narcissistically defined self.

One reaction on the part of a girl, in her attempt to liberate herself from her mother, is the development of penis envy or desire for the penis—in Chasseguet-Smirgel's view, also a dual (narcissistic and libidinal) affair. Early narcissistic injuries and anger at maternal

---

*Following them, she also calls the preoedipal mother "phallic." Her discussion, however, suggests that being phallic is a way of talking about power, and not so much a physiological characteristic of a mother who will then come to be recognized as what she really is, that is, "castrated."

omnipotence provide the preoedipal history and psychodynamic specificity which make a penis and masculinity important to a girl. According to her, a girl without a penis has

nothing with which to oppose the mother, no narcissistic virtue the mother does not also possess. She will not be able to "show her" her independence. So she will envy the boy his penis and say that he can "do everything." I see penis envy *not as "a virility claim" to something one wants for its own sake, but as a revolt against the person who caused the narcissistic wound: the omnipotent mother.* . . . The narcissistic wound aroused by the child's helplessness and penis envy are closely related.[37]

This view places the narcissistic desire for the penis on the proper metaphoric level: The penis, or phallus, is a symbol of power or omnipotence, whether you have one as a sexual organ (as a male) or as a sexual object (as her mother "possesses" her father's). A girl wants it for the powers which it symbolizes and the freedom it promises from her previous sense of dependence, and not because it is inherently and obviously better to be masculine: "Basically, penis envy is the symbolic expression of another desire. Women do not wish to become men, but want to detach themselves from the mother and become complete, autonomous *women*."[38] A girl's wish to liberate herself from her mother engenders penis envy.*

There is also an internal dynamic in a girl's turn to her father. A girl, having introjected a preambivalent (where "good" and "bad" are still undifferentiated) preoedipal mother-image in relation to herself, splits this internal image into good and bad aspects. Because she wants to justify her rejection of her mother, and because she experiences her mother as overwhelming, she then projects all the good-object qualities of her internalized mother-image and the inner relationship to her onto her father as an external object and onto her relationship to him. She retains all the bad-object characteristics for her mother, both as internal object and external. Secondarily, she also splits her image of her father, transferring all its bad aspects onto her mother as well.

Chasseguet-Smirgel's interpretation here illuminates the way in which, as Freud claims, a girl's attachment to her father grows out of and depends on her attachment to her mother. It also points to ways that the feminine oedipus complex is as much a change in a girl's inner relational stance toward her mother as it is a change from

---

*As I noted earlier, Chasseguet-Smirgel agrees with Horney, Klein, and Jones that a girl also comes to desire and love her father because of innate heterosexuality, and not only as a secondary reaction to her real desire to be masculine and possess a penis.

mother to father. An oedipal girl's "rejection" of her mother is a defense against primary identification, hence her own internal affair as much as a relational affair in the world. Insofar as a girl is identified with her mother, and their relationship retains qualities of primary identification and symbiosis, what she is doing, in splitting her internal maternal image, is attempting by fiat to establish boundaries between herself and her mother. She does this by projecting all that feels bad in their unity onto her mother and retaining all that is good for herself (to be brought into other, good relationships). She arbitrarily transfers these good and bad aspects of a fused internal object onto two different persons in relation to split aspects of herself.

Chasseguet-Smirgel, hence, gives us part of the necessary historical account: A girl's preoedipal experience of self, and of self in relation to mother, leads her to look for a symbol of her own autonomy and independence, and a relationship which will help her to get this. But her account retains Klein's (like Freud's) mistaken instinctual determinism, as well as Klein's blindness to the positive components of object-relationships. Oedipal daughters, in Chasseguet-Smirgel's view, are not even ambivalent about their mothers, but simply hate and fear them. There is no place here for a little girl's love for her mother, a love which Freud and most analysts probably take for granted, even while talking of hostility.

An alternate view of how a girl comes to envy the possession of a penis and to turn to her father speaks to this other side of a girl's ambivalence to her mother. Alice Balint, Brunswick, Lampl-de Groot, and anthropologist Gayle Rubin all suggest that *love* for the mother, rather than, or in addition to, hostility toward her, leads directly to penis envy.[39] All agree with Freud that the girl's castration complex is an important step in the development of her heterosexuality. They suggest, however, that we cannot assume that the origins of this castration complex are self-evident. Chasseguet-Smirgel has pointed to the origins of penis envy in ego issues, in the development of a girl's self-esteem, sense of autonomy, and experience of self. These theorists embed its origins in more immediately object-oriented causes: "The person of the mother herself has a special significance here. It is the *love for the mother* that causes the gravest difficulty for the little girl."*[40]

*All four agree on this component in the development of penis envy, though they vary in how they weigh it in comparison to other components. Brunswick is closest to Freud, in seeing the original basis of penis envy as narcissistic, with an "object root" added on. Balint and Lampl-de Groot tend to put more emphasis on the object-relational root, and to assume equivalent narcissistic threats to children of both genders. Rubin assigns to penis envy an almost exclusively object-oriented root.

Envy and narcissistic grievance, experienced by children of both genders, are insufficient to account for the strength of a girl's anger at her mother, especially if the girl knows that her mother has no penis either. What a girl comes to realize is that her common genital arrangement with her mother does not work to her advantage in forming a bond with her mother, does not make her mother love her more. Instead, she finds out her mother *prefers* people like her father (and brother) who have penises. She comes to want a penis, then, in order to win her mother's love:

If the little girl comes to the conclusion that such an organ is really indispensable to the possession of the mother, she experiences in addition to the narcissistic insults common to children of both sexes, still another blow, namely, a feeling of inferiority of her genitals.[41]

The wish to be a boy stems therefore not only from hurt narcissism, but perhaps even more from the *wounded love of the little girl for the mother*, whom she wants for herself just as much as a boy does.[42]

The psychoanalysts assume that this inequality in boys and girls is inevitable, because they assume heterosexuality. Rubin reminds us that a mother's heterosexuality is not an inevitable given, but has also been constructed in her own development one generation previously. It is not simply "the person of the mother herself," but the heterosexual person of the mother, who leads a girl to devalue her own genitals: "If the pre-Oedipal lesbian were not confronted by the heterosexuality of the mother, she might draw different conclusions about the relative status of her genitals."[43] In the view of Balint et al. then, a girl turns to her father in defense, feeling angry, like a rejected lover. She wants from him both the special love which she cannot get from her mother and a penis which will allow her to get this love—she both wants her father and wants her mother too. These accounts still stress that the intensity and ambivalence of her feelings cause a girl's turning from her mother, but they emphasize the positive side of her ambivalence—her feelings of love—rather than its negative aspects.

RELATIONAL COMPLEXITIES
IN THE FEMALE OEDIPUS SITUATION

Psychoanalysts offer various interpretations of the girl's turn to her father, but all these accounts share an important argument. They all claim that the oedipal situation is for a girl at least as much a mother-daughter concern as a father-daughter concern. A girl generally does turn to her father as a primary love object, and does feel hostile and rivalrous toward her mother in the process. This "change of object" may be partly a broadening of innate sexual drives, and it is probably in part a reaction to her heterosexual father's behavior and feelings toward her and his preoccupation with her (hetero-) sexuality. The turn to the father, however, is embedded in a girl's external relationship to her mother and in her relation to her mother as an internal object. It expresses hostility to her mother; it results from an attempt to win her mother's love; it is a reaction to powerlessness vis-à-vis maternal omnipotence and to primary identification. Every step of the way, as the analysts describe it, a girl develops her relationship to her father while looking back at her mother—to see if her mother is envious, to make sure she is in fact separate, to see if she can in this way win her mother, to see if she is really independent. Her turn to her father is both an attack on her mother and an expression of love for her.

Fairbairn, discussing the oedipus situation in general, suggests that this maternal primacy must result, given the structural situation of parenting in which women care for infants:

It is not difficult to see that the maternal components of both the internal objects have, so to speak, a great initial advantage over the paternal components; and this, of course, applies to children of both sexes. . . . *A sufficiently deep analysis of the Oedipus situation invariably reveals that this situation is built around the figures of an internal exciting mother and an internal rejecting mother.*[44]

The structural and affective form of the girl's oedipus complex grows out of the structural and affective form of her preoedipal object-relations. These relations, rooted in a particular family structure and ideology, center on her mother. Lampl-de Groot says, "The Oedipus complex is the final product of the pre-oedipal development. . . .[45] As the Oedipus complex carries along with it its previous history, the pre-oedipal phase, the events of the latter period determine the shape of the Oedipus constellation and thus play an important part in the ultimate formation of personality."[46]

A girl's "rejection" of her mother, and oedipal attachment to her father, therefore, do not mean the termination of the girl's affective relationship to her mother. Rather, a girl's dual internal and external mother-infant world becomes triadic. This process is encouraged by her father's role. He *has* probably interacted with her in ways that encourage her forming a heterosexual/feminine attachment to him. At the same time, because of his extrafamilial involvements, his own personality, and socialization as a father, he is not as likely to be involved in the family and in constant contact with his children as is his wife. Nor is the quality of this developing relationship to his daughter likely to have the same overwhelming impact on her as the earlier relation to her mother, since it does not concern whether or not she is a separate person.

Thus, a girl is likely to maintain both her parents as love objects and rivals throughout the oedipal period. Freud calls this a "complete Oedipus complex," and suggests that a boy also goes through phases of cathecting his father and wanting to replace his mother.[47] However, for most boys, this variant is but a weak echo of the reverse and does not really compete with it. In both cases, a boy is faced with the same choice between giving up his penis and giving up his parental object (since he can only take a "feminine" stance vis-à-vis his father if he is already castrated). In both cases he makes his choices fast. Usually he opts for his penis, which means that he opts for mother over father, and for repression, so that he will not be subject to castration by his father.

For a girl, however, there is no single oedipal mode or quick oedipal resolution, and there is no absolute "change of object." Psychoanalytic accounts make clear that a girl's libidinal turning to her father is not at the expense of, or a substitute for, her attachment to her mother. Nor does a girl give up the internal relationship to her mother which is a product of her earlier development. Instead, a girl develops important oedipal attachments to her mother *as well as* to her father. These attachments, and the way they are internalized, are built upon, and do not replace, her intense and exclusive preoedipal attachment to her mother and its internalized counterpart. If there is an absolute *component* to the change of object, it is at most a concentration on her father of a girl's genital, or erotic, cathexis. But a girl never gives up her mother as an internal or external love object, even if she does become heterosexual.

The male and female oedipus complex are asymmetrical. A girl's love for her father and rivalry with her mother is always tempered by love for her mother, even against her will. According to Brunswick, a girl, embittered and hostile toward her mother, does "seek to transfer her libido to the father," but "this transference is beset by difficulties arising from the tenacity of the active and passive preoedipal mother-attachment."[48] Thus, a girl's relational ambivalence toward her mother continues. This is also true for a girl's internal defensive operations, like object-splitting and projection.* The internal

*This splitting and projection can never be a permanent solution to experienced merging (as Alice Balint suggests, it maintains the connection with a negative sign).

relation and connection to the mother tend to persist in spite of her daughter's defensive maneuvers.

Analysts stress the lack of "final success" in the girl's turn to her father. Deutsch says that the girl does normally make a tentative choice in favor of her father, turning to him "with greater intensity, although still not exclusively."[49] Brunswick explains the possible variations in this outcome. She points to the number of adult women who come for analytic treatment who have "total lack of contact with the man," and suggests that this situation is only an exaggeration of the typical girl's oedipal resolution:

Between the exclusive attachment to the mother on the one hand and the complete transfer of the libido to the father on the other hand, the innumerable gradations of normal and abnormal development are to be found. It might also be said that partial success is the rule rather than the exception, so great is the proportion of women whose libido has remained fixed to the mother.[50]

Brunswick, Deutsch, and Freud here conflate several separable elements: conscious heterosexual erotic orientation—what we usually mean by *heterosexuality*, that is, being sexually attracted to people of a different gender; heterosexual love—forming a deep emotional attachment to a person of a different gender with whom one is sexually involved; and general, nonsexualized emotional attachments and their internalized object-relational counterparts—which do not speak to conscious sexual involvement or attraction. They focus their concern on conscious sexual orientation, and the possibility of women becoming erotically homosexual. What they are really describing, however, is not so specifically the genesis of sexual orientation as the genesis of emotional commitments and possibilities for love and emotional satisfaction. A girl's father does not serve as a sufficiently important object to break her maternal attachment, given his physical and emotional distance in conjunction with a girl's desperate need to separate from her mother but simultaneous love for her. While the father in most cases does activate heterosexual genitality in his daughter, he does not activate exclusive heterosexual love or exclusive generalized attachment. This "failure" is because of his own emotional qualities, because he is not her primary caretaker but comes on the scene after his daughter's relationship to this caretaker (her mother) is well established, and because he is not so involved with his children, however idealized and seductive he may be. A father is a different —and less available—oedipal object than a mother, and the differential involvement of the two parents with their child produces differences in her attachment to them.

A girl's internal oedipus situation is multilayered. Her relationship of dependence, attachment, and symbiosis to her mother continues, and her oedipal (triangular, sexualized) attachments to her mother and then her father are simply added. Freud, Brunswick, Deutsch, and Fairbairn imply that the relationship to the father is at most emotionally equal to that of the mother, that the relationships which compose the oedipus situation compete for primacy. Deutsch argues and offers abundant clinical examples in her *Psychology of Women* that the oedipal girl alternates between positive attraction to her father as escape from her mother, and reseeking of her mother as a safe and familiar refuge against her father's frustrating and frightening aspects: "Analytic experience offers abundant evidence of this bi-sexual oscillation between father and mother."[51]

A girl does "turn" to her father, and experiences her mother as a rival. This change of object, however, is founded on a lack of change. It is based in a girl's relation to her mother, both as this has become part of her internal object-world and ego defenses and as this relationship continues to be important and to change externally as much as, or maybe more than, her relationship to her father. Moreover, this "turn" cannot be absolute because of the depth of her maternal attachment and because of the emotional and physical distance of her father (now and previously). An oedipal girl, according to psychoanalysts, oscillates between attachment to her mother and to her father.

Two things stand out here. One is the external and internal relational complexity of the feminine oedipus complex, and the resulting complexities of cathectic orientations. A boy also may experience a "complete" oedipus complex, but his oscillation is usually not so pronounced, nor his heterosexual resolution so chancy (both treatment as a sexual other and his mother's generally greater emotional involvement mean that he is likely to get emotional satisfactions and involvements, as well as heterosexual genitality, from her that a girl does not get from her father). Second, fathers, given the normal situation of parenting and masculine and feminine personality, do not become the same kind of emotionally exclusive oedipal object for girls that mothers do for boys.

8

Oedipal Resolution and Adolescent Replay

In boys . . . the complex is not simply repressed, it is literally smashed to pieces by the shock of threatened castration.
FREUD,
"Some Psychical Consequences of the
Anatomical Distinction Between the Sexes"

Girls remain in it for an indeterminate length of time; they demolish it late and, even so, incompletely.
FREUD,
"Femininity"

The amicable loosening of the bond between daughter and mother is one of the most difficult tasks of education.
ALICE BALINT,
The Early Years of Life

A girl's longer preoedipal period, and her history of entry into the oedipus complex and different oedipal configuration, produce a third and final difference between a girl's oedipus complex and that of a boy: the manner in which each resolves it. Freud stresses the absolute finality of the boy's resolution of his oedipus complex.[1] He uses this observation as the basis for unwarranted and incorrect conclusions about women's lesser moral character, lesser ability to be objective, and lesser capacities for sublimation,[2] and both Freud's clinical accounts and those of others indicate that his characterization of the masculine resolution is idealized.* Nonetheless, a boy's repression of his oedipal maternal attachment (and his preoedipal dependence) seems to be *more* complete than a girl's. Neither mode of resolution

---

*It is not easy for boys to give up their intense mother-attachment, to come to terms with their father, and to recognize their mother's and father's relationship. In addition to oedipal tasks themselves, moreover, boys must deny dependence, deal with paternal fantasies about masculinity which often entail what they experience as rejecting behavior (fathers who cannot hold or be affectionate with even quite little boys), maintain precarious individuation, and develop in adulthood satisfactory relationships with women and men. These complexities in masculine development are not the immediate subject of my account here.

is intrinsically better, though each has distinct consequences. An examination of why boys and girls resolve their oedipus complex differently gives insight into these consequences, and into differences in masculine and feminine personality which result from the current structure and process of parenting.

THE ONGOINGNESS OF THE
FEMALE OEDIPUS SITUATION

In "The Dissolution of the Oedipus Complex," Freud held that a girl, since she is already castrated, has no motive for breaking up her infantile sexual organization.[3] She retains, therefore, a less repressed desire for her father. A boy, on the other hand, can be castrated and is more likely to fear paternal retaliation for his wishes. Therefore, he does repress love for his mother. Freud can come up with this theory, it is clear, by holding that only the presence of male genitalia matters to children of either gender. As Jones points out, children of either gender can feel threatened with the physical or psychical extinction of their sexuality.[4] He and Klein suggest further that a girl may very well fear retaliation by her mother in the form of internal destruction, and that in this respect a girl may have even more cause for fear, in that she cannot check as easily to make sure that her genitalia remain intact.[5] Moreover, as Freud also holds, superego formation and identification result from loss of love and fear of loss of a loved object,[6] and on this score a girl is just as likely to have fears, and has the same to lose, as a boy.

There are reasons other than the presence or absence of a penis which can account for the clinical finding that boys repress and resolve their oedipus complex in a way that girls do not. I read the clinical account as showing that the difference between a boy's oedipal relation to his mother and that of a girl toward her father produce this gender difference in processes of oedipal resolution. Compared to a girl's love for her father, a boy's oedipal love for his mother, because it is an extension of the intense mother-infant unity, is more overwhelming and threatening for his ego and sense of (masculine) independence. Reciprocally, as we have seen, a mother is invested in her baby boy (and probably baby girl) in a way that it is unlikely that a father will be invested in his young daughter, since his relationship to her does not have the same preoedipal roots. This mother-son love threatens her husband and causes him to resent his son. The intensity of the oedipal mother-son bond (and of the father-son rivalry) thus causes its repression in the son.

By contrast, as we have seen, a girl's attachment to her father does not become exclusive, nor is it as intense as that of a boy's to his mother. It is mitigated by her attachment to and dependence on her mother and is not reciprocated by her father with such intensity. Several analysts, in fact, stress the likelihood that a girl's oedipal love will *not* be reciprocated.[7] Moreover, because a girl's oedipal attachment to her mother and father comes later than a boy's to his mother, and because of the genesis of her attachment to her father as a reaction to maternal omnipotence, this attachment is less likely to be characterized by ambivalence and defensive anger. Since she has split and repressed these threatening components and negative feelings, and since her involvement is less intense in the first place, she is less likely to fear paternal or maternal retaliation, and therefore does not need as much to repress her oedipal love itself.

Sociologists give further insight into reasons for the difference in modes of masculine and feminine oedipal resolution. One primary goal of socialization, they argue, is to instill a taboo on nuclear family incest. Talcott Parsons, followed by Miriam Johnson, argues that mother-son incest is the most potentially regressive form of incest, because it threatens a son's returning to infantile dependency just when he should be initiating erotic and nonerotic relationships outside his family of origin. Father-daughter incest does not threaten a daughter in the same way because, presumably, her father is a less exclusive object.[8] They imply, using teleological reasoning, that mother-son incest is therefore most tabooed. The logic of their analyses points in a different direction, however. It is certainly the case that societies (and parents) enforce a taboo on incestuous relationships. However, given the organization of parenting, mother-son and mother-*daughter* incest* are the major threats to the formation of new families (as well as to the male-dominant family itself) and not, equivalently, mother-son and *father*-daughter incest. Mother-daughter incest may be the most "socially regressive," in the sense of a basic threat to species survival, since a mother and son can at least produce a child. But the threat of mother-daughter incestuous and exclusive involvement has been met by a girl's entry into the oedipus situation and her change of genital erotic object.

If we are looking for teleologically derived normative "tasks," an oedipal girl has fulfilled hers by becoming erotically heterosexual, while an oedipal boy—who is supposed to separate out and give up

---

*Or, since we are talking about more than actual commission of the sin, "incestuous" relationships—relationships that are not consummated but sufficiently emotionally and libidinally involved to keep son or daughter from forming nonfamilial sexual relationships.

his particular attachment to his mother while remaining heterosexual, and who is supposed to become masculine-identified while not becoming oriented sexually toward men—has yet to do so. For all the reasons I have suggested, the oedipal girl is very unlikely to have the intense investment in her relationship with her father that a boy has in the relationship with his mother. Accordingly, a girl does not have to give up her attachment to her father as radically, because this attachment was never so threatening to her future commitment to other men. Psychoanalytic theorists describe the ways some men go constantly from one woman to another, always searching for the perfect woman, an idealized mother-figure, and do not mention such a syndrome to be characteristic of women.[9] Freud and others suggest that a woman's relationship to men is as likely to take its character from her relation to her *mother* as to her father;[10] and sociologist Robert Winch reports that marked attachment to the opposite gender parent retards courtship progress for male college students and accelerates it for females.[11]

Girls, as Freud suggests, do eventually resolve their oedipus complex, but they do not "smash it to pieces." They do give up to some extent the intense, immediately sexualized investment in or overwhelming anger toward both parents, and transfer these into less emotion-laden and conflictual attachments and love. They certainly develop the identifications which lead to superego formation. However, the organization of parenting generates a relational situation in a girl's oedipus complex in which she does not need to repress her oedipal attachments so thoroughly as a boy does. Her attachment to her father in particular is more idealized and less intense than a boy's to his mother. Given this less charged attachment, and given her ongoing relation to her mother, she is less likely to fear maternal retaliation, and maternal retaliation fantasies are less likely than paternal retaliation fantasies toward a son.

MOTHERS, DAUGHTERS, AND ADOLESCENCE

My reading of the psychoanalytic account of the feminine oedipus complex suggests that the asymmetrical structure of parenting generates a feminine oedipus complex with particular characteristics. Because mothers are the primary love object and object of identification for children of both genders, and because fathers come into the relational picture later and differently, the oedipus complex in girls is characterized by the continuation of preoedipal attachments and preoccupations, sexual oscillation in an oedipal triangle, and the lack of either absolute change of love object or absolute oedipal resolution. Clinical descriptions and theory concerning the girl's object-relations during puberty and adolescence show how a girl revives these issues at this time and how they move with her into adulthood.

In going from oedipal resolution to adolescence, I am jumping over what psychoanalysts call the "latency" period (the period between the oedipal resolution and puberty). This period was originally thought to be one in which sexuality recedes as an issue (is repressed and/or sublimated), only to reemerge with the fresh impetus brought by puberty. More recently, Peter Blos has suggested that a better way to conceptualize latency is as a period in which no *new* instinctual urges or issues develop, rather than as one in which no sexual concerns exist at all.[12] New concerns, in this view, emerge at puberty.* I am assuming, in line with my object-relational reformulation of the drive theory and from my reading of clinical accounts, that in our society latency is also not typically a period of major crises and conflicts in object-relations but a period of learning and living in the world (school, peers, and so forth). Much of the conscious learning and role-training that feminists, role theorists, and social psychologists have described occurs at this time.

In moving in my discussion to adolescence then, I am moving to a period of renewed crises and conflict, in which new object-relational and ego resolutions are made. I do not mean to consider general issues about adolescence *qua* adolescence, as these have been developed in the social psychological literature. I am concerned only to draw out further the developmental lines I have been discussing, those related to the structure of parenting, mother-daughter relationships, and the construction of the feminine psyche in its object-world. Peter Blos, in his classic psychoanalytic study of adolescence, claims that the main issue of early adolescence and adolescence is "object relinquishment and object finding."[13] That is, a child of either gender must give up its incestuous love objects (parents, siblings, parent substitutes) in favor of other primary objects in order to be able to go out into the nonfamilial relational world.

As we might expect, most boys in this situation are in a favorable position compared to most girls. Most boys have had to (that is, felt that they had to) repress and renounce their oedipal wishes more radically, to "resolve" their oedipal complex. They are therefore more ready to turn to the nonfamilial external world in a search for important objects. (I say *most* boys, here, because the form of this re-

---

*For Freud, puberty is the time when eroticization of the vagina occurs in girls; the end of the oedipus complex involves simply giving up their clitoris as an organ of pleasure.

nouncing varies. As I have suggested, a man is also more likely to take his oedipal search into adulthood, perhaps just because he had to give up his heterosexual oedipal object—his mother—so precipitously and because she has so much general significance for him, compared to the significance that a girl's heterosexual oedipal object—her father—has for her.)

By contrast, a girl's transition from her oedipus complex has not been so precipitous. This has enabled (or required) her to maintain affective connections to her familial objects, as well as a conflictual and less-resolved inner object-world. Before she can fully develop extrafamilial commitments, therefore, a girl must confront her entanglement in familial relationships themselves. It is not surprising, then, that as Blos and other analysts point out, the pubertal/adolescent transition is more difficult and conflictual for girls than for boys, and that issues during this period concern a girl's relationship to her mother: "The girl struggles with object relations more intensely during her adolescence: in fact, the prolonged and painful severence from the mother constitutes the major task of this period."[14]

This struggle occurs in the context of a mutually engaged relationship with a girl's mother. Both Deutsch and Alice Balint discuss the way a mother reciprocates her daughter's involvement with her.[15] Mothers feel ambivalent toward their daughters, and react to their daughters' ambivalence toward them. They desire both to keep daughters close and to push them into adulthood. This ambivalence in turn creates more anxiety in their daughters and provokes attempts by these daughters to break away. Deutsch suggests that this spiral, laden as it is with ambivalence, leaves mother and daughter convinced that any separation between them will bring disaster to both. Balint concurs and points to the expressions of this ambivalence in mothers:

The mother's ambivalence, too, is apt to manifest itself partly by an exaggerated (because guilty) tenderness, and partly in open hostility. In either case the danger arises that the daughter, instead of finding the path away from the mother towards men, remains tied to the mother. Coldness on the mother's part may, because of the child's unappeased love for her, prevent the requisite loosening of the bond between them. The child will still eternally seek, even when grown up, for a mother-substitute, and bring a childish, immature love to the relationship. Yet on the other hand, excessive tenderness—since it allows for no discharge of hostile feelings—keeps the child in a perpetual emotional slavery to the mother, hemmed in by potential guilt.[16]

Against this collusive binding, or along with it, a girl takes what steps she can toward internal feelings of individuation and relational stability and external independence. Deutsch perceptively describes these processes.* (Later clinical accounts confirm her interpretations and the developmental account she derives from them.[17]) Deutsch demonstrates that a girl's object-relational experiences and issues during the prepubertal period and during puberty recapitulate her never-resolved preoedipal and oedipal conflicts.

During her prepubertal period, the central issue for the girl is a two-person issue—a struggle for psychological liberation from her mother. Her father—loved or rejected, experienced as powerful or weak—is emotionally in the background. It is not simply that a girl is preoccupied with her attachment to her mother, however. This attachment, as Deutsch and Blos describe it, reproduces its two-person preoedipal counterpart in its ambivalence, its binding quality, its nonresolution, and often in its involvement with food and body issues (at this later time, this involvement is often around weight, clothes, and so forth). A girl tends to retain elements of her preoedipal primary love and primary identification. This has been compounded through the years by reinforcement from a more conscious gender-role identification with her mother. The ease of this identification and the feeling of continuity with her mother conflict with a girl's felt need to separate from her and to overcome her ambivalent and dependent preoedipally-toned relationship.

The conflating of ambivalent primary identification, ambivalent secondary identification, and ambivalent object choice specifies the prepubertal (as preoedipal) girl's relationship to her mother.** That is, a daughter acts as if she is and feels herself unconsciously one with her mother. Puberty helps here because a girl, at this time, confronts all the social and psychological issues of being a woman (relations to men, menstruation and feminine reproductive functions, and so forth). In a society in which gender differences are central, this confrontation emphasizes her tie to and identification with her mother. So does whatever reciprocal unconscious or conscious proprietary interest in her daughter's developing sexuality a mother has. By this

---

*I cannot repeat this clinical detail here, but recommend the account (Chapters 1–3 in volume 1, especially) to anyone interested in understanding adolescent mother-daughter relationships. Deutsch has been ignored and criticized by feminist theorists because her theory of feminine personality is more Freudian than Freud's (passivity, narcissism and masochism as the biological core of femininity; women's "service to the species," and so on) and also because it is harder to plough through a theory of development elaborated through extensive clinical example than to read Freud's summary distillation.

**In Deutsch's terminology, the girl tries to break her "identification" with her mother. However, her actual account and her other comments about the girl's object-relationships indicate that she is talking about more than what we normally think of as identification. She is in fact talking about ambivalent feelings of both primary identification and attachment.

time, the daughter has gone through many years of conscious identification with her mother and women. Finally, daughters are apt still
to feel dependent on and attached to their mother.

The conflict at the prepubertal period is not *exactly* the same as
the preoedipal. In the earlier period, the construction of ego boundaries, individuation, and emergence from primary love were completely open. In the later period, the issue is usually not individuation
in its infantile sense: Most girls can act in the world according to the
reality principle, know cognitively that they are differentiated. In relation to their mother, however (and similarly, the mother in relation
to her daughters), they experience themselves as overly attached,
unindividuated, and without boundaries. Their conflict concerns
"preoedipal" issues, though it is replayed at a later time, informed by
the development which has gone on and the conflicts which have
emerged since the early period. (This duality is also characteristic of
the subsequent pubertal/oedipal replay.)

Deutsch describes a variety of ploys which prepubertal girls use
to effect their individuation and independence.[18] A girl often becomes very critical of her family, especially of her mother, and may
idealize the mother or the family of a friend. As earlier, she tries to
solve her ambivalent dependence and sense of oneness by projection
and by splitting the good and bad aspects of objects; her mother and
home represent bad, the extrafamilial world, good. Alternatively, she
may try in every way to be unlike her mother. (She may idealize a
woman teacher, another adult woman or older girl, or characters in
books and films, and contrast them to her mother.*) In this case her
solution again involves defensive splitting, along with projection, introjection, and the creation of arbitrary boundaries by negative identification (I am what she is not). In both cases she has fled to intense
identification-idealization-object loves, trying to merge herself with
anyone other than her mother, all the while expressing her feelings
of dependence on and primary identification with this mother. Another solution, Deutsch suggests, and one adopted by many prepubertal girls, is to find a "best friend" whom she loves, with whom she
is identified, with whom she shares everything.** This friend in part
counteracts the feelings of self-diffusion which result from the in-

---

*Behaviorally, this conscious identification with images of femininity is like a boy's
conscious use of cultural sources and adult men other than his father to construct a
sense of masculinity. The reasons are different, however: A girl is not trying to figure
out how to be feminine, but how not to be her mother. Gender-*role* identification is
not so involved, whereas it is *the* central issue in the masculine case.

**Deutsch describes and interprets the feminine form of what Sullivan calls the
preadolescent "chum" relationship, but which he describes entirely as a masculine
phenomenon.[19]

tensely experienced random identification-attachments in which the girl has engaged. Her friendship permits her to continue to experience merging, while at the same time denying feelings of merging with her mother.

All these attempts involve oscillations in emotions and ambivalence. A girl alternates between total rejection of a mother who represents infantile dependence and attachment to her, between identification with anyone other than her mother and feeling herself her mother's double and extension. Her mother often mirrors her preoccupations.[20]

Just as object-relations during the prepubertal period repeat elements of the preoedipal period, the object-relations of puberty and adolescence resemble those of the oedipus situation. During early puberty, a girl usually moves from preoccupation with her relationship to her mother to concern with her father and males. This period is characterized by bisexual wavering and indecisiveness about the relative importance to the girl of females (mother/girl friends) and males (father/boys). She may feel guilty toward her mother for loving her father more, thus keeping her conflicts within the family. Or she and her best friend may develop an attachment together to a male —a teacher, a boy they know—outside the family. Later puberty tends to be for most girls a time of greater resolution in favor of heterosexuality. In the adolescent case, however, unlike the oedipal, a girl must not only turn to her father but must also give up her oedipal father-attachment in favor of attachment to other males. In this sense, it is, as Deutsch puts it, "a new edition of the oedipus complex."[21]

As in the oedipal period, the choice of heterosexuality is not simply a natural development, but occurs in the context of her relationships. It is particularly dependent on the behavior of her father. As noted previously, social psychologists have found that fathers "sex-type" their children ("feminize" their daughters) more than mothers do.[22] "Sex-typing," however, remains an extremely vague concept. It is riddled with simplistic assumptions about gender roles, especially when measured by masculinity-femininity scales which are unidimensional (you cannot be both instrumental and expressive, for instance) and produce different results among different classes.[23]

Miriam Johnson and E. Mavis Hetherington formulate the meaning of the father-daughter relationship more precisely.[24] Hetherington, in one of the few studies of the effects of father-absence on girls, found that adolescent girls from father-absent homes were uncomfortable and insecure with men and boys. Yet they had no other deviations from traditional gender-typing in their behavior, preferences, or sense of identity. They were slightly more dependent on adult women, but father-absent and father-present girls related to women in basically the same way. Johnson, drawing on this and other studies, suggests that we can understand the father's role in his daughter's development if we divide femininity, as it develops in the family and is relevant for a girl's future family roles, into two components—the maternal and the heterosexual.* When social psychologists claim that fathers "feminize" daughters and produce the appropriate gender-role development, she suggests, they are not talking about gender-role learning in general but about heterosexual aspects of the feminine role in particular ("passivity" and "dependence," for instance, as these are behaviors oriented toward men).

These findings confirm the psychoanalytic account. This account, which centers on the development of heterosexuality in women (in psychoanalytic discussion, femininity equals female sexuality equals sexual orientation to men, passivity, and so on), claims that the father's role is to shape his daughter's sexuality (without getting too involved in it).**

The two periods when a father is most crucial to his daughter's development are the oedipal period and early adolescence—both times when a girl is supposed to be negotiating her transition to heterosexuality. Going one step further than Freud, who suggests that "the constitution will not adopt itself to its function without a struggle,"[26] Deutsch suggests that this struggle takes place against an "environment" which socializes a girl into her biologically engendered feminine role (for Deutsch, recall, femininity means heterosexual orientation, passivity, and relinquishment of clitoris for vagina). Deutsch points out that "the environment exerts an inhibiting influence as regards both [a girl's] aggressions and her activity," and "offers the woman's ego a kind of prize or bribe for renouncing them."[27] The environment here is social and ideological, and, as in the social psychological accounts, her father mediates it:

The bribe offered to the little girl by the father, as a representative of the environment, is love and tenderness. . . . The father is a representative of the environment, which later will again and again exert this inhibiting influence on the woman's activity and drive her back into her constitutionally predetermined passive role.[28]

*"Those aspects of femininity that are oriented to [both sexual and more general] interaction with males in terms of their 'masculinity.' "[25]

**Johnson, following Parsons and several psychoanalysts, also speaks to the father's role in individuation and emancipating children from primary love, but this role, as I point out in Chapter 4, could be played by *any* secondary parenting figure of either gender. It is played by fathers only because of our organization of parenting.

Deutsch summarizes the complexity and difficulty of a girl's adolescent tasks:

Thus the task of adolescence is not only to master the oedipus complex, but also to continue the work begun during prepuberty and early puberty, that is, to give adult forms to the old, much deeper, and much more primitive ties with the mother, and to end all bisexual wavering in favor of a definite heterosexual orientation.[29]

But the adolescent period is reminiscent of the feminine oedipus complex even in its final moment. In Deutsch's view, as in Freud's, a woman is "biologically destined" to submit passively to intercourse with men in order to produce children. Their clinical account makes clear that nothing inevitable leads a girl to this destiny: Girls do not give up their attachment to their mother, and do not make final and absolute commitments to heterosexual *love*, as emotional commitment, whether or not they make final commitments of genital object-choice. Deutsch contrasts this finding to Freud's original views:

Freud raised the problem regarding the manner in which the girl's love object changes from the mother, hitherto the only object of her attachment, to father. Numerous attempts to explain this, on the part of Freud and other authors, have been based on the assumption that this change is accomplished during childhood, but, according to my view, it is never completely achieved.[30]

Adolescent girls in our society tend to remain attached to their mothers and preoccupied with preoedipal and oedipal issues in relation to her even while becoming "heterosexual." These preoccupations persist not for biological reasons, but because their mother is their primary caretaker. Her father has never presented himself to a girl with the same force as her mother. He is not present as much, and is not involved with his children in the same way. Even if he is idealized, adored, and an object of internal fantasy, he is not the same primary, internal object as her mother and therefore cannot, finally, counteract his daughter's primary identification with and attachment to her mother. Mothers, especially in isolated nuclear family settings without other major occupations, are also invested in their daughters, feel ambivalence toward them, and have difficulty in separating from them.

Girls in our society have normally remained externally and internally in relationships with their preoedipal mother and have been preoccupied with issues of separation, identification without merging, mitigation of dependency, freedom from ambivalence. Girls cannot and do not "reject" their mother and women in favor of their father and men, but remain in a bisexual triangle throughout childhood and into puberty. They usually make a sexual resolution in favor of men and their father, but retain an internal emotional triangle.

9

Freud: Ideology and Evidence

"Anatomy is Destiny," to vary a saying of Napoleon's.

FREUD,
"The Dissolution of the Oedipus Complex"

Freud and psychoanalysts who follow him locate the origins of gender differentiation in personality in the oedipal period and in the issues and developmental tasks of this period. As Freud saw it, the oedipus complex constitutes the ultimate formative cause of both health and neurosis. A discussion of this period, then, has led us to the center of early psychoanalytic theory. My account agrees that crucial features of gender personality emerge out of the oedipal crisis. However, the traditional psychoanalytic account is open to significant criticism, and it (unintentionally) misrepresents what it can claim to show. Here I consider these criticisms and this misrepresentation.

BIAS IN THE FREUDIAN ACCOUNT

Anyone who draws on psychoanalysis to explain the psychology of women today is aware of the extensive criticism in most feminist literature of the Freudian account of female development and the development of sex differences. Mitchell has put forth a major counterargument to these criticisms and has led many feminists to take Freud seriously once again.[1] However, her otherwise provocative and important discussion includes a zealous defense of every claim Freud makes. She implies that all have equal empirical and methodological status and are always valid. Therefore (I think unfortunately) she has sometimes failed to convince others, since she often seems another apologist for Freud's misogyny and patriarchal distortions. Mitchell defends uncritically Freud's work, sharply criticizes that of his contemporaries (both supporters, like Deutsch, and opponents, like Horney and Jones), and ignores most later developments in psychoanalytic theory. These positions put her well to one extreme of the views expressed by psychoanalysts, some of whom have been much more critical of the traditional formulations and have attempted to develop them in different directions.[2]

Unlike Mitchell, I feel that much of this criticism is justified. Feminist critics of Freud, as well as psychoanalysts, have engaged in an important and necessary critical task in exposing the ideological biases in what has, after all, come to be our cultural psychology. We must face up to the Freudian excesses. Freud was only sometimes describing how women develop in a patriarchal society. At other times, he was simply making unsupported assertions which should be taken as no more than that, or as statements about how women (and men) ought to be. I have mentioned some of these claims in the previous chapters. Most have no clinical warrant; they are not grounded in clinical experience or interpretation nor, as in the case of penis envy I have discussed, are they interpreted in ways that follow psychoanalytic methodological principles. Rather, they grow from unexamined patriarchal cultural assumptions, from Freud's own blindnesses, contempt of women, and misogyny, from claims about biology which Freud was in no position to demonstrate from his own research, from a patriarchal value system and an evolutionary theory to rationalize these values.

We do a disservice to the psychoanalytic cause Freud professed if we accept his claims unquestioningly. Psychoanalytic theory remains the most coherent, convincing theory of personality development available for an understanding of fundamental aspects of the psychology of women in our society, in spite of its biases. The critique I propose is meant to show by elimination and specification just what the Freudian account can with justification claim to tell us. It is not meant as an exhaustive evaluation of the scientific "validity" of early Freudian claims.[3]

What strikes an attuned reader when reading Freud is his failure to deal with women at all in the major part of his writing, even when it specifically concerns issues of gender. Freud is explicit when he says, "In its simplified form the case of a male child may be described," or "In order to simplify my presentation I shall discuss only [the boy's] identification with the father."[4] This sort of remark often goes along with an admission (reiterated in many psychoanalytic defenses of Freud) that he did not know very much about women and did not really understand them. In his essay "The Dissolution of the Oedipus Complex," for example, Freud says, "It must be admitted, however, that in general our insight into these developmental processes in girls is unsatisfactory, incomplete, and vague."[5] His final major formulation on "femininity" concludes with the admission that his knowledge is "incomplete and fragmentary."[6] If we had only statements such as these to go on, we might accuse him of no more than the normal tendency in most social and psychological thought to equate maleness with humanness. We would need, to right the situation, to do research concerning women on the questions he treats.

These admissions, however, are in Freud's case part of an obvious condescension, if not misogyny, toward women and a virtual dismissal of interest in them. In his essay on the "psychical consequences of the anatomical distinction between the sexes," Freud explains how girls do not demolish their oedipus complex in the same way as do boys, and therefore do not develop an equally severe superego. He concludes (endearing himself to a generation of feminists), "I cannot evade the notion (though I hesitate to give it expression) that for women the level of what is ethically normal is different from what it is in men. Their super-ego is never so inexorable, so impersonal, so independent of its emotional origins as we require it to be in men."[7] Here, and in his later lecture on "femininity," he claims that women have less sense of justice than men, are overwhelmed by jealousy and shame, are vain, are unable to submit to life's requirements, and have made no contribution to civilization.* Most of these traits, he implies, are not discovered through his clinical work. They are "character-traits which critics of every epoch have brought up against women,"[9] and which Freud can deduce logically from his theory of the psychic effects of genital differences. However, given his admissions of ignorance about women, and given that these are not claims formulated in psychological terms, we do better, methodologically, to take them as gratuitous. Freud does not seem particularly concerned to find evidence, nor to formulate his claims theoretically. The man who wanted psychoanalysis to be as scientifically rigorous as his earlier neurological research, and whose theory is founded on the discovery that our experiences are not what they seem, suggests three seemingly equivalent ways to find out more about women: "Enquire from your experiences of life, or turn to the poets, or wait until science can give you deeper and more coherent information."[10]

Freud's conclusions here are not accidental, nor is he unconscious of the purposes they serve. He is aware in all his writing about women of the political setting in which he is working and is unambiguous about which side he supports. In several major statements on mas-

---

*With the exception of weaving and plaiting—which women developed on the model of their pubic hair to further cover their genital deficiency from the world![8]

culinity and femininity, he anticipates a feminist response in a way which makes it unclear whether he or feminists first chose to make psychoanalysis a center of ideological struggle. He argues that "the feminist demand for equal rights between the sexes does not take us far";[11] that "we must not allow ourselves to be deflected from such conclusions [about women's sense of justice and so forth] by the denials of feminists, who are anxious to force us to regard the two sexes as completely equal in position and worth";[12] and that "feminists are not pleased when we point out to them the effects of this factor [superego development again] upon the average feminine character."[13] By these last years, feminism appears to have crept into the psychoanalytic ranks themselves. In his essay on "Female Sexuality" he, uncharacteristically, reviews all other recent work on this topic, specifying exactly with whom he agrees and disagrees.[14] In his later lecture on the same topic, he smugly replies to female analysts who had presumed to criticize him and other male analysts in their characterization of femininity: "We . . . standing on the ground of bisexuality, had no difficulty in avoiding impoliteness. We had only to say: 'This doesn't apply to *you*. You're the exception; on this point you're more masculine than feminine.' "[15] None of these attitudes, moreover, needs any explanation by Freud. As we know, a central outcome of the masculine oedipus complex is, and is expected to be, "what we have come to consider the normal male contempt for women."[16]

Explicit statements of the sort I have mentioned are not difficult to isolate and criticize. However, the assumptions they embody are not random or contingent to the main point of psychoanalysis, but are embedded in what is directly a theory of gender itself. These assumptions, which form the basis of psychoanalytic theory, range from those which grow out of unsubstantiated sexist assumptions to others which reflect serious distortions of reality. They have serious therapeutic implications for what is taken to be a possible goal of therapy, and for what is taken to be normal development.

Horney's early observation that the picture of feminine development propounded by Freud is completely isomorphic with the traditional psychoanalytic picture of the four-year-old boy's view of girls is correct.[17] Freud and his orthodox followers often unwittingly translate clinically derived accounts of fantasy into their own scientific account of reality. This is most obvious in relation to accounts of the relative valuation of male and female genitals and characteristics and the accompanying description of female anatomy. Thus, Freud does not tell us only that a little girl *thinks* or *imagines* that she is castrated*

---

*We should note that the psychoanalytic use of "castration" here is itself a misconception a child might have. Castration in men means removal of the testes and not amputation of the penis.

or mutilated, or that she *thinks* she is inferior or an incomplete boy. Rather, she *is* so. Freud mentions, for example, the girl's "discovery that she *is* castrated,"[18] her refusal "to accept the *fact* of being castrated,"[19] the woman's need to conceal her "genital deficiency."[20] In a similar vein, Brunswick implies that a normal mother *is* castrated, in her suggestion that the concept of the phallic mother is a product of "pure fantasy," while "both the active and the castrated mother exist *in point of fact*."[21] Abraham, finally, speaks not so much of what these organs *are* as what they can *do*: "We must keep in view *the fact that* sexual activity is essentially associated with the male organ, that the woman is only in the position to excite the man's libido or respond to it, and that otherwise she is compelled to adopt a waiting attitude."[22] He even manages to imply that males have a more important role than females in childbirth, suggesting that girls often prefer the stork myth to the more accurate knowledge they have gained about procreation, because "the stork tale has the advantage that in it children originate without the man's part being a more privileged one than theirs in respect of activity."[23]

Freud's discussion of these anatomical differences is not simply concerned with *difference*—difference in this case is equated with relations of superiority and inferiority. Thus, he persistently refers to women's "genital deficiency," and sees no need to explain that a girl, on discovering her penislessness, "develops, like a scar [a psychic scar to match the physical one?], a sense of inferiority."[24] This holds as well for Freud's characterological claims. Schafer points out that even if we grant Freud's account of differences in superego formation and ego development (and Schafer questions whether we have reason for doing so in the first place), Freud can *at most* claim to be talking about different "modes of response or configurations of attitude and behavior"[25] in moral activity and ego processes:

Modes may be described, and different modes may be contrasted, but only a taken-for-granted patriarchal value system could lead to Freud's unqualified statement about women's relative mental incompetence. . . . One must conclude that Freud's estimates of women's morality and objectivity are logically and empirically indefensible. In large part these estimates implement conventional patriarchal values and judgments that have been misconstrued as being disinterested, culture-free scientific observations.[26]

Freud's androcentric view of development more subtly manifests this valuational and evidential bias. His view is that children, when they begin to conceive of physiological gender differentiation, do so in terms of the presence or absence of masculinity: "For both sexes, only one kind of genital, namely the male, comes into account."[27] He arrives at this conclusion by definitional fiat, however, and not by clinical discovery. A little girl, he claims, does not recognize any female genitalia other than her clitoris. This clitoris, according to Freud, is not feminine but masculine because it involves active sexuality and can bring gratification without penile penetration, whereas Freud has *defined* femininity as vaginal and passive sexuality. Thus, he and Deutsch talk of "the atrophied penis, a girl's clitoris"[28] which is "in reality [again!] so inadequate a substitute for the penis."[29] Because of this definition, Freud can argue that a little girl's physical and psychical manifestations of genital activity are just like a boy's.

We could formulate this by suggesting that the sexes are in some respects originally undifferentiated, or that sexual behavior is originally without distinction of gender, or that all children, if parented by women, are originally actively matrisexual—all these formulations seem plausible. But Freud, beginning from his male norm, takes another position, one in which the account he provides moves from sexist bias into the distortion of reality. It all follows logically, but, as we have seen, its original premise is arbitrary. All children, he claims, are originally masculine: "We are now obliged to recognize that the little girl is a little man,"[30] or as Brunswick puts it, "At the beginning of her sexual life the little girl is to all intents and purposes a little boy."[31] A little girl is confronted with the strange task of literally changing her sex. Freud says, as if this conception were unproblematic, "As she changes in sex, so must the sex of her love object change."[32] Femaleness, according to Freud's account, does not become an issue for children of either sex until puberty:

At the stage of the pregenital sadistic-anal organization, there is as yet no question of male and female; the antithesis between *active* and *passive* is the dominant one. At the following stage of infantile genital organization, which we now know about, maleness exists, but not femaleness. The antithesis here is between having *a male genital* and being *castrated*. It is not until development has reached its completion at puberty that the sexual polarity coincides with *male* and *female*.[33]

These claims rest on several unexamined assumptions. One is the notion that children learn about gender differences through learning about genital differences. Brunswick suggests, for instance, that before the discovery of genital differences, "the child makes personal but not sexual differentiation between the individuals of its immediate world."[34] At this time, children assume that their own sexual constitution is universal. When they first see sex differences, they retain their original postulate that there is only one kind of genital and assume that everyone is supposed to have a penis. Boys stubbornly insist that everyone has a penis; girls, that everyone has a penis but them. Final recognition of their own gender identity comes with learning that genital differences between the sexes are systematic. A second assumption is that sexual orientation and mode define gender. A little girl is a little man or boy because she loves a woman, and her sexuality is active and clitoral. "Changing sex," as Freud puts it, means giving up her clitoris and her activity. Third is a *definitional* assumption about what constitutes female sexuality—that it is oriented to men, passive, and vaginal. This definition remains phallocentric: "Maleness combines [the factors of] subject, activity and possession of the penis; femaleness takes over [those of] object and passivity. The vagina is now valued as a place of shelter for the penis; it enters into the heritage of the womb."[35]

These assumptions of the primacy of maleness distort the Freudian view of gender and female psychological life, especially by downplaying anything associated with motherhood and refusing to recognize that desires to be a mother can develop other than as a conversion of penis envy and a girl's desire to be masculine. The baby, Freud says, is to a woman a symbolic substitute for a penis, which she really wants more. Freud here is again not simply reporting empirical observation, nor discussing a possible psychical component of a wish for babies. He admits that there are other ways that women come to want babies but then makes clear that any baby will not do, that a girl does not have a properly *feminine* wish for a baby until her femininity includes as a fundamental component the wish to be masculine. Penis envy here is no longer even an inevitable outcome of the anatomical difference between the sexes, but becomes a developmental task:

It has not escaped us that the girl has wished for a baby earlier, in the undisturbed phallic phase: that, of course, was the meaning of her playing with dolls. But that play was not in fact an expression of her femininity, it served as an identification with her mother. . . . Not until the emergence of the wish for a penis does the doll-baby become a baby from the girl's father, and thereafter the aim of the most powerful feminine wish. . . . Perhaps we ought rather to recognize this wish for a penis as being *par excellence* a feminine one.[36]

Freud's assumption that women's function is to have babies becomes subsumed under his view that femininity has to do only with sexual orientation and mode and the wish to be masculine. He seems to fear that in spite of his endeavors it might be possible to think of women independently from men if one focused on childbearing and motherhood too much (playing with dolls is only an identification with her mother). This orientation suggests how psychoanalysts could have made so little of what is in some ways the final goal of the development they describe. Sexuality in the psychoanalytic view has many aspects, much meaning, involves important conscious and un-

conscious transformations and enormous complexities in object-relations, whereas mothering is either ignored or dismissed in an aside
about a girl's identification with her mother.

These biases in the Freudian account did not go unnoticed. Against
Freud's hypothesis that all prepubertal genitality is masculine, Horney suggested, "I do not see why, in spite of its past evolution, it
should not be conceded that the clitoris legitimately belongs to and
forms an integral part of the female genital apparatus."[37] She points
out that analysts have bolstered their claims of male superiority by
focusing on genital differences to the exclusion of differences in the
reproductive functions of the two sexes. When they have paid attention to reproduction, it has been treated as compensation for genital
deficiency—for narcissistic penis envy or, in Ferenczi's case, because
a woman does not have a penis with which she can herself return,
through coitus, to her mother's womb. Anticipating Freud's suggestion that we "enquire of our own experience," Horney exclaims,

At this point I, as a woman, ask in amazement, and what about motherhood?
And the blissful consciousness of bearing a new life within oneself? And the
ineffable happiness of the increasing expectation of the appearance of this
new being? And the joy when it finally makes its appearance and one holds
it for the first time in one's arms? And the deep pleasurable feeling of satisfaction in suckling it and the happiness of the whole period when the infant
needs her care?[38]

Later she dares to suggest, against Freud, that female reproductive
functions are originally female, and not male: "The special point
about Freud's conception is rather that it views the wish for motherhood not as an innate formation, but as something that can be reduced psychologically to its ontogenetic elements and draws its energy originally from homosexual or phallic instinctual urges."[39]

I suggested earlier that Horney here is trapped, like Freud, in a
form of biological determination. They have equal problems of evidence: Horney needs to show an innate wish for motherhood, Freud
needs to justify his decision to consider as evidence only that which
supports the position that only a wish for a baby which emerges out
of penis envy is the real thing. Yet Horney's claim, beginning from
the assumption that there are two physiological sexes, each defined
by the genitalia and reproductive organs it possesses, and psychical
consequences possibly emergent from each, seems at least to lead logically in the right direction. Freud is certainly incorrect *biologically*

when he suggests that the clitoris is an atrophied penis or masculine organ. It is biologically the homologue of the penis, and we might ascribe to both the same character, but we cannot consider this character either feminine or masculine: The organ is "masculinized" into a penis through the input of androgens at the proper fetal time—whatever the chromosomal sex of the fetus—and if not androgenized becomes a clitoris—again regardless of chromosomal sex.[40]

Although we might dispute the extent to which feminine biology shapes psychic life without mediation of culture, it does seem plausible to look for drives toward pregnancy and lactation in femininity, rather than defining away anything which is not the result of blocked masculinity. Biologically, also, there is no justification for ascribing superiority or inferiority as a general feature of masculine or feminine genitalia or reproductive organs, though these organs have different capacities for particular functions (penetration, parturition, lactation).

It is argued by Freud's supporters that he had nothing *biological* in mind in this theory of sexual monism.[41] Instead, he was referring to psychoanalytic clinical findings that people (especially children) of both genders regard the clitoris as an inferior or atrophied penis and women as castrated men, and to clinical findings that children originally see sex as presence or absence and do not know about vaginas. From the moment they learn of the sexual difference, girls think their own organs are inferior, want to be boys, and think they can be if they get a penis.

But Horney, Jones, and Klein also bring clinical argument to bear against Freud. They ascribe a different history to children's fantasies and feelings about gender and genital differences. They agree with Freud that little girls love their mothers, but not that this makes them masculine. They agree that girls come to experience penis envy, but claim that this is reactive to earlier experiences, and not primary—girls do not originally think their own genitals are inferior and that they are castrated, but come to think so defensively. Similarly, they argue, girls have both conscious and unconscious awareness of their inner genital area and early vaginal sensations, and boys have intuitive or actual knowledge of the existence of vaginas. Both may then repress this knowledge from consciousness. As Horney put it, *"Behind the 'failure to discover' the vagina is a denial of its existence."*[42]

Both sides of the original argument base their claims more on interpretation and reconstruction from analyses of adults than on observations or analyses of children. Both must, I think, be accorded their own clinical claims. The opposition view, like Freud's, is limited by its own form of biological determinism. But its clinical evidence does lead to the conclusion that Freud's account is not inevitable or necessary, as he postulates.

Between the two, Freud's account is perhaps the more strained. His "argument" against those who claim early knowledge of the vagina is inconsistent, illogical, and simply ignores their evidence:

> We believe we are justified in assuming that for many years the vagina is virtually nonexistent and possibly does not produce sensations until puberty. It is true that an increasing number of observers report that vaginal impulses are present even in these early years. In women, therefore, the main genital occurrences of childhood must take place in relation to the clitoris.[43]

Chasseguet-Smirgel argues convincingly that Freud's clinical account contradicts his assertion that the vagina does not become known until puberty, pointing especially to Freud's study of Little Hans. A reading of Little Hans supports the view that Hans knew unconsciously and often consciously about vaginas and uteruses. He has a variety of thinly veiled dreams and fantasies about penetration, and almost certainly understood and remembered his mother's pregnancy with his sister.* Chasseguet-Smirgel argues, with Horney, that the denial of the vagina and "sexual monism"—a child's notion (and Freud's) that there is only one genital, which people either have or are missing— is a way a child defends itself psychologically against the overwhelming importance of its early mother image. This "sexual monism" is a reaction to the infant's feelings of helplessness and dependence on its mother.**

Research on the development of gender identity and gender identity disturbances further qualifies the Freudian clinical claim.[46] These studies confirm that gender identity is with rare exception firmly and irreversibly established for both sexes by the time a child is around three. Gender identity receives its major input from social ascription of sex that begins at birth and is cognitively learned concomitantly with language. Physical experience, and a child's perception of its genitals and body, help to create a gendered body-ego but not in unmediated or inevitable ways. Thus, most girls early establish an unequivocally female gender identity with realistic perception of their own genital organs. Even a girl's or woman's discovery that she has

---

*Alternately, little Hans may have been denying the knowledge of genital and reproductive differences through splitting of the ego, so one part knew one thing, one part another. Chasseguet-Smirgel cites Little Hans:

[Father]: "But you know quite well that boys can't have children."
Hans: "Well, yes. But I believe they can, all the same."[44]

**Psychoanalysts continue to find evidence of unconscious and conscious early vaginal awareness in girls, which supports the view that such knowledge is later repressed by girls who then "discover" their vagina.[45]

chromosomal abnormalities or is missing inner genitalia or reproductive organs will not cause her to doubt her fundamental femaleness, if she has already developed an unambiguous gender identity
which her parents have never doubted. It is, moreover, almost always
easier for a person who has been "mistakenly" ascribed to the "wrong"
gender (according to chromosomal or hormonal sex, because of a sexual morphology which looked like the opposite sex's) to create sur-
gically the missing organ of the assigned sex than to change gender.

Stoller argues that both core gender identity and basic morphology may be best understood as female for both sexes. A boy's sense
of maleness—his sense that an enduring feature of his being in the
world is as a male—is more problematically attained than a girl's sense
of femaleness, because children of both sexes are cared for by women.
Thus, there are many more biologically normal males whose gender
is unambiguously female—that is, male transsexuals—than vice versa.
Stoller argues further that a sense of one's gender is independent of
sexual orientation or identification; sexual orientation and identification develop as a result of being treated as and having accepted
assignation as a person of a particular gender. Therefore, those issues
which Freudians make the center of their account—penis envy, love
for the mother, the "very circuitous path" to the "normal" feminine
oedipus complex with father as love-object[47]—are later phenomena
and do not involve a girl's fundamental sense of being female.

This research questions Freud's claim concerning the psychological primacy of maleness and masculinity. It also suggests, as is clear
from Freud's account though denied by his theory, that the development of gender identity is a precondition of the oedipus complex.
In order for a girl to have the oedipal experience she supposedly has,
she would have to know her own gender (and about gender differences) in order to connect herself to her mother, to be vulnerable to
differences in sexual morphology, and to think these matter. In fact,
what occurs for both sexes during the oedipal period is a product of
this knowledge about gender and its social and familial significance,
rather than the reverse (as the psychoanalytic accounts have it).*

Freud's differential evaluation of male and female genitals and
masculine and feminine character, his androcentric view of development, and his equation of that which is female with heterosexuality

---

*This interpretation of the genesis of the oedipus complex receives some support
from recent psychoanalytic clinical findings. This research suggests an early genital
phase in the child's second year, which connects the development of a gendered body-
ego and classically "oedipal" conflicts about castration, and penis envy, to the earliest
development of sense of self separated from mother.[48]

and resentment at not being male, all have significant implications for therapy and for assumptions about "normality." In looking at these implications, it is important to keep in mind that psychoanalytic accounts tend to agree about a *clinical* picture likely to characterize women. "Dissidents" (Klein, Horney, Jones, Thompson, more recently Chasseguet-Smirgel, Stoller) like "orthodox" Freudians (Bonaparte, Deutsch, Brunswick, Lampl-de Groot, more recently Greenacre) agree that many women patients express "penis envy," and that analysts meet with masochism (aggressiveness turned upon the self and pleasure in pain), narcissism (the need to be loved), and passivity in women. All agree, moreover, that these are early developed, unconscious, complex psychic formations, transformed and often built into fundamental character, and are not simply conscious attitudes imposed by a patriarchal society, to be dealt with by reassurance, pointing to the effects of patriarchy, or convincing women to feel better.

Where the "dissidents" disagree with Freud is in the extent to which they think these characteristics can be treated. Freud's view, and that shared by some of his early colleagues, is that penis envy comes out of a girl/woman's bisexuality (just as attraction to other men and castration anxiety come out of men's bisexuality). This bisexuality is a basic physiological fact and therefore inevitable. Therefore, all character traits which derive from it—narcissism, masochism, envy, and so on—are also inevitable. As a result, these traits are all-pervasive; penis envy persists throughout women's psychic existence.[49] Moreover, psychoanalysis can affect only the psychic, and Freud suggests that women's penis envy and men's rejection of their own femininity, resting as they do on a biological basis, are exceedingly difficult to overcome. As Freud tells us in "Analysis Terminable and Interminable,"

We often have the impression that with the wish for a penis and the masculine protest we have penetrated through all the psychological strata and have reached bedrock, and thus our activities are at an end. This is probably true, since, for the psychical field, the biological field does in fact play the part of the underlying bedrock. The repudiation of femininity can be nothing else than a biological fact, a part of the great riddle of sex.[50]

The bedrock, moreover, is less mutable in women (and girls), because giving up penis envy gains them nothing immediately positive, in Freud's view. (A baby and heterosexuality are, recall, roundabout ways to get a penis—a real penis from fathers and men, a symbolic penis in the form of a baby.) A man, by contrast, gets the direct reward of his penis and masculinity for his efforts:

We must not overlook the fact that [the wish to have attributes of the other sex] cannot, by its very nature, occupy the same position in both sexes. In males the striving to be masculine is completely ego-syntonic from the first. . . . In females, too, the striving to be masculine is ego-syntonic at a certain period. . . . But it then succumbs to the momentous process of repression.[51]

I have mentioned what Schafer calls Freud's remarkable lack of curiosity here, a lack inconsistent with Freud's methodology. What Freud gains, however, is justification for giving up on women without seeking either developmental or social explanations for their neuroses and problems. These were an inevitable outcome of women's bisexuality in the particular asymmetric form bisexuality takes. His cavalier dismissal is appalling:

A man of about thirty strikes us as a youthful, somewhat unformed individual, whom we expect to make powerful use of the possibilities for development opened up to him by analysis. A woman of the same age, however, often frightens us by her psychical rigidity, and unchangeability. Her libido has taken up final positions and seems incapable of exchanging them for others. There are no paths open to further development; it is as though the whole process had already run its course and remains thenceforward insusceptible to influence—as though, indeed, the difficult development to femininity had exhausted the possibilities of the person concerned.[52]

In a similar vein, Abraham complains vindictively that women in analysis who wish for some autonomy have extremely obstinate, anal characters and are beyond help: "They want, for example, to find out everything in their psycho-analysis by themselves without the help of the physician. They are as a rule women who through their obstinacy, envy, and self-overestimation destroy all their relationships with their environment, and indeed their whole life."[53]

Once again, these conclusions are derived from a logical process resting on faulty assumptions; once again, there is an opposed tradition from early in psychoanalytic thought, beginning with Horney and Jones. Freud's hypothesis of bisexuality included within it a contradictory assumption of masculine and male primacy, which led him to accept as natural the desire in women to have masculine physiological or social prerogatives, though these desires were usually painful, made women unhappy, and led to character traits and neuroses which Freud otherwise thought should be treated. Horney and Jones, by contrast, and those who have followed their line of argument, do not see these phenomena as inevitable (and desirable) consequences of biology. They see them as undesirable, contingent, and open to analysis. As is clear from their clinical writing, many orthodox analysts also have not accepted Freud's and Abraham's position, and recent psychoanalytic writing certainly moves away from it. However, the early dissenters had no theoretical justification for not following Freud, and recent analysts only begin to do so. These unwarranted assumptions on Freud's part have never been systematically refuted within the psychoanalytic tradition in a manner that presents a coherent alternative theory.*

BIOLOGICAL DETERMINISM

Psychoanalysis developed out of the discovery that there was nothing inevitable in the development of sexual object choice, mode, or aim, nor was there innate masculinity or femininity. How one understands, fantasizes, symbolizes, internally represents and feels about her or his physiology is a product of developmental experience in the family, is related in many possible ways to this physiology, and perhaps is shaped by considerations completely apart from it. At the same time, Freud often sounds, in matters concerning the sexes, like a biological determinist. He argues that "the feminist demand for equal rights for the sexes does not take us far, for the morphological distinction is bound to find expression in differences of psychical development,"[54] and he titles an important article, "Some Psychical Consequences of the Anatomical Distinction Between the Sexes."

Freud is a biological determinist only in a specific sense—a sense, however, which has profound implications for the development of his theory. It is not, according to Freud, that people of either gender naturally develop in particular ways as a result of their physiology. Rather, psychoanalysis looks at this development in terms of a particular interpretation of the meaning of sexual differentiation. Underlying the psychoanalytic position is the assumption that this differentiation is meant to serve biological reproduction.[55] Anatomy is destiny, then, in a *functional* sense. The psychoanalytic discovery that "the constitution will not adapt itself to its function without a struggle"[56]—that anatomy is *not* destiny in the maturational sense—only makes the path to this destiny more problematic.

This particular biologically determinist position is responsible for the apparently contradictory way that Freud appears both as a per-

---

*Schafer's argument that we need to look for the *history* of an oedipal girl's reaction to her penislessness is certainly a beginning. Robert Stoller's work, which brings his research on the development of gender identity to bear on psychoanalytic theory, is the basis for such a full substitute developmental account. However, Stoller's research has not been accorded that kind of significance in the psychoanalytic community as a whole. Stoller explicitly rejects some of Freud's basic claims, whereas analysts generally tend to search diligently to show that whatever reformulation they are engaged in is really based in some passage, article, or footnote of Freud's. This forthrightness may have hurt Stoller's cause.

petrator of patriarchal hegemony and as an astute analyst of patriarchal culture. On one level, psychoanalysis does describe and interpret how people come to value themselves and their genitals, and how they come to have particular sexual predilections, neuroses, character traits, and inner object worlds. On another level, however, psychoanalysis and psychoanalytic descriptions of development assume the desirability and rightness of traditional gender roles in the family, of debilitating personality characteristics in women, and of heterosexuality, because these seem to serve functional goals of biological reproduction.

Both Deutsch and Freud, for instance, explicitly link aspects of femininity that serve biological ends and are goals of feminine development (passivity and masochism) to the social purposes these serve. Freud claims,

It is our impression that more constraint has been applied to the libido when it is pressed into the service of the feminine function, and that—to speak teleologically—Nature takes less careful account of its [that function's] demands than in the case of masculinity. And the reason for this may lie— thinking once again teleologically—in the fact that the accomplishment of the aim of biology has been entrusted to the aggressiveness of men and has been made to some extent independent of women's consent.[57]

Deutsch accepts the Freudian clinical picture and Freud's functional teleological explanation for it, and uses these to support a sexual status quo on which, she suggests, depends the very continuation of the species. Feminine masochism, according to Deutsch, is biologically required for women's "service to the species." That is, women's experiences in intercourse and childbirth become tied to masochistic pleasure, and even the mother-child relation is based on feminine masochism: "In the deepest experience of the relation of mother to child it is masochism in its strongest form which finds gratification in the bliss of motherhood."[58] This masochism has its social counterpart, and is the fortuitous reason that women put up with their oppression. In concluding her account of feminine masochism, Deutsch states,

Women would never have suffered themselves throughout the epochs of history to have been withheld by social ordinances on the one hand from possibilities of sublimation, and on the other from sexual gratifications, were it not that in the function of reproduction they have found magnificent satisfaction for both urges.[59]

Deutsch's statement expresses a prevalent psychoanalytic expectation, derived from unquestioned observation of the sexual status quo: Women's lives should be and inevitably are totally centered on reproductive functions, and on the particular sexuality (heterosexual and vaginal) which produces reproduction. (The third part of the triad—passivity—is not so obviously related to reproduction and finds its bioteleological justification only through the tenuous biological assumption in Freud's statement that heterosexual coitus by definition involves male aggressiveness and hence female acquiescence in aggression.*)

Psychoanalysts also assume that men will perform their reproductive part—that is, will be heterosexual and genital (and "active") as well—but they do not assume that this is the exclusive center of masculine life. Rather, they assume that men will do other—cultural, social, productive—things as well. The repressions and machinations necessary to produce heterosexual genitality in men also produce the capacities for these other activities.

The functionalist stance of psychoanalysis, and the intertwining of descriptive and normative themes characteristic of functionalism, are apparent in the theory of the oedipus complex. Psychoanalysts always talk about the "tasks" of this period, claim that a girl "has to change" her erotogenic zone and her object in order to "pass from her masculine phase to the feminine one to which she is biologically destined."[61] Feminine oedipal experience and its psychic outcomes are measured against what a girl "has to" or "must" do. The psychoanalytic account not only shows how parents act and children respond. It also assumes that mothers and fathers *should* play certain kinds of parental roles *in order to* make their children heterosexual. Polar orientations (active and initiating versus passive and receptive) should emerge in heterosexual relationships whose goal is reproduction (thus, genitality is the goal for both sexes, and genital means vaginal for women). Psychoanalyst Charles Sarlin unintendedly betrays the potentially coercive underpinnings of Freud's insistence on the psychological primacy of the vagina. Sarlin directly equates Freud's goal with enforced clitoridectomy: "Among some aboriginal tribes the pubertal rite of clitoridectomy represents a crude physical attempt to accomplish in a primitive and direct fashion the very same objective which Freud established as the necessary precondition on a psychological level for the establishment of a feminine identity."[62]

---

*A relatively recent psychoanalytic article on "feminine identity," which I expected to broaden this restricted and restricting view (identity, after all, seems in our day to imply so much), exemplifies it perfectly. Identity for women, it implies, is simply the self-image counterpart to traditional teleological views of women's role and function: "The feminine representation of self must become established upon a female basis [i.e., the body image must be female, and not male or phallic, and the representations of libidinal drives must be primarily genital and vaginal], and the representation of her sexual object must be of the opposite sex, if her biologically fixed goals are to be achieved."[60]

Both Freudians and the Horney-Jones-Klein opposition remain bound to a theory of development and an account of the oedipus complex which stress libidinal and instinctual shifts and biology even while emphasizing difficulties in the attainment of biological destiny. For them, the female oedipus complex arises out of physical erotic sensations (whether vaginal, "phallic," or even oral) and concerns the development of female (hetero-) sexuality. The "change of object" is important only because it is the way a girl becomes heterosexual. Similarly, the change from activity to passivity and the shift of primary organ of sexual gratification from clitoris to (or back to) vagina are necessary for the requisite heterosexual stance. These theories see people (in this case women) as appendages of their drives and genitalia. The task of the oedipal period is to put the libido on its proper (functionally determined but constitutionally opposed) track.

The senses of femininity (as passivity toward men and inferiority) and masculinity, and varied superego formation are meant to assist this libidinal development in the patriarchal and evolutionary form that Freud believes is necessary. It is necessary in Freud's model that men have a stronger superego, because their oedipal task is to give up their mother as a sexual object (to internalize the incest taboo) and as an object of identification (to become "masculine" beings who will be active and superior toward women—which Freud took to be part of the male biological task). By contrast, the major oedipal task for a girl is to become heterosexual (which is accomplished both by seductiveness on the part of her heterosexual father and rejection as a sexual object by her heterosexual mother). This change of object prevents the most threatening form of incest to men—that between mother and daughter. Furthermore, the attachment to her father is tenuous, so there is less need to get her to internalize a taboo against incestuous involvement with him. Feminine superego formation is thus less important in the teleological picture. Freud accordingly deduces (from his assumptions that castration is all-important to both sexes and that the male genital is inherently superior) that women in fact have weaker superegos and less moral sense.

I have argued that the Freudian edifice stands on shaky ground. The assumptions it begins with are questionable, and it ignores or defines away clinical evidence and reasoning which contradict it. The classic Freudian account of the oedipus complex is imbued with an inexorable logic following from two basic assumptions about sex and gender: first, Freud defines gender and sexual differentiation as presence or absence of masculinity and the male genital rather than as two different presences; second, Freud maintains a functional/

teleological view of the "destiny" reserved for anatomical differences between the sexes. Patriarchal assumptions about passivity and activity, and the necessity for men to aggress sexually, are cloaked in the idiom of "nature." The psychoanalytic opposition, in postulating a (possibly unconscious) primary recognition of female and male organs and sexuality in children, takes issue only with the first of these assumptions, and agrees with Freud's assumption that gender differentiation and gender identity arise from genital difference.

We can reformulate the traditional theory of the oedipus complex to take account of the considerations I have raised. We can put Freud's functionalism in its proper teleological place and eliminate that which comes from assumptions of the automatically innate superiority and primacy of maleness, both biological and psychological. We can conclude that the establishment of an unambiguous and unquestioned gender identity and realistically sexed body-ego is a preoedipal phenomenon. Moreover, there may well be preoedipal conflicts around genital issues and sexual knowledge that contribute to the oedipal experience itself.

10

Conclusions on Post-Oedipal Gender Personality

The final result, an Oedipus complex—an internally felt and phantasized sit-uation that has become a persisting structural feature of a given individual mind—by no means corresponds exactly to the real outer parental situation. It is more akin to a final summary form in which the problem relationships of the child's infancy-life come to be preserved in his mental make-up.

HARRY GUNTRIP,
Personality Structure and Human Interaction

Freud treated the oedipus complex as a product and experience of childhood fantasy resulting from the accession to primacy of the gen-ital libidinal drives. Thus, a girl's original attachment to her mother and her difficulty in breaking this attachment, children's differential evaluations of the sexes and guilt about fantasies concerning their parents, are all seen largely as instinctual issues. Both libidinal and aggressive fantasies and projections go from child to parent, and pa-rental behavior is unimportant or secondary.

Oedipal object-relations are subordinate and derivative in these early accounts, as are their effects on the ego, its forms of defense, and its internalized object-world. From the account itself, however, it seems clear that the oedipal situation is not at all one way, nor is it a direct product of biology. It is an object-relational experience, in which what is going on among family members is causally important for a child's development. The psychological processes and the fea-tures of gender personality that grow out of the oedipus complex are grounded in family structure and family relations. Here I discuss parental participation in the oedipus complex as a final basis for my reformulation of the theory. My reformulation accepts the method-ologically consistent clinical findings of the traditional account but not its assumptions about sex, gender, and innate determining drives. I conclude with a review of this new account.

159

FAMILY RELATIONS AND OEDIPAL EXPERIENCE

Freud's neglect of parental participation in the oedipal experience and his theory of parental innocence are particularly evident in the case of fathers. Mothers, he admits, are really the child's first seducer, though even this occurs as a by-product of their ministering to infantile needs for feeding and cleansing rather than as an expression of intentional (if unconscious) seductiveness. Mothers, furthermore, are the parents who threaten their sons with castration, and whom their daughters blame for their lack of a penis.

Fathers, however, are by and large victims of childhood fantasy. Sons, for instance, come to fear castration by their father, even though their mother uttered such threats. According to Freud, daughters develop fantasies of their father as sexual seducer as a by-product of the feminine change of object, and not because of anything the father himself does or feels: "The fact that the mother so unavoidably initiates the child into the phallic phase is, I think, the reason why in the fantasies of later years, the father so regularly appears as the sexual seducer. When the girl turns away from the mother she also makes over to her father her introduction into sexual life."[1]

Freud's original reason for exonerating fathers was his well-known discovery that reported parental seductions by women patients with hysterical neuroses were in fact fantasy. This perspective was also probably supported by Freud's own personality. His (recognized) overwhelming anger at his own father led to his first formulation of the oedipus complex. In his later intense, largely denied resentment of younger colleagues, he again never saw himself as contributing to their disagreements, upsets, or breaks.[2]

Whatever the reasons, Freud's account is inconsistent. In the case of fathers and daughters, Freud claims to distinguish between a daughter's fantasies of seduction and actual seduction by her father, but he ignores the reciprocal possibility—that absence of actual paternal seduction is not the same thing as absence of seductive fantasies toward a daughter or behavior which expresses such fantasy. In the case of fathers and sons, Freud's phylogenetic theory, developed in *Totem and Taboo*,[3] suggests that the original aggression was from father to sons, in the primal father's monopolization of sexual rights over women based on his physical power. His clinical and theoretical account of the oedipus complex, by contrast, locates the direction of these aggressive feelings entirely from son to father. He claims that these arise out of a son's libidinal situation, and not at all out of participation in a two-way relational experience.

These contradictions in Freud's account suggest that a child's inner object constellation, which Freud makes into the whole of his account, is an aspect of a larger situation. This includes an internal oedipus situation on the part of a child's parents, derived largely from their own childhood oedipal experience. It also includes mutual meanings with which the parents have invested their marital relationship, and external reciprocal interaction which both results from and shapes parental and childish fantasies and internal oedipus situations. To understand this total picture, it is useful to explore further the ways that parents initiate their child into the oedipus situation.

Benedek and Gregory Zilboorg suggest that incestuous libidinal fantasies may arise initially in parents rather than children. Zilboorg is particularly concerned with the paternal fantasies of seduction which Freud so energetically denies.[4] He assumes that such fantasies are widespread and develops a provocative phylogenetic theory of development, following "motherright" theories, which suggests that the original matrilineal system in fact served patriarchy by forbidding all forms of nuclear family incest except that between father and daughter. Benedek develops her account in more clinical directions. Given that the hormonal and physiological equipment of the child does not permit the realization of its oedipal strivings, Benedek asks what accounts for the intensity and significance of castration fear, and fear of punishment for a sin which the child cannot commit. In answer, she points out that it is "not the child but the parent [who] is in possession of the mental and physiological equipment which stimulates sexual impulses and the fear of its consequences."[5] She suggests that parental feelings about these impulses are communicated to the child and themselves engender the intensity of the child's own emotions. Sexual drives toward a child are common, particularly if there has been a gratifying preoedipal parent-child relationship which has strengthened parental love. Society does not approve these incestuous wishes, and for the most part a parent's superego requires their repression. However, a child often senses its parents' unconscious feelings and fantasies. In this case, these are feelings laden with guilt and conflict, which makes them even more powerful and overwhelming to a child. Thus, the reawakened, guilt-laden, and conflictual oedipus situation in parents helps to reproduce a similar oedipus situation in their child.

Aggressive oedipal fantasies, as well as libidinal ones, may also arise earlier and more strongly in parents than in children, and especially in fathers rather than in sons. Zilboorg argues that the *Totem and Taboo* myth demonstrates the primal father's narcissistic and sadistic motives for establishing sexual control over women, and his concern for the ways that the mother-child bond and children in general diminished his primacy. Children, Zilboorg argues, awakened not feelings of tender paternity but feelings of resentment at intrusion: "These are the deep phylogenetic roots of that hostility which even the civilized father of today harbors against his own offspring. The unconscious hostility against one's own children is well nigh a universal clinical finding among men."[6]

David Bakan also refutes the Freudian account by appealing to important mythic exemplifications of paternal hostility.[7] He points out that even in the original Oedipus myth, it is Oedipus's father, Laius, who first tries to kill Oedipus. The fact that this is in response to a prophecy that Oedipus would grow up and kill him supports Bakan's account, since this prophecy was, after all, a grown man's fantasy (whether of Laius, the prophet, or the teller of the myth) and not in the unborn infant's head at all. It serves as an excuse (based on projection) for Laius's attempted infanticide. Bakan also suggests that paternal infanticide is a central theme in the Old Testament. (The Abraham-Isaac story is most prominent, especially given Bakan's report of variants in which Abraham actually does kill Isaac. God even lets his son Jesus be killed, if not executing the act himself.) This theme, according to Bakan, reflects major contradictions in male life concerning the inevitable replacement of a man by his son, the primacy of the mother-child bond compared to that of the father and child (and sometimes to father and mother), and the impossibility of complete certainty about the paternity of a child.[8]

Benedek agrees with Zilboorg and Bakan, but claims that we do not need a phylogenetic/mythic explanation for a son's fear of punishment for a sin which he cannot yet commit. She argues that there is sufficient clinical evidence to support the assumption that fathers consider their growing sons as rivals, and therefore begrudge and fear the virility they at the same time bequeath them. When a father has to restrict his aggressive impulses toward his son because of his superego demands, especially while restricting libidinal impulses toward his daughters, Benedek suggests, he conveys to this son that any impulses which arise in him may be very dangerous. The strength of a son's castration fears, therefore, correspond to the strictures of the paternal superego, which are based, in turn, on the father's own fears of punishment.

These accounts suggest that the oedipus complex in a child is not primarily a product of the effects of endogenously changing erotogenic zones and component drives, though it does come to have an independent psychological reality that results from the child's mental and emotional activities. It is rather the product of social structure and family relations; the latter are shaped in a major way by parental superego and psychic conflicts. Moreover, in contrast to Freud, who exonerates fathers even more than mothers from any responsibility for creating oedipal feelings in children, Benedek, Bakan, and Zilboorg give more attention to father-to-son (or father-to-child) hostility than that of a mother to her daughter or children.

I think the emphasis on paternal hostility is probably a feature of the developmental period they discuss rather than an absolute statement about which parent is ultimately more ambivalent about or hostile toward children. Maternal hostility and ambivalence, if we are to believe the clinical account, are more likely to be expressed and have their effect in the early mother-infant relationship. The entrance of a father (or anyone who mitigates the intensity of the mother-child bond) at the same time mitigates the impact of these feelings on a child. Nevertheless, if a father's hostile oedipal fantasies are more absolute and implacable, this may be another factor in accounting for the more total repression of the male than the female oedipus complex.

The implication of these accounts is that members of both generations come to have significant conscious and unconscious conflicts about libidinal and aggressive feelings and fantasies, and about the inevitable coming to sexual maturity of the younger generation and its replacement of the elder.[9] At the same time, both generations come to have a stake in ensuring that this sexual maturity will be non-incestuous and heterosexual. Parents have feelings, fantasies, and ways of behaving that communicate to their children views about sexuality and possibly about the relative value of female and male genitals. Parents and children participate together here in an affect-laden, object-relational experience constructed out of fantasy and perceptions of reality.

The oedipus complex is one manifestation, growing out of a particular family structure, of a more generalized phenomenon which Guntrip characterizes as a "family complex":[10] After a child grows out of primary love and identification built on relationships with its primary caretaker or caretakers, it internalizes and organizes a more complex constellation of familial object-relationships. These relationships tend to be particularly conflictual and ambivalent, and to this extent a child represses them in defense, with associated affects, fantasies, and commitments. That is, the child represses the oedipus complex itself into its unconscious. In Fairbairn's terms, its central ego banishes and represses those aspects of itself involved in these conflictual attachments. The oedipus complex thus engenders splits in the ego and its object-world that come to constitute a basic fixing of personality.

The oedipus complex leaves in a child unconscious inner representations of feelings about its position in relation to both parents, and potentially other primary figures as well. Whether or not this fixing and these inner relationships are heterosexual, focused on masculinity or femininity, uniquely preoccupied with love for an opposite sex parent or rivalry with a parent of the same sex, depends on the quality of the child's object-relations and family constellation, on societal norms, on parental personality, and on the inner object-world, repressions, ego splits, conflicts, and ego defenses which a child brings to and uses during the oedipal period.

This final oedipal stance, because it is now unconscious and was conceived at a period when the child felt particularly helpless and vulnerable, continues to exert powerful influence in later life. Further change in a person's inner ego and object-world and sense of relational self can certainly take place after the oedipal period, especially at times which reawaken and bring to prominence a complex of major life-cycle relations and social definitions.* But in all cases, much of the fantasy brought to a new situation and the issues and relationships invested with conflict and ambivalence gain their significance from the internalized and repressed oedipal situation.

POST-OEDIPAL GENDER PERSONALITY: A RECAPITULATION

Children of both sexes are originally matrisexual, though, as many accounts suggest, they have different kinds of relationships to their mother and later their father. Girls, for many overdetermined reasons, do develop penis envy and may repress knowledge of their vagina because they cannot otherwise win their heterosexual mother; because of exhibitionistic desires; because the penis symbolizes independence from the (internalized) powerful mother; as a defense against fantasies of acting on sexual desires for their father and anxiety at the possible consequence of this; because they have received either conscious or unconscious communication from their parents that penises (or being male) are better, or sensed maternal conflict about the mother's own genitals; and because the penis symbolizes

---

*I have discussed its resuscitation in adolescence for girls. Bibring describes a similar process in pregnancy, as does Benedek for "parenthood as a developmental phase."[11] Loewald suggests that the process of analysis also leads to the reexternalization of internalized or introjected objects and their reworking through and reinternalization, in such a way that there is often a radical change in mental structure.[12]

the social privileges of their father and men. The only psychoanalytic account of the origin of penis envy that seems inconceivable is Freud's original claim that a girl "makes her judgment and her decision in a flash"—that as soon as she learns about genitals different from hers, she wants a penis. Yet there is little to suggest either that penis envy completely permeates women's lives, or that the envy, jealousy, vanity, and pettiness that supposedly result from penis envy are characteristic of women. Similarly, most contemporary analysts agree that passivity, masochism, and narcissism are psychological defenses found in both women and men, and have the same object-relational origins in each, in the early mother-infant relationship. To the extent that these are (or were) more characteristically women's solutions to anxiety or guilt, this is not because of female biology but because the particular generating mother-child pattern is more characteristic of women's than men's early experience.[13]

The oedipus complex, according to the psychoanalytic paradigm, is a time of major developmental differentiation in personality and of a relative fixing of personality structure for girls and boys. For the traditional psychoanalyst, the major developmental outcomes of the oedipus complex are erotic heterosexuality and superego formation, masculinity and femininity. Even within this traditional account, however, with its teleological formulation of conscious parental and social goals arising from their own assumptions about appropriate gender roles, and unconscious goals arising from unconscious parental attitudes to gender and sexuality and their own oedipal stance, it is clear that what is being negotiated and what needs explaining is different for boys and girls as a result of the asymmetrical structure of parenting. For boys, gender identifications are more the issue; for girls, psychosexual development. Because both are originally involved with their mother, the attainment of heterosexuality—achieved with the feminine change of object—is the major traditional oedipal goal for girls. For boys the major goal is the achievement of personal masculine identification with their father and sense of secure masculine self, achieved through superego formation and disparagement of women. Superego formation and further identification with their mother also happen for girls, and giving up the original attachment to their mother is also an issue for boys. Yet the ways these happen, the conflicts and defenses involved, and typical gender differences between them are not elaborated in the psychoanalytic account. (These differences include varying forms of superego operation; differences in what identification with the parent of the same gender means; differences in what doubt about femininity and doubt about masculinity consist in; the particular ways in which each does and does not give up the mother as a love object; and implications for asymmetries in modes of libidinal relationship and heterosexual love.)

My account suggests that these gender-related issues may be influenced during the period of the oedipus complex, but they are not its only focus or outcome. The negotiation of these issues occurs in the context of broader object-relational and ego processes. These broader processes have equal influence on psychic structure formation, and psychic life and relational modes in men and women. They account for differing modes of identification and orientation to heterosexual objects, for the more asymmetrical oedipal issues psychoanalysts describe. These outcomes, like more traditional oedipal outcomes, arise from the asymmetrical organization of parenting, with the mother's role as primary parent and the father's typically greater remoteness and his investment in socialization especially in areas concerned with gender-typing.

The oedipal period is a nodal time of the creation of psychic reality in a child and of important internalizations of objects in relation to the ego. The main importance of the oedipus complex, I argue, is not primarily in the development of gender identity and socially appropriate heterosexual genitality, but in the constitution of different forms of "relational potential" in people of different genders.[14] The oedipus complex is the form in which the internal interpersonal world will later be imposed on and help to create the external. Postoedipal (and, in the girl, postpubertal) personality is the relatively stable foundation upon which other forms of relational development will build.

A girl continues a preoedipal relationship to her mother for a long time. Freud is concerned that it takes the girl so long to develop an oedipal attachment to her father and the "feminine" sexual modes that go with this attachment. The stress is on the girl's attachment as *pre*oedipal rather than on the attachment itself.

It is important to stress the other side of this process. Mothers tend to experience their daughters as more like, and continuous with, themselves. Correspondingly, girls tend to remain part of the dyadic primary mother-child relationship itself. This means that a girl continues to experience herself as involved in issues of merging and separation, and in an attachment characterized by primary identification and the fusion of identification and object choice. By contrast, mothers experience their sons as a male opposite. Boys are more likely to have been pushed out of the preoedipal relationship, and to have had to curtail their primary love and sense of empathic tie with their mother. A boy has engaged, and been required to engage, in a more emphatic individuation and a more defensive firming of experienced ego boundaries. Issues of differentiation have become intertwined with sexual issues. This does not mean that women have "weaker" ego boundaries than men or are more prone to psychosis. Disturbances in the early relation to a caretaker have equally profound effects on each, but these effects differ according to gender. The earliest mode of individuation, the primary construction of the ego and its inner object-world, the earliest conflicts and the earliest unconscious definitions of self, the earliest threats to individuation, and the earliest anxieties which call up defenses, all differ for boys and girls because of differences in the character of the early mother-child relationship for each.

Girls emerge from this period with a basis for "empathy" built into their primary definition of self in a way that boys do not. Girls emerge with a stronger basis for experiencing another's needs or feelings as one's own (or of thinking that one is so experiencing another's needs and feelings). Furthermore, girls do not define themselves in terms of the denial of preoedipal relational modes to the same extent as do boys. Therefore, regression to these modes tends not to feel as much a basic threat to their ego. From very early, then, because they are parented by a person of the same gender (a person who has already internalized a set of unconscious meanings, fantasies, and self-images about this gender and brings to her experience her own internalized early relationship to her own mother), girls come to experience themselves as less differentiated than boys, as more continuous with and related to the external object-world and as differently oriented to their inner object-world as well.

Differences in the oedipal experience have important implications. As we have seen, a girl does not turn absolutely from her mother to her father, but adds her father to her world of primary objects. She defines herself, as Deutsch says, in a relational triangle; this relational triangle is imposed upon another inner triangle involving a girl's preoccupation alternately with her internal oedipal and internal preoedipal mother. Most importantly, this means that there is greater complexity in the feminine endopsychic object-world than in the masculine. It also means that although most women emerge from their oedipus complex erotically heterosexual—that is, oriented to their father and men as primary *erotic* objects (which the psychoanalysts seem not so sure of)—heterosexual love and emotional commitment are less exclusively established. Men tend to remain *emotionally* secondary, though this varies according to the mother-daughter relationship, the quality of the father's interaction with his daughter, and the mother-father relationship. This contrasts to the greater primacy and exclusivity of the oedipal boy's emotional tie to his mother and women.

There is a developmental distinction between the genesis of genital heterosexual impulses (or decision to engage in heterosexual erotic relationships) and heterosexual love as a psychological and emotional phenomenon that involves varieties of commitment, fantasy, and experiences of the other person. The former are activated to some extent by seductive behavior on the part of a girl's father. But since girls growing up with and without men, with and without paternal interaction, also tend to become genitally heterosexual, this may also result either from (something like) constitutional bisexuality or from self-convincing and learning of the appropriate role.*

Finally, girls do not "resolve" their oedipus complex to the same extent as do boys. They neither repress nor give up so absolutely their preoedipal and oedipal attachment to their mother, nor their oedipal attachment to their father. This means that girls grow up with more ongoing preoccupations with both internalized object-relationships and with external relationships as well. These ongoing preoccupations in a girl grow especially out of her early relationship to her mother. They consist in an ambivalent struggle for a sense of separateness and independence from her mother and emotional, if not erotic, bisexual oscillation between mother and father—between preoccupation with "mother-child" issues and "male-female" issues.

This account explains conventional psychoanalytic notions about women's psyche, which traditional accounts explain in terms of constitutional or anatomic factors like passivity[15] and inner space.[16] Thus, Deutsch speaks of women's proneness to identification—in my account, a product of the continuing importance of the preoedipal stance of the ego; women's stronger fantasy life—in my account this grows from the lack of repression of oedipal attachment to the father; women's "subjectivity"—in my account this comes from continuity of the preoedipal "lack of reality principle" and primary identification; and women's greater intuition and inner perception—growing, my

---

*Such a distinction is important when we are faced with explaining the development and persistence of heterosexual bonding in societies characterized by a high degree of segregation and antagonism between the sexes, and where neither love nor companionship is expected to be, and is not, a primary component of the husband-wife relationship. In such societies where men may have separate eating, living, and even sleeping space from women and children, it is hard to conceive how a girl could become genitally heterosexual if such development depended on forming a *love* relationship with her father. What seems to happen, and is consistent with the distinction I am drawing, is that most women become genitally heterosexual but do not develop strong heterosexual object love.

account argues, from their richer inner object-world and the greater continuity in their external object-relations.

My conclusions provide a context for understanding Freud's account of superego formation in men and women, without imposing the value judgments he insisted on. Denial of sense of connectedness and isolation of affect may be more characteristic of masculine development and may produce a more rigid and punitive superego, whereas feminine development, in which internal and external object-relations and affects connected to these are not so repressed, may lead to a superego more open to persuasion and the judgments of others, that is, not so independent of its emotional origins.*

Women's mothering, then, produces asymmetries in the relational experiences of girls and boys as they grow up, which account for crucial differences in feminine and masculine personality, and the relational capacities and modes which these entail. Women and men grow up with personalities affected by different boundary experiences and differently constructed and experienced inner object-worlds, and are preoccupied with different relational issues. Feminine personality comes to be based less on repression of inner objects, and fixed and firm splits in the ego, and more on retention and continuity of external relationships. From the retention of preoedipal attachments to their mother, growing girls come to define and experience themselves as continuous with others; their experience of self contains more flexible or permeable ego boundaries. Boys come to define themselves as more separate and distinct, with a greater sense of rigid ego boundaries and differentiation. The basic feminine sense of self is connected to the world, the basic masculine sense of self is separate.

From their oedipus complex and its resolution, women's endopsychic object-world becomes a more complex relational constellation than men's, and women remain preoccupied with ongoing relational issues (both preoedipal mother-child issues and the oedipal triangles) in a way that men do not. Men's endopsychic object-world tends to be more fixed and simpler, and the masculine heritage of the oedipus complex is that relational issues tend to be more repressed. Masculine personality, then, comes to be defined more in terms of denial of relation and connection (and denial of femininity), whereas feminine personality comes to include a fundamental definition of self in relationship. Thus, relational abilities and preoccupations have been extended in women's development and curtailed in men's. Boys and

---

*Of course, extremes in either direction—implacability and overrigidity, or instant dependence on the superego strictures of another—provide their own problems.

girls experience the sexual wishes and fantasies of their oedipal triangles differently, and thus emerge with differently constructed sexual needs and wants. This points to boys' preparation for participation in nonrelational spheres and to girls' greater potential for participation in relational spheres. It points also to different relational needs and fears in men and women.

PART III

Gender Personality and the Reproduction of Mothering

11

The Sexual Sociology
of Adult Life

Hence, there is a typically asymmetrical relation of the marriage pair to the occupational structure.

This asymmetrical relation apparently both has exceedingly important positive functional significance and is at the same time an important source of strain in relation to the patterning of sex roles.

TALCOTT PARSONS,
"The Kinship System of the Contemporary United States"

Girls and boys develop different relational capacities and senses of self as a result of growing up in a family in which women mother. These gender personalities are reinforced by differences in the identification processes of boys and girls that also result from women's mothering. Differing relational capacities and forms of identification prepare women and men to assume the adult gender roles which situate women primarily within the sphere of reproduction in a sexually unequal society.

GENDER IDENTIFICATION
AND GENDER ROLE LEARNING

All social scientists who have examined processes of gender role learning and the development of a sense of identification in boys and girls have argued that the asymmetrical organization of parenting in which women mother is the basic cause of significant contrasts between feminine and masculine identification processes.[1] Their discussions range from concern with the learning of appropriate gender role behavior—through imitation, explicit training and admonitions, and cognitive learning processes—to concern with the development of basic gender identity. The processes these people discuss seem to be universal, to the extent that all societies are constituted around a structural split, growing out of women's mothering, between the private, domestic world of women and the public, social world of men.[2] Because the first identification for children of both genders has always been with their mother, they argue, and because children are first around women, women's family roles and being feminine are more available and often more intelligible to growing children than masculine roles and being masculine. Hence, male development is more complicated than female because of the difficult shifts of identification which a boy must make to attain his expected gender identification and gender role assumption. Their view contrasts sharply to the psychoanalytic stress on the difficulties inherent in feminine development as girls make their convoluted way to heterosexual object choice.*

Because all children identify first with their mother, a girl's gender and gender role identification processes are continuous with her earliest identifications and a boy's are not. A girl's oedipal identification with her mother, for instance, is continuous with her earliest primary identification (and also in the context of her early dependence and attachment). The boy's oedipal crisis, however, is supposed to enable him to shift in favor of an identification with his father. He gives up, in addition to his oedipal and preoedipal attachment to his mother, his primary identification with her.

What is true specifically for oedipal identification is equally true for more general gender identification and gender role learning. A boy, in order to feel himself adequately masculine, must distinguish and differentiate himself from others in a way that a girl need not —must categorize himself as someone apart. Moreover, he defines masculinity negatively as that which is not feminine and/or connected to women, rather than positively.[3] This is another way boys come to deny and repress relation and connection in the process of growing up.

These distinctions remain even where much of a girl's and boy's socialization is the same, and where both go to school and can participate in adulthood in the labor force and other nonfamilial institutions. Because girls at the same time grow up in a family where mothers are the salient parent and caretaker, they also can begin to identify more directly and immediately with their mothers and their

---

*The extent of masculine difficulty varies, as does the extent to which identification processes for boys and girls differ. This variance depends on the extent of the public-domestic split in a subculture or society—the extent to which men, men's work, and masculine activities are removed from the home, and therefore masculinity and personal relations with adult men are hard to come by for a child.

mothers' familial roles than can boys with their fathers and men. Insofar as a woman's identity remains primarily as a wife/mother, moreover, there is greater generational continuity in role and life-activity from mother to daughter than there can be from father to son. This identity may be less than totally appropriate, as girls must realistically expect to spend much of their life in the labor force, whereas their mothers were less likely to do so. Nevertheless, family organization and ideology still produce these gender differences, and generate expectations that women much more than men will find a primary identity in the family.

Permanent father-absence, and the "father absence" that is normal in our society, do not mean that boys do not learn masculine roles or proper masculine behavior, just as there is no evidence that homosexuality in women correlates with father absence.[4] What matters is the extent to which a child of either gender can form a personal relationship with their object of identification, and the differences in modes of identification that result from this. Mitscherlich, Slater, Winch, and Lynn all speak to these differences.[5] They suggest that girls in contemporary society develop a personal identification with their mother, and that a tie between affective processes and role learning—between libidinal and ego development—characterizes feminine development. By contrast, boys develop a positional identification with aspects of the masculine role. For them, the tie between affective processes and role learning is broken.

Personal identification, according to Slater and Winch, consists in diffuse identification with someone else's general personality, behavioral traits, values, and attitudes. Positional identification consists, by contrast, in identification with specific aspects of another's role and does not necessarily lead to the internalization of the values or attitudes of the person identified with. According to Slater, children preferentially choose personal identification because this grows out of a positive affective relationship to a person who is there. They resort to positional identification residually and reactively, and identify with the perceived role or situation of another when possibilities for personal identification are not available.

In our society, a girl's mother is present in a way that a boy's father, and other adult men, are not. A girl, then, can develop a personal identification with her mother, because she has a real relationship with her that grows out of their early primary tie. She learns what it is to be womanlike in the context of this personal identification with her mother and often with other female models (kin, teachers, mother's friends, mothers of friends). Feminine identification, then, can be based on the gradual learning of a way of being familiar in everyday life, exemplified by the relationship with the person with whom a girl has been most involved.

A boy must attempt to develop a masculine gender identification and learn the masculine role in the absence of a continuous and ongoing personal relationship to his father (and in the absence of a continuously available masculine role model). This positional identification occurs both psychologically and sociologically. Psychologically, as is clear from descriptions of the masculine oedipus complex, boys appropriate those specific components of the masculinity of their father that they fear will be otherwise used against them, but do not as much identify diffusely with him as a person. Sociologically, boys in father-absent and normally father-remote families develop a sense of what it is to be masculine through identification with cultural images of masculinity and men chosen as masculine models.

Boys are taught to be masculine more consciously than girls are taught to be feminine. When fathers or men are not present much, girls are taught the heterosexual components of their role, whereas boys are assumed to learn their heterosexual role without teaching, through interaction with their mother.[6] By contrast, other components of masculinity must be more consciously imposed. Masculine identification, then, is predominantly a gender role identification. By contrast, feminine identification is predominantly *parental*: "Males tend to identify with a cultural stereotype of the masculine role; whereas females tend to identify with aspects of their own mother's role specifically."[7]

Girls' identification processes, then, are more continuously embedded in and mediated by their ongoing relationship with their mother. They develop through and stress particularistic and affective relationships to others. A boy's identification processes are not likely to be so embedded in or mediated by a real affective relation to his father. At the same time, he tends to deny identification with and relationship to his mother and reject what he takes to be the feminine world; masculinity is defined as much negatively as positively. Masculine identification processes stress differentiation from others, the denial of affective relation, and categorical universalistic components of the masculine role. Feminine identification processes are relational, whereas masculine identification processes tend to deny relationship.

These distinctions do not mean that the development of femininity is all sugar and spice for a girl, but that it poses different *kinds* of problems for her than the development of masculinity does for a boy.

The feminine identification that a girl attains and the masculine identification about which a boy remains uncertain are valued differently.
In their unattainability, masculinity and the masculine role are fantasized and idealized by boys (and often by girls), whereas femininity
and the feminine role remain for a girl all too real and concrete. The
demands on women are often contradictory—for instance, to be passive and dependent in relation to men, and active and independently
initiating toward children. In the context of the ego and object-relational issues I described in the preceding chapters, moreover, it is
clear that mother-identification presents difficulties. A girl identifies
with and is expected to identify with her mother in order to attain
her adult feminine identification and learn her adult gender role.
At the same time she must be sufficiently differentiated to grow
up and experience herself as a separate individual—must overcome
primary identification while maintaining and building a secondary
identification.

Studies suggest that daughters in American society have problems
with differentiation from and identification with their mothers.[8] Slater
reports that all forms of personal parental identification (cross-gen-
der and same-gender) correlate with freedom from psychosis or neurosis except personal identification of a daughter with her mother.
Johnson reports that a boy's identification with his father relates to
psychological adjustment, whereas a girl's with her mother does not.
The implication in both accounts is that for a girl, just as for a boy,
there can be too much of mother. It may be easy, but possibly too
easy, for a girl to attain a feminine gender identification.*

Gender and gender-role identification processes accord with my
earlier account of the development of psychic structure. They reinforce and replicate the object-relational and ego outcomes which I
have described. Externally, as internally, women grow up and remain
more connected to others. Not only are the roles which girls learn
more interpersonal, particularistic, and affective than those which
boys learn. Processes of identification and role learning for girls also
tend to be particularistic and affective—embedded in an interpersonal relationship with their mothers. For boys, identification processes and masculine role learning are not likely to be embedded in
relationship with their fathers or men but rather to involve the denial
of affective relationship to their mothers. These processes tend to be
more role-defined and cultural, to consist in abstract or categorical
role learning rather than in personal identification.

*Recall also Deutsch's description of the prepubertal girl's random attempts to
break her identification with her mother.

FAMILY AND ECONOMY

Women's relatedness and men's denial of relation and categorical self-definition are appropriate to women's and men's differential participation in nonfamilial production and familial reproduction. Women's roles are basically familial, and concerned with personal, affective ties. Ideology about women and treatment of them in this society, particularly in the labor force, tend to derive from this familial location and the assumptions that it is or should be both exclusive and primary for women, and that this exclusivity and primacy come from biological sex differences. By contrast, men's roles as they are defined in our society are basically not familial. Though men are interested in being husbands and fathers, and most men do occupy these roles during their lifetime, ideology about men and definitions of what is masculine come predominantly from men's nonfamilial roles. Women are located first in the sex-gender system, men first in the organization of production.

We can reformulate these insights to emphasize that women's lives, and beliefs about women, define them as embedded in social interaction and personal relationships in a way that men are not. Though men and women participate in both the family and the nonfamilial world, the sexual division of labor is such that women's first association is within the family, a relational institution, and men's is not. Women in our society are primarily defined as wives and mothers, thus in particularistic relation to someone else, whereas men are defined primarily in universalistic occupational terms. These feminine roles and women's family functions, moreover, stress especially affective relationship and the affective aspects of family life. As I discuss in Chapter 1, being a mother and wife are increasingly centered on emotional and psychological functions—women's work is "emotion work."⁹ By contrast, men's occupational roles, and the occupational world in general, are increasingly without room for affect and particularistic commitments. Women's two interconnected roles, their dual relatedness to men and children, replicate women's internalized relational triangle of childhood—preoccupied alternately with male-female and mother-child issues.

The definitional relatedness of being a wife and mother, and women's intrafamilial responsibility for affectively defined functions, receive further support from the way the family is related socially to the extrafamilial world. Parsons and many feminist theorists point out that it is the husband/father whose occupational role is mainly determinant of the class position and status of the whole family, and sociologists who measure socioeconomic status by *paternal* occupation and education seem to concur. The husband/father thus formally articulates the family in the larger society and gives it its place. And although families increasingly depend on income from both spouses, class position derives ideologically from what the male spouse does. The wife, accordingly, is viewed as deriving her status and class position mainly from her husband, even if she also is in the labor force and contributes to the maintenance of the family's life style. She is seen as a representative of her family, whereas her husband is seen as an independent individual.

The wife/mother role draws on women's personality in another way, as a result of the fundamentally different modes of organization of the contemporary sex-gender system and contemporary capitalism. The activities of a wife/mother have a nonbounded quality. They consist, as countless housewives can attest and as women poets, novelists, and feminist theorists have described, of diffuse obligations. Women's activities in the home involve continuous connection to and concern about children and attunement to adult masculine needs, both of which require connection to, rather than separateness from, others. The work of maintenance and reproduction is characterized by its repetitive and routine continuity, and does not involve specified sequence or progression. By contrast, work in the labor force—"men's work"—is likely to be contractual, to be more specifically delimited, and to contain a notion of defined progression and product.

Even when men and women cross into the other's sphere, their roles remain different. Within the family, being a husband and father is different from being a wife and mother; as women have become more involved in the family, men have become less so. Parsons's characterization of men's instrumental role in the family may be too extreme, but points us in the right direction. A father's first responsibility is to "provide" for his family monetarily. His emotional contribution is rarely seen as of equal importance. Men's work in the home, in all but a few households, is defined in gender-stereotyped ways. When men do "women's" chores—the dishes, shopping, putting children to bed—this activity is often organized and delegated by the wife/mother, who retains residual responsibility (men "babysit" their own children; women do not). Fathers, though they relate to their children, do so in order to create "independence."[10] This is facilitated by a father's own previous socialization for repression and denial of relation, and his current participation in the public nonrelational world. Just as children know their fathers "under the sway of the reality principle,"*,11 so also do fathers know their children more as separate people than mothers do.

Outside the family, women's roles and ideology about women are more relational than nonfamilial male roles and ideology about men. Women's work in the labor force tends to extend their housewife, wife, or mother roles and their concern with personal, affective ties (as secretaries, service workers, private household workers, nurses, teachers). Men's work is less likely to have affective overtones—men are craft workers, operatives, and professional and technical workers.

Rosaldo claims that all these aspects of women's position are universal.12 She suggests that feminine roles are less public or "social," that they exhibit less linguistic and institutional differentiation, and that the interaction they involve is more likely to be kin-based and to cross generations, whereas men's interaction remains within a single generation and cuts across kin units on the basis of universalistic categories. Women's roles are thus based on what are seen as personal rather than "social" or "cultural" ties. The corollary to this is that women's roles typically tend to involve the exercise of influence in face-to-face, personal contexts rather than legitimized power in contexts which are categorical and defined by authority. Finally, women's roles, and the biological symbolism attached to them, share a concern with the crossing of boundaries: Women mediate between the social and cultural categories which men have defined; they bridge the gap and make transitions—especially in their role as socializer and mother —between nature and culture.

Women's role in the home and primary definition in social reproductive, sex-gender terms are characterized by particularism, concern with affective goals and ties, and a diffuse, unbounded quality. Masculine occupational roles and men's primary definition in the sphere of production are universalistically defined and recruited, and are less likely to involve affective considerations. This nonrelational, economic and political definition informs the rest of their lives. The production of feminine personalities oriented toward relational issues and masculine personalities defined in terms of categorical ties and the repression of relation fits these roles and contributes to their reproduction.

MOTHERING, MASCULINITY, AND CAPITALISM

Women's mothering in the isolated nuclear family of contemporary capitalist society creates specific personality characteristics in men that

---

*Conscious of him as a separate person, verbally rather than preverbally.

reproduce both an ideology and psychodynamic of male superiority and submission to the requirements of production. It prepares men for participation in a male-dominant family and society, for their lesser emotional participation in family life, and for their participation in the capitalist world of work.

Masculine development takes place in a family in which women mother and fathers are relatively uninvolved in child care and family life, and in a society characterized by sexual inequality and an ideology of masculine superiority. This duality expresses itself in the family. In family ideology, fathers are usually important and considered the head of the household. Wives focus energy and concern on their husbands, or at least think and say that they do. They usually consider, or at least claim, that they love these husbands. Mothers may present fathers to children as someone important, someone whom the mother loves, and may even build up their husbands to their children to make up for the fact that these children cannot get to know their father as well as their mother. They may at the same time undercut their husband in response to the position he assumes of social superiority or authority in the family.

Masculinity is presented to a boy as less available and accessible than femininity, as represented by his mother. A boy's mother is his primary caretaker. At the same time, masculinity is idealized or accorded superiority, and thereby becomes even more desirable. Although fathers are not as salient as mothers in daily interaction, mothers and children often idealize them and give them ideological primacy, precisely because of their absence and seeming inaccessibility, and because of the organization and ideology of male dominance in the larger society.

Masculinity becomes an issue in a way that femininity does not. Masculinity does not become an issue because of some intrinsic male biology, nor because masculine roles are inherently more difficult than feminine roles, however. Masculinity becomes an issue as a direct result of a boy's experience of himself in his family—as a result of his being parented by a woman. For children of both genders, mothers represent regression and lack of autonomy. A boy associates these issues with his gender identification as well. Dependence on his mother, attachment to her, and identification with her represent that which is not masculine; a boy must reject dependence and deny attachment and identification. Masculine gender role training becomes much more rigid than feminine. A boy represses those qualities he takes to be feminine inside himself, and rejects and devalues women and whatever he considers to be feminine in the social world.

Thus, boys define and attempt to construct their sense of masculinity largely in negative terms. Given that masculinity is so elusive, it becomes important for masculine identity that certain social activities are defined as masculine and superior, and that women are believed unable to do many of the things defined as socially important. It becomes important to think that women's economic and social contribution cannot equal men's. The secure possession of certain realms, and the insistence that these realms are superior to the maternal world of youth, become crucial both to the definition of masculinity and to a particular boy's own masculine gender identification.[13]

Freud describes the genesis of this stance in the masculine oedipal crisis. A boy's struggle to free himself from his mother and become masculine generates "the contempt felt by men for a sex which is the lesser"[14]—"What we have come to consider the normal male contempt for women."[15]

Both sexes learn to feel negatively toward their mother during the oedipal period. A girl's negative feelings, however, are not so much contempt and devaluation as fear and hostility: "The little girl, incapable of such contempt because of her own identical nature, frees herself from the mother with a degree of hostility far greater than any comparable hostility in the boy."[16] A boy's contempt serves to free him not only from his mother but also from the femininity within himself. It therefore becomes entangled with the issue of masculinity and is generalized to all women. A girl's hostility remains tied more to her relationship to her mother (and/or becomes involved in self-depreciation).

A boy's oedipus complex is directly tied to issues of masculinity, and the devaluation of women is its "normal" outcome. A girl's devaluation of or hostility toward her mother may be a part of the process, but its "normal" outcome, by contrast, entails acceptance of her own femininity and identification with her mother. Whatever the individual resolution of the feminine oedipus complex, however, it does not become institutionalized in the same way.

Freud "explains" the development of boys' contempt for mothers as coming from their perception of genital differences, particularly their mother's "castration." He takes this perception to be unmediated by social experience, and not in need of explanation. As many commentators have pointed out, it did not occur to Freud that such differential valuation and ensuing contempt were not in the natural order of things. However, the analysis of "Little Hans," which provides the most direct (reported) evidence that Freud had for such an assumption, shows that in fact Hans's father perpetuated and created such beliefs in his son—beliefs about the inferiority of female genitalia, denial of the feminine role in gestation and parturition, views that men have something and women have nothing, rather than having something different.[17]

Karen Horney, unlike Freud, does take masculine contempt for and devaluation of women as in need of interactive and developmental explanation.[18] According to her, these phenomena are manifestations of a deeper "dread of women"—a masculine fear and terror of maternal omnipotence that arises as one major consequence of their early caretaking and socialization by women. Psychoanalysts previously had stressed boys' fears of their fathers. Horney argues that these fears are less severe and therefore less in need of being repressed. Unlike their fears of a mother, boys do not react to a father's total and incomprehensible control over his child's life at a time when the child has no reflective capacities for understanding: "Dread of the father is more actual and tangible, less uncanny in quality."[19] Moreover, since their father is male like them, boys' fears of men do not entail admission of feminine weakness or dependency on women: "Masculine self-regard suffers less in this way."[20]

Dread of the mother is ambivalent, however. Although a boy fears her, he also finds her seductive and attractive. He cannot simply dismiss and ignore her. Boys and men develop psychological and cultural/ideological mechanisms to cope with their fears without giving up women altogether. They create folk legends, beliefs, and poems that ward off the dread by externalizing and objectifying women: "It is not . . . that I dread her; it is that she herself is malignant, capable of any crime, a beast of prey, a vampire, a witch, insatiable in her desires . . . the very personification of what is sinister."[21] They deny dread at the expense of realistic views of women. On the one hand, they glorify and adore: "There is no need for me to dread a being so wonderful, so beautiful, nay, so saintly."[22] On the other, they disparage: "It would be too ridiculous to dread a creature who, if you take her all round, is such a poor thing."[23]

Unfortunately, Horney does not point to developmental implications of the mother's overwhelming power for girls. We can apply here the difference I noted earlier. A girl may well develop a fear or dread of her mother. However, this dread does not become tied up for her with the assertion of genderedness. Because she is also female, and presumably does not feel herself dreadful or fearsome, but rather the reverse, it is likely that a girl will not generalize her dread to all females. Moreover, because women's and girls' experiences take place in a male-dominant society, whatever fear or dread individual women do experience is less likely to gain cultural or normative import.

Horney's article implicitly claims that fear and disparagement of women and assertions of masculine superiority are universal. This claim needs further specification, since the extent of men's "dread of women" and need to assert masculine superiority varies widely among different societies.[24] Horney noticed the dread of women because it was salient in her own society. Tendencies in contemporary family organization have produced a mother-son relationship that leads to disparagement and fear of women. Direct patriarchal authority and paternal salience in the family have declined as a result of men's steady loss of autonomy in work, and the growing submission of their lives to work requirements (whether the work of bureaucratized and salaried professionals and managers, or of proletarianized craft workers and small entrepreneurs).[25]

Grete Bibring provides a suggestive clinical account. She describes the fathers and mothers in "matriarchal" families in the United States.*[26] As described by their grown sons and daughters (Bibring's patients), the mothers in these households were active and strong, efficient household managers, and generally seemed superior and more competent than their husbands. Fathers were generally ineffectual in the home and uninvolved in family life. (Bibring seems to be talking about professional, middle- and upper-middle-class husbands. What she says, however, would seem to apply equally to working-class households, where fathers have jobs which keep them away even longer hours, may exhaust them even more, and where much social life is sex-segregated.) Bibring summarizes the situation:

At closer investigation it seems evident that in all these cases the father did not participate essentially in the upbringing of his children, that social as well as moral standards, religious and aesthetic values were mostly conveyed by the mother. The same holds true of praise and reprimands. The setting of goals and the supervision of the boy's development lay in her hands. The father appears in all these instances as a friendly onlooker rather than as an important participant.[27]

The sons in these families considered their mothers to be rejecting, punitive, ambitious, and cold. But the women who grew up in this "matriarchal" setting were less likely to reject the feminine role than female patients coming from patriarchal family settings. Bibring concludes, guided by the sons' concrete descriptions of their mothers' behavior, that the mothers were thoughtful and responsible and that

---

*Horkheimer suggests, in contrast to Bibring, that in Germany at least this decline in real paternal authority and power was accompanied by a rise in what we might call pseudo-authority.

the fathers' "absence," rather than anything the mother actually did, was the "major factor in determining these attitudes in the sons."[28] For these sons, whatever the social reality and however their mother acted, there was simply "too much of mother."[29]

Sons in this situation inevitably experience their mother as overwhelming and resent her for this. They both admire and fear her, experience her as both seductive and rejecting. In such a situation, mothers themselves may also reciprocate and encourage their sons' incestuous wishes as well as their infantile dependence. As Bibring puts it, they are "as much in need of a husband as a son is of his father."[30] Moreover, because there is no mediator to his oedipal wishes—no father to protect him—a boy's wishes also build. He often projects both these and the fears they engender onto his mother, making her both a temptress and hostile punisher. Sons take these fears with them into adulthood and experience the world as filled with "dangerous, cold, cutting women."[31]

Too much of mother results from the relative absence of the father and nearly exclusive maternal care provided by a woman isolated in a nuclear household. It creates men's resentment and dread of women, and their search for nonthreatening, undemanding, dependent, even infantile women—women who are "simple, and thus safe and warm."[32] Through these same processes men come to reject, devalue, and even ridicule women and things feminine.

Women's mothering produces a psychological and ideological complex in men concerning women's secondary valuation and sexual inequality. Because women are responsible for early child care and for most later socialization as well, because fathers are more absent from the home, and because men's activities generally have been removed from the home while women's have remained within it, boys have difficulty in attaining a stable masculine gender role identification. Boys fantasize about and idealize the masculine role and their fathers, and society defines it as desirable.

Given that men control not only major social institutions but the very definition and constitution of society and culture, they have the power and ideological means to enforce these perceptions as more general norms, and to hold each other accountable for their enforcement. (This is not solely a matter of force. Since these norms define men as superior, men gain something by maintaining them.[33]) The structure of parenting creates ideological and psychological modes which reproduce orientations to and structures of male dominance in individual men, and builds an assertion of male superiority into the definition of masculinity itself.

The same repressions, denials of affect and attachment, rejection of the world of women and things feminine, appropriation of the world of men and identification with the father that create a psychology of masculine superiority also condition men for participation in the capitalist work world. Both capitalist accumulation and proper work habits in workers have never been purely a matter of economics. Particular personality characteristics and behavioral codes facilitated the transition to capitalism. Capitalists developed inner direction, rational planning, and organization, and workers developed a willingness to come to work at certain hours and work steadily, whether or not they needed money that day.

Psychological qualities become perhaps even more important with the expansion of bureaucracy and hierarchy: In modern capitalism different personality traits are required at different levels of the bureaucratic hierarchy.*[34] Lower level jobs are often directly and continuously supervised, and are best performed by someone willing to obey rules and conform to external authority. Moving up the hierarchy, jobs require greater dependability and predictability, the ability to act without direct and continuous supervision. In technical, professional, and managerial positions, workers must on their own initiative carry out the goals and values of the organization for which they work, making those goals and values their own. Often they must be able to draw on their interpersonal capacities as a skill. Parental child-rearing values and practices (insofar as these latter reflect parental values) reflect these differences: Working class parents are more likely to value obedience, conformity to external authority, neatness, and other "behavioral" characteristics in their children; middle-class parents emphasize more "internal" and interpersonal characteristics like responsibility, curiosity, self-motivation, self-control, and consideration.[35]

These behavioral and personality qualities differentiate appropriately according to the requirements of work in the different strata. But they share an important commonality. Conformity to behavioral rules and external authority, predictability and dependability, the ability to take on others' values and goals as one's own, all reflect an orientation external to oneself and one's own standards, a lack of autonomous and creative self-direction. The nuclear, isolated, neolocal family in which women mother is suited to the production in children of these cross-class personality commitments and capacities.

*It is certainly possible that these same characteristics apply in all extensively bureaucratic and hierarchical settings (in the U.S.S.R. and Eastern Europe, for instance); however, the work I am drawing on has investigated only the capitalist West, and especially the United States.

Parsonsians and theorists of the Frankfurt Institute for Social Research have drawn on psychoanalysis to show how the relative position of fathers and mothers in the contemporary family helps to create the foundations of men's psychological acquiescence in capitalist domination.* They discuss how the family prepares men for subordination to authority, for participation in an alienated work world, for generalized achievement orientation.[36] These complementary and overlapping accounts discuss personality traits required of all strata, centering on lack of inner autonomy and availability to manipulation. Yet their differences of emphasis point to variation among strata as well. Parsonsians discuss more how middle-class families prepare boys to be white-collar bureaucrats, professionals, technicians, and managers; Frankfurt theorists discuss more the genesis of working-class character traits. Parsonsians start from the growing significance of the mother, and her sexualized involvement with her male infant. Frankfurt theorists start from the historical obverse, from the decline in the father's role and his growing distance, unavailability, and loss of authority in the family.

In American families, Parsons argues, where mothers tend not to have other primary affective figures around, a mutual erotic investment between son** and mother develops—an investment the mother can then manipulate. She can love, reward, and frustrate him at appropriate moments in order to get him to delay gratification and sublimate or repress·erotic needs. This close, exclusive, preoedipal mother-child relationship first develops dependency in a son, creating a motivational basis for early learning and a foundation for dependency on others. When a mother "rejects" her son or pushes him to be more independent, the son carries his still powerful dependence with him, creating in him both a general need to please and conform outside of the relationship to the mother herself and a strong assertion of independence. The isolated, husband-absent mother thus helps to create in her son a pseudo-independence masking real dependence, and a generalized sense that he ought to "do well" rather than an orientation to specific goals. This generalized sense can then be

---

*I do not mean to suggest here that a psychological account gives a complete explanation for the reproduction of workers. The main reason people go to work is because they need to in order to live. The family creates the psychological *foundations* of acquiescence in work and of work skills. But even reinforced by schools and other socializing institutions, it is clear that socialization for work never works well enough to prevent all resistance.

**Parsons and his colleagues talk of the "mother-child" relationship. However, they focus on erotic, oedipal attachment as motivating, and on the development of character traits which are appropriate to masculine work capacity and not to feminine expressive roles. It is safe to conclude, therefore, that the child they have in mind is male.

used to serve a variety of specific goals—goals not set by these men themselves. The oedipus complex in the contemporary family creates a " 'dialectical' relationship between dependency, on the one hand, independence and achievement on the other."[37]

In an earlier period of capitalist development, individual goals were important for more men, and entrepreneurial achievement as well as worker discipline had to be based more on inner moral direction and repression. Earlier family arrangements, where dependency was not so salient nor the mother-child bond so exclusive, produced this greater inner direction. Today, with the exception of a very few, individual goals have become increasingly superseded by the goals of complex organizations: "Goals can no longer be directly the individual's responsibility and cannot be directly specified to him as a preparation for his role."[38] The contemporary family, with its manipulation of dependency in the mother-child relationship, and its production of generalized achievement orientation rather than inner goals and standards, produces personalities "that have become a fully fluid resource for societal functions."[39]

Slater extends Parsons's discussion. People who start life with only one or two emotional objects, he argues, develop a "willingness to put all [their] emotional eggs in one symbolic basket."[40] Boys who grow up in American middle-class nuclear families have this experience.* Because they received such a great amount of gratification from their mother relative to what they got from anyone else, and because their relationship to her was so exclusive, it is unlikely that they can repeat such a relationship. They relinquish their mother as an object of dependent attachment and deny their dependence on her, but, because she was so uniquely important, they retain her as an oedipally motivated object to win in fantasy—they retain an unconscious sense that there is one finally satisfying prize to be won. They turn their lives into a search for a success that will both prove their independence and win their mother. But because they have no inner sense of goals or real autonomy apart from this unconscious, unattainable goal from the past, and because success in the external world does not for the most part bring real satisfactions or real independence, their search is likely to be never-ending. They are likely to continue to work and to continue to accept the standards of the situation that confronts them.

This situation contrasts to that of people who have had a larger number of pleasurable relationships in early infancy. Such people are more likely to expect gratification in immediate relationships and

---

*Again, girls do as well, and both genders transfer it to monogamic, jealous tendencies. But Slater is talking about the sexually toned oedipal/preoedipal relationship that is more specific to boys.

maintain commitments to more people, and are less likely to deny themselves now on behalf of the future. They would not be the same kind of good worker, given that work is defined in individualist, non-cooperative, outcome-oriented ways, as it is in our society.

Horkheimer and other Frankfurt theorists focus on the oedipal relationship of son to father, rather than son to mother, and on the internalization of paternal authority. The family in every society transmits orientation to authority. However, the nature of this orientation changes with the structure of authority in the economic world. During the period of early capitalist development, when independent craftspeople, shopkeepers, farmers, and professionals were relatively more important, more fathers had some economic power in the world.* This paternal authority expressed itself also in the family. Sons could internalize their father's authority through a classic oedipal struggle. They could develop inner direction and self-motivation and accept "realistic" limits on their power: "Childhood in a limited family [became] an habituation to authority."[41] But with the growth of industry, fathers became less involved in family life. They did not just physically leave home, however. As more fathers became dependent on salaries and wages, on the vagaries of the labor market and the authority of capitalists and managers, the material base for their family authority was also eroded. Fathers reacted by developing authoritarian modes of acting. But because there was no longer a real basis for their authority, there could be no genuine oedipal struggle. Instead of internalizing paternal authority, and developing a sense of self with autonomous inner principles, sons remained both fearful of and attracted to external authority. These characteristics were appropriate to obedience and conformity on the job and in the world at large.

Contemporary family structure produces not only malleability and lack of internalized standards, but often a search for manipulation. These character traits lend themselves to the manipulations of modern capitalism—to media and product consumerism, to the attempt to legitimate a polity that serves people unequally, and finally to work performance. The decline of the oedipal father creates an orientation to external authority and behavioral obedience. Exclusive maternal involvement and the extension of dependence create a generalized need to please and to "succeed," and a seeming independence. This need to succeed can help to make someone dependable and reliable.

---

*The Frankfurt theorists are not explicit and in their implicit account are inconsistent about class. The reading of their account that is to me most consistent with the changes in work and the family they describe is that they are talking about the proletarianization of the traditionally independent middle strata.

Because it is divorced from specific goals and real inner standards but has involved the maintenance of an internal dependent relationship, it can also facilitate the taking of others' goals as one's own, producing the pseudo-independent organization man.

An increasingly father-absent, mother-involved family produces in men a personality that both corresponds to masculinity and male dominance as these are currently constituted in the sex-gender system, and fits appropriately with participation in capitalist relations of production. Men continue to enforce the sexual division of spheres as a defense against powerlessness in the labor market. Male denial of dependence and of attachment to women helps to guarantee both masculinity and performance in the world of work. The relative unavailability of the father and overavailability of the mother create negative definitions of masculinity and men's fear and resentment of women, as well as the lack of inner autonomy in men that enables, depending on particular family constellation and class origin, either rule-following or the easy internalization of the values of the organization.

Thus, women's and men's personality traits and orientations mesh with the sexual and familial division of labor and unequal ideology of gender and shape their asymmetric location in a structure of production and reproduction in which women are in the first instance mothers and wives and men are workers. This structure of production and reproduction requires and presupposes those specific relational modes, between husband and wife, and mother and children, which form the center of the family in contemporary society. An examination of the way that gender personality is expressed in adulthood reveals how women and men create, and are often committed to creating, the interpersonal relationships which underlie and reproduce the family structure that produced them.

12

The Psychodynamics of the Family

Let us recall that we left the pubescent girl in a triangular situation and expressed the hope that later she would dissolve the sexually mixed triangle . . . in favor of heterosexuality. This formulation was made for the sake of simplification. Actually, whether a constitutional bisexual factor contributes to the creation of such a triangle or not, this triangle can never be given up completely. The deepest and most ineradicable emotional relations with both parents share in its formation. It succeeds another relation, even older and more enduring—the relationship between mother and child, which every man or woman preserves from his birth to his death. It is erroneous to say that the little girl gives up her first mother relation in favor of the father. She only gradually draws him into the alliance, develops from the mother-child exclusiveness toward the triangular parent-child relation and continues the latter, just as she does the former, although in a weaker and less elemental form, all her life. Only the principal part changes; now the mother, now the father plays it. The ineradicability of affective constellations manifests itself in later repetitions.

HELENE DEUTSCH,
The Psychology of Women

A woman is her mother
That's the main thing

ANN SEXTON,
"Housewife"

OEDIPAL ASYMMETRIES
AND HETEROSEXUAL KNOTS[1]

The same oedipally produced ideology and psychology of male dominance, repression, and denial of dependence that propel men into the nonfamilial competitive work world place structural strains on marriage and family life. Because women mother, the development and meaning of heterosexual object-choice differ for men and women. The traditional psychoanalytic account of femininity and masculinity begins from this perception. In our society, marriage has assumed a larger and larger emotional weight, supposedly offsetting the strains of increasingly alienated and bureaucratized work in the paid economy. It no longer has the economic and political basis it once had, and the family has collapsed in upon its psychological and personal functions as production, education, religion, and care for the sick and aged have left the home. In this context, the contradictions between women's and men's heterosexuality that result from women's performing mothering functions stand out clearly.

According to psychoanalytic theory, heterosexual erotic orientation is a primary outcome of the oedipus complex for both sexes. Boys and girls differ in this, however. Boys retain one primary love object throughout their boyhood. For this reason, the development of masculine heterosexual object choice is relatively continuous: "In males the path of this development is straightforward, and the advance from the 'phallic' phase does not take place in consequence of a complicated 'wave of repression' but is based upon a ratification of that which already exists. . . ."[2] In theory, a boy resolves his oedipus complex by repressing his attachment to his mother. He is therefore ready in adulthood to find a primary relationship with someone *like* his mother. When he does, the relationship is given meaning from its psychological reactivation of what was originally an intense and exclusive relationship—first an identity, then a "dual-unity," finally a two-person relationship.

Things are not so simple for girls: "Psychoanalytic research discovered at the very outset that the development of the infantile libido to the normal heterosexual object-choice is in women rendered difficult by certain peculiar circumstances."[3] These "peculiar circumstances" are universal facts of family organization. Because her first love object is a woman, a girl, in order to attain her proper heterosexual orientation, must transfer her primary object choice to her father and men. This creates asymmetry in the feminine and masculine oedipus complex, and difficulties in the development of female sexuality, given heterosexuality as a developmental goal.

For girls, just as for boys, mothers are primary love objects. As a result, the structural inner object setting of female heterosexuality differs from that of males. When a girl's father does become an important primary person, it is in the context of a bisexual relational triangle. A girl's relation to him is emotionally in reaction to, interwoven and competing for primacy with, her relation to her mother. A girl usually turns to her father as an object of primary interest from the exclusivity of the relationship to her mother, but this libidinal turning to her father does not substitute for her attachment to her mother. Instead, a girl retains her preoedipal tie to her mother (an intense tie involved with issues of primary identification, primary love, dependence, and separation) and builds oedipal attachments to both her mother and her father upon it. These attachments are characterized by eroticized demands for exclusivity, feelings of competition, and jealousy. She retains the internalized early relationship, including its implications for the nature of her definition of self, and internalizes these other relationships in addition to and not as replacements for it.

For girls, then, there is no absolute change of object, nor exclusive attachment to their fathers. Moreover, a father's behavior and family role, and a girl's relationship to him, are crucial to the development of heterosexual orientation in her. But fathers are comparatively unavailable physically and emotionally. They are not present as much and are not primary caretakers, and their own training for masculinity may have led them to deny emotionality. Because of the father's lack of availability to his daughter, and because of the intensity of the mother-daughter relationship in which she participates, girls tend not to make a total transfer of affection to their fathers but to remain also involved with their mothers, and to oscillate emotionally between mother and father.

The implications of this are twofold. First, the nature of the heterosexual relationship differs for boys and girls. Most women emerge from their oedipus complex oriented to their father and men as primary *erotic* objects, but it is clear that men tend to remain *emotionally* secondary, or at most emotionally equal, compared to the primacy and exclusivity of an oedipal boy's emotional tie to his mother and women. Second, because the father is an additional important love object, who becomes important in the context of a relational triangle, the feminine inner object world is more complex than the masculine. This internal situation continues into adulthood and affects adult women's participation in relationships. Women, according to Deutsch, experience heterosexual relationships in a triangular context, in which men are not exclusive objects for them. The implication of her statement is confirmed by cross-cultural examination of family structure and relations between the sexes, which suggests that conjugal closeness is the exception and not the rule.[4]

Because mother and father are not the same *kind* of parent, the nature and intensity of a child's relationship to them differ as does the relationship's degree of exclusiveness. Because children first experience the social and cognitive world as continuous with themselves and do not differentiate objects, their mother, as first caretaking figure, is not a separate person and has no separate interests. In addition, this lack of separateness is in the context of the infant's total dependence on its mother for physical and psychological survival.

The internalized experience of self in the original mother-relation remains seductive and frightening: Unity was bliss, yet meant the loss of self and absolute dependence. By contrast, a child has always differentiated itself from its father and known him as a separate person with separate interests. And the child has never been totally dependent on him. Her father has not posed the original narcissistic threat (the threat to basic ego integrity and boundaries) nor provided the original narcissistic unity (the original experience of oneness) to a girl. Oedipal love for the mother, then, contains both a threat to selfhood and a promise of primal unity which love for the father never does. A girl's love for her father and women's attachment to men reflect all aspects of these asymmetries.

Men cannot provide the kind of return to oneness that women can. Michael Balint argues that the return to the experience of primary love—the possibility of regressing to the infantile stage of a sense of oneness, no reality testing, and a tranquil sense of well-being in which all needs are satisfied—is a main goal of adult sexual relationships: "This primary tendency, I shall be loved always, everywhere, in every way, my whole body, my whole being—without any criticism, without the slightest effort on my part—is the final aim of all erotic striving."[5] He implies, though, that women can fulfill this need better than men, because a sexual relationship with a woman reproduces the early situation more completely and is more completely a return to the mother. Thus, males in coitus come nearest to the experience of refusion with the mother—"The male comes nearest to achieving this regression during coitus: with his semen in reality, with his penis symbolically, with his whole self in phantasy."[6]

Women's participation here is dual. (Balint is presuming women's heterosexuality.) First, a woman identifies with the man penetrating her and thus experiences through identification refusion with a woman (mother). Second, she *becomes* the mother (phylogenetically the all-embracing sea, ontogenetically the womb). Thus, a woman in a heterosexual relationship cannot, like a man, recapture *as herself* her own experience of merging. She can do so only by identifying with someone who can, on the one hand, and by identifying with the person with whom she was merged on the other. The "regressive restitution" (Balint's term) which coitus brings, then, is not complete for a woman in the way that it is for a man.

Freud speaks to the way that women seek to recapture their relationship with their mother in heterosexual relationships.[7] He suggests that as women "change object" from mother to father, the mother remains their primary internal object, so that they often impose on their relation to their father, and later to men, the issues which preoccupy them in their internal relation to their mother. They look in relations to men for gratifications that they want from a woman. Freud points to the common clinical discovery of a woman who has apparently taken her father as a model for her choice of husband, but whose marriage in fact repeats the conflicts and feelings of her relationship with her mother. For instance, a woman who remains ambivalently dependent on her mother, or preoccupied internally with the question of whether she is separate or not, is likely to transfer this stance and sense of self to a relationship with her husband.[8] Or she may identify herself as a part-object of her male partner, as an extension of her father and men, rather than an extension of her mother and women.*

But children seek to escape from their mother as well as return to her. Fathers serve in part to break a daughter's primary unity with and dependence on her mother. For this and a number of other reasons, fathers and men are idealized.[9] A girl's father provides a last ditch escape from maternal omnipotence, so a girl cannot risk driving him away. At the same time, occupying a position of distance and ideological authority in the family, a father may be a remote figure understood to a large extent through her mother's interpretation of his role. This makes the development of a relationship based on his real strengths and weaknesses difficult. Finally, the girl herself has not received the same kind of love from her mother as a boy has. Mothers experience daughters as one with themselves; their relationships to daughters are "narcissistic," while those with their sons are more "anaclitic."

Thus, a daughter looks to her father for a sense of separateness and for the same confirmation of her specialness that her brother receives from her mother. She (and the woman she becomes) is willing to deny her father's limitations (and those of her lover or husband) as long as she feels loved.[10] She is more able to do this because his distance means that she does not really know him. The relationship, then, because of the father's distance and importance to her, occurs largely as fantasy and idealization, and lacks the grounded reality which a boy's relation to his mother has.

These differences in the experience of self in relation to father and mother are reinforced by the different stages at which boys and girls are likely to enter the oedipal situation. Girls remain longer in the preoedipal relationship, enter the oedipus situation later than boys, and their modes of oedipal resolution differ. Bibring, Slater,

---

*This is obviously only one side of the psychological matter. Chasseguet-Smirgel, who points this out, notes that men also gain satisfaction and security from turning their all-powerful mother into a part-object attachment.

and John Whiting have suggested that in the absence of men, a mother sexualizes her relationship with her son early, so that "oedipal" issues of sexual attraction and connection, competition and jealousy, become fused with "preoedipal" issues of primary love and oneness. By contrast, since the girl's relationship to her father develops later, her sense of self is more firmly established. If oedipal and preoedipal issues are fused for her, this fusion is more likely to occur in relation to her mother, and not to her father. Because her sense of self is firmer, and because oedipal love for her father is not so threatening, a girl does not "resolve" her oedipus complex to the same extent as a boy. This means that she grows up more concerned with both internalized and external object-relationships, while men tend to repress their oedipal needs for love and relationship. At the same time, men often become intolerant and disparaging of those who can express needs for love, as they attempt to deny their own needs.*[11]

Men defend themselves against the threat posed by love, but needs for love do not disappear through repression. Their training for masculinity and repression of affective relational needs, and their primarily nonemotional and impersonal relationships in the public world make deep primary relationships with other men hard to come by.[12] Given this, it is not surprising that men tend to find themselves in heterosexual relationships.

These relationships to women derive a large part of their meaning and dynamics from the men's relation to their mothers. But the maternal treatment described by Bibring, Slater, and Whiting creates relational problems in sons. When a boy's mother has treated him as an extension of herself and at the same time as a sexual object, he learns to use his masculinity and possession of a penis as a narcissistic defense. In adulthood, he will look to relationships with women for narcissistic-phallic reassurance rather than for mutual affirmation and love. Because their sexualized preoedipal attachment was encouraged, while their oedipal-genital wishes were thwarted and threatened with punishment, men may defensively invest more exclusively in the instinctual gratifications to be gained in a sexual relationship in order to avoid risking rejection of love.

Women have not repressed affective needs. They still want love and narcissistic confirmation and may be willing to put up with limitations in their masculine lover or husband in exchange for evidence

---

*Chasseguet-Smirgel argues that what Freud and Brunswick call the boy's "normal contempt" for women, and consider a standard outcome of the oedipus complex, is a pathological and defensive reaction to the sense of inescapable maternal omnipotence rather than a direct outcome of genital differences.

of caring and love. This can lead to the denial of more immediately felt aggressive and erotic drives. Chasseguet-Smirgel suggests that a strong sexuality requires the expression of aggressive, demanding impulses fused with erotic love impulses and idealization. To the extent that women feel conflict and fear punishment especially over all impulses they define as aggressive, their sexuality suffers.*

As a result of the social organization of parenting, then, men operate on two levels in women's psyche. On one level, they are emotionally secondary and not exclusively loved—are not primary love objects like mothers. On another, they are idealized and experienced as needed, but are unable either to express their own emotional needs or respond to those of women. As Grunberger puts it, "The tragedy of this situation is that the person who could give [a woman] this confirmation, her sexual partner, is precisely the one who, as we have just seen, has come to despise narcissistic needs in an effort to disengage himself from them."[13]

This situation is illuminated by sociological and clinical findings. Conventional wisdom has it, and much of our everyday observation confirms, that women are the romantic ones in our society, the ones for whom love, marriage, and relationships matter. However, several studies point out that men love and fall in love romantically, women sensibly and rationally.[14] Most of these studies argue that in the current situation, where women are economically dependent on men, women must make rational calculations for the provision of themselves and their (future) children. This view suggests that women's apparent romanticism is an emotional and ideological response to their very real economic dependence. On the societal level, especially given economic inequity, men are exceedingly important to women. The recent tendency for women to initiate divorce and separation more than men as income becomes more available to them (and as the feminist movement begins to remove the stigma of "divorcee") further confirms this.

Adult women are objectively dependent on men economically, just as in childhood girls are objectively dependent on their fathers to escape from maternal domination. Their developed ability to romanticize rational decisions (to ignore or even idealize the failings of their father and men because of their dependence) stands women in good stead in this adult situation.

---

*She suggests that this reaction, in which aggressive and erotic drives opposed to idealization are counter-cathected and repressed, better explains feminine frigidity and what Marie Bonaparte and Deutsch consider to be the "normal" feminine spiritualization of sex. Bonaparte explains these in terms of women's lesser libidinal energy, and Deutsch explains them as constitutional inhibition.

There is another side to this situation, however. Women have acquired a real capacity for rationality and distance in heterosexual relationships, qualities built into their earliest relationship with a man. Direct evidence for the psychological primacy of this latter stance comes from findings about the experience of loss itself. George Goethals reports the clinical finding that men's loss of at least the first adult relationship "throws them into a turmoil and a depression of the most extreme kind"[15]—a melancholic reaction to object-loss of the type Freud describes in "Mourning and Melancholia"—in which they withdraw and are unable to look elsewhere for new relationships. He implies, by contrast, that first adult loss may not result in as severe a depression for a woman, and claims that his women patients did not withdraw to the same extent and were more able to look elsewhere for new relationships. Zick Rubin reports similar findings.[16] The women he studied more frequently broke up relationships, and the men, whether or not they initiated the break-up, were more depressed and lonely afterward. Jessie Bernard, discussing older people, reports that the frequency of psychological distress, death, and suicide is much higher among recently widowed men than women, and indicates that the same difference can be found in a comparison of divorced men and women.[17]

These studies imply that women have other resources and a certain distance from their relationships to men. My account stresses that women have a richer, ongoing inner world to fall back on, and that the men in their lives do not represent the intensity and exclusivity that women represent to men. Externally, they also retain and develop more relationships. It seems that, developmentally, men do not become as emotionally important to women as women do to men.

Because women care for children, then, heterosexual symbiosis has a different "meaning" for men and women. Freud originally noted that "a man's love and a woman's are a phase apart psychologically."[18] He and psychoanalytic thinkers after him point to ways in which women and men, though usually looking for intimacy with each other, do not fulfill each other's needs because of the social organization of parenting. Differences in female and male oedipal experiences, all growing out of women's mothering, create this situation. Girls enter adulthood with a complex layering of affective ties and a rich, ongoing inner object world. Boys have a simpler oedipal situation and more direct affective relationships, and this situation is repressed in a way that the girl's is not. The mother remains a primary internal object to the girl, so that heterosexual relationships are on the model of a nonexclusive, second relationship for her, whereas for the boy they recreate an exclusive, primary relationship.

As a result of being parented by a woman, both sexes look for a return to this emotional and physical union. A man achieves this directly through the heterosexual bond, which replicates the early mother-infant exclusivity. He is supported in this endeavor by women, who, through their own development, have remained open to relational needs, have retained an ongoing inner affective life, and have learned to deny the limitations of masculine lovers for both psychological and practical reasons.

Men both look for and fear exclusivity. Throughout their development, they have tended to repress their affective relational needs, and to develop ties based more on categorical and abstract role expectations, particularly with other males. They are likely to participate in an intimate heterosexual relationship with the ambivalence created by an intensity which one both wants and fears—demanding from women what men are at the same time afraid of receiving.

As a result of being parented by a woman and growing up heterosexual, women have different and more complex relational needs in which an exclusive relationship to a man is not enough. As noted previously, this is because women situate themselves psychologically as part of a relational triangle in which their father and men are emotionally secondary or, at most, equal to their mother and women. In addition, the relation to the man itself has difficulties. Idealization, growing out of a girl's relation to her father, involves denial of real feelings and to a certain extent an unreal relationship to men. The contradictions in women's heterosexual relationships, though, are due as much to men's problems with intimacy as to outcomes of early childhood relationships. Men grow up rejecting their own needs for love, and therefore find it difficult and threatening to meet women's emotional needs. As a result, they collude in maintaining distance from women.

THE CYCLE COMPLETED: MOTHERS AND CHILDREN

Families create children gendered, heterosexual, and ready to marry. But families organized around women's mothering and male dominance create incompatibilities in women's and men's relational needs. In particular, relationships to men are unlikely to provide for women satisfaction of the relational needs that their mothering by women and the social organization of gender have produced. The less men participate in the domestic sphere, and especially in parenting, the more this will be the case.

Women try to fulfill their need to be loved, try to complete the relational triangle, and try to reexperience the sense of dual unity they had with their mother, which the heterosexual relationship tends to fulfill for men. This situation daily reinforces what women first experienced developmentally and intrapsychically in relation to men. While they are likely to become and remain erotically heterosexual, they are encouraged both by men's difficulties with love and by their own relational history with their mothers to look elsewhere for love and emotional gratification.

One way that women fulfill these needs is through the creation and maintenance of important personal relations with other women. Cross-culturally, segregation by gender is the rule: Women tend to have closer personal ties with each other than men have, and to spend more time in the company of women than they do with men. In our society, there is some sociological evidence that women's friendships are affectively richer than men's.[19] In other societies, and in most sub-cultures of our own, women remain involved with female relatives in adulthood.[20] Deutsch suggests further that adult female relationships sometimes express a woman's psychological participation in the re-lational triangle. Some women, she suggests, always need a woman rival in their relationship to a man; others need a best friend with whom they share all confidences about their heterosexual relation-ships. These relationships are one way of resolving and recreating the mother-daughter bond and are an expression of women's general relational capacities and definition of self in relationship.

However, deep affective relationships to women are hard to come by on a routine, daily, ongoing basis for many women. Lesbian re-lationships do tend to recreate mother-daughter emotions and con-nections,[21] but most women are heterosexual. This heterosexual pref-erence and taboos against homosexuality, in addition to objective economic dependence on men, make the option of primary sexual bonds with other women unlikely—though more prevalent in recent years. In an earlier period, women tended to remain physically close to their own mother and sisters after marriage, and could find rela-tionships with other women in their daily work and community. The development of industrial capitalism, however—and the increasingly physically isolated nuclear family it has produced—has made these primary relationships more rare and has turned women (and men) increasingly and exclusively to conjugal family relationships for emo-tional support and love.[22]

There is a second alternative, made all the more significant by the elimination of the first, which also builds both upon the nature of women's self-definition in a heterosexual relationship and upon the primary mother-child bond. As Deutsch makes clear, women's psyche consists in a layering of relational constellations. The preoedipal mother-child relation and the oedipal triangle have lasted until late in a woman's childhood, in fact throughout her development. To the extent that relations with a man gain significance for a woman, this experience is incomplete. Given the triangular situation and emotional asymmetry of her own parenting, a woman's relation to a man *requires* on the level of psychic structure a third person, since it was originally established in a triangle. A man's relation to women does not. His relation to his mother was originally established first as an identity, then as a dual unity, then as a two-person relationship, before his father ever entered the picture.

On the level of psychic structure, then, a child completes the relational triangle for a woman. Having a child, and experiencing her relation to a man in this context, enables her to reimpose intrapsychic relational structure on the social world, while at the same time resolving the generational component of her oedipus complex as she takes a new place in the triangle—a maternal place in relation to her own child.

The mother-child relationship also recreates an even more basic relational constellation. The exclusive symbiotic mother-child relationship of a mother's own infancy reappears, a relationship which all people who have been mothered want basically to recreate. This contrasts to the situation of a man. A man often wants a child through his role-based, positional identification with his father, or his primary or personal identification with his mother. Similarly, a woman has been involved in relational identification processes with her mother, which include identifying with a mother who has come to stand to both sexes as someone with unique capacities for mothering. Yet on a less conscious, object-relational level, having a child recreates the desired mother-child exclusivity for a woman and interrupts it for a man, just as the man's father intruded into his relation to his mother. Accordingly, as Benedek, Zilboorg, and Bakan suggest, men often feel extremely jealous toward children.* These differences hold also on the level of sexual and biological fantasy and symbolism. A woman, as I have suggested, cannot return to the mother in coitus as directly as can a man. Symbolically her identification with the man can help. However, a much more straightforward symbolic return occurs through her identification with the child who is in her womb: "Ferenczi's 'maternal regression' is realized for the woman in equating coitus with the situation of sucking. The last act of this regression (return into the uterus) which the man accomplishes by the act of

---

*This is not to deny the conflicts and resentments which women may feel about their children.

introjection in coitus, is realized by the woman in pregnancy in the complete identification between mother and child."[23]

For all these reasons, it seems psychologically logical to a woman to turn her marriage into a family, and to be more involved with these children (this child) than her husband. By doing so, she recreates for herself the exclusive intense primary unit which a heterosexual relationship tends to recreate for men. She recreates also her internalized asymmetrical relational triangle. These relational issues and needs predate and underlie her identifications, and come out of normal family structure regardless of explicit role training. Usually, however, this training intensifies their effects. In mothering, a woman acts also on her personal identification with a mother who parents and her own training for women's role.

This account indicates a larger structural issue regarding the way in which a woman's relation to her children recreates the psychic situation of the relationship to her mother. This relationship is recreated on two levels: most deeply and unconsciously, that of the primary mother-infant tie; and upon this, the relationship of the bisexual triangle. Because the primary mother-infant unit is exclusive, and because oscillation in the bisexual triangle includes a constant pull back to the mother attachment, there may be a psychological contradiction for a woman between interest in and commitment to children and that to men. Insofar as a woman experiences her relationship to her child on the level of intrapsychic structure as exclusive, her relationship to a man may therefore be superfluous.

Freud points tentatively to this (to him, unwelcome) situation, in contrasting men's and women's object-love. In his essay "On Narcissism," he claims that "complete object-love of the attachment type is, properly speaking, characteristic of the male."[24] Women, by contrast, tend to love narcissistically—on one level, to want to be loved or to be largely self-sufficient; on another, to love someone as an extension of their self rather than a differentiated object. He implies here that the necessary mode of relating to infants is the normal way women love. Yet he also claims that women do attain true object-love, but only in relation to their children—who are both part of them and separate. Freud's stance here seems to be that of the excluded man viewing women's potential psychological self-sufficiency vis-à-vis *men*. This situation may be the basis of the early psychoanalytic claim that women are more narcissistic than men, since clinically it is clear that men have just as many and as serious problems of fundamental object-relatedness as do women.[25]

Clinical accounts reveal this contradiction between male-female and mother-child love. Fliess and Deutsch point to the extreme case where children are an exclusively mother-daughter affair.[26] Some women fantasize giving their mother a baby, or even having one from her. These are often teenage girls with extreme problems of attachment and separation in relation to their mothers, whose fathers were more or less irrelevant in the home. Often a girl expresses this fantasy through either not knowing who the father of her baby is, or knowing and not caring. Her main object is to take her baby home to her mother.

Deutsch points out that in women's fantasies and dreams, sexuality and erotism are often opposed to motherhood and reproduction.[27] She reports clinical and literary cases of women who choose either sexuality or motherhood exclusively, mothers for whom sexual satisfactions become insignificant, women with parthenogenic fantasies. Benedek and Winnicott observe that the experience of pregnancy, and the anticipation of motherhood, often entail a withdrawal of a woman's interest from other primary commitments to her own body and developing child. As Benedek puts it, "The woman's interest shifts from extraverted activities to her body and its welfare. Expressed in psychodynamic terms: the libido is withdrawn from external, heterosexual objects, becomes concentrated upon the self."[28]

This libidinal shift may continue after birth. Psychological and libidinal gratifications from the nursing relationship may substitute for psychological and libidinal gratifications formerly found in heterosexual involvements.[29] The clinical findings and theoretical claims of Bakan, Benedek, and Zilboorg concerning men's jealousy of their children confirm this as a possibility.

On the level of the relational triangle also, there can be a contradiction between women's interest in children and in men. This is evident in Freud's suggestion that women oscillate psychologically between a preoedipal and oedipal stance (he says between periods of "masculinity" and "femininity") and that women's and men's love is a phase apart psychologically (that a woman is more likely to love her son than her husband). Deutsch points out that a man may or may not be psychologically necessary or desirable to the mother-child exclusivity. When she is oriented to the man, a woman's fantasy of having children is "I want a child by him, *with him*"; when men are emotionally in the background, it is "I want a *child*."[30]

Women come to want and need primary relationships to children. These wants and needs result from wanting intense primary relationships, which men tend not to provide both because of their place in women's oedipal constellation and because of their difficulties with intimacy. Women's desires for intense primary relationships tend not to be with other women, both because of internal and external taboos on homosexuality, and because of women's isolation from their primary female kin (especially mothers) and other women.

As they develop these wants and needs, women also develop the capacities for participating in parent-child relationships. They develop capacities for mothering. Because of the structural situation of parenting, women remain in a primary, preoedipal relationship with their mother longer than men. They do not feel the need to repress or cut off the capacity for experiencing the primary identification and primary love which are the basis of parental empathy. Also, their development and oedipal resolution do not require the ego defense against either regression or relation which characterizes masculine development. Women also tend to remain bound up in preoedipal issues in relation to their own mother, so that they in fact have some unconscious investment in reactivating them. When they have a child, they are more liable than a man to do so. In each critical period of their child's development, the parent's own development conflicts and experiences of that period affect their attitudes and behavior.[31] The preoedipal relational stance, latent in women's normal relationship to the world and experience of self, is activated in their coming to care for an infant, encouraging their empathic identification with this infant which is the basis of maternal care.

Mothering, moreover, involves a double identification for women, both as mother *and* as child. The whole preoedipal relationship has been internalized and perpetuated in a more ongoing way for women than for men. Women take both parts in it. Women have capacities for primary identification with their child through regression to primary love and empathy. Through their mother identification, they have ego capacities and the sense of responsibility which go into caring for children. In addition, women have an investment in mothering in order to make reparation to their own mother (or to get back at her). Throughout their development, moreover, women have been building layers of identification with their mothers upon the primary internalized mother-child relationship.[32]

Women develop capacities for mothering from their object-relational stance. This stance grows out of the special nature and length of their preoedipal relationship to their mother; the nonabsolute repression of oedipal relationships; and their general ongoing mother-daughter preoccupation as they are growing up. It also develops because they have not formed the same defenses against relationships as men. Related to this, they develop wants and needs to be mothers from their oedipal experience and the contradictions in heterosexual love that result.

The *wants and needs* which lead women to become mothers put them in situations where their mothering *capacities* can be expressed. At the same time, women remain in conflict with their internal mother and often their real mother as well. The preoccupation with issues of separation and primary identification, the ability to recall their early relationship to their mother—precisely those capacities which enable mothering—are also those which may lead to over-identification and pseudoempathy based on maternal projection rather than any real perception or understanding of their infant's needs.[33] Similarly, the need for primary relationships becomes more prominent and weighted as relationships to other women become less possible and as father/husband absence grows. Though women come to mother, and to be mothers, the very capacities and commitments for mothering can be in contradiction one with the other and within themselves. Capacities which enable mothering are also precisely those which can make mothering problematic.

GENDER PERSONALITY
AND THE REPRODUCTION OF MOTHERING

In spite of the apparently close tie between women's capacities for childbearing and lactation on the one hand and their responsibilities for child care on the other, and in spite of the probable prehistoric convenience (and perhaps survival necessity) of a sexual division of labor in which women mothered, biology and instinct do not provide adequate explanations for how women come to mother. Women's mothering as a feature of social structure requires an explanation in terms of social structure. Conventional feminist and social psychological explanations for the genesis of gender roles—girls and boys are "taught" appropriate behaviors and "learn" appropriate feelings—are insufficient both empirically and methodologically to account for how women become mothers.

Methodologically, socialization theories rely inappropriately on individual intention. Ongoing social structures include the means for their own reproduction—in the regularized repetition of social processes, in the perpetuation of conditions which require members' participation, in the genesis of legitimating ideologies and instititutions, and in the psychological as well as physical reproduction of people to perform necessary roles. Accounts of socialization help to explain the perpetuation of ideologies about gender roles. However, notions of appropriate behavior, like coercion, cannot in themselves produce parenting. Psychological capacities and a particular object-relational stance are central and definitional to parenting in a way that they are not to many other roles and activities.

Women's mothering includes the capacities for its own reproduction. This reproduction consists in the production of women with, and men without, the particular psychological capacities and stance which go into primary parenting. Psychoanalytic theory provides us with a theory of social reproduction that explains major features of personality development and the development of psychic structure, and the differential development of gender personality in particular. Psychoanalysts argue that personality both results from and consists in the ways a child appropriates, internalizes, and organizes early experiences in their family—from the fantasies they have, the defenses they use, the ways they channel and redirect drives in this object-relational context. A person subsequently imposes this intrapsychic structure, and the fantasies, defenses, and relational modes and preoccupations which go with it, onto external social situations. This reexternalization (or mutual reexternalization) is a major constituting feature of social and interpersonal situations themselves.

Psychoanalysis, however, has not had an adequate theory of the reproduction of mothering. Because of the teleological assumption that anatomy is destiny, and that women's destiny includes primary parenting, the ontogenesis of women's mothering has been largely ignored, even while the genesis of a wide variety of related disturbances and problems has been accorded widespread clinical attention. Most psychoanalysts agree that the basis for parenting is laid for both genders in the early relationship to a primary caretaker. Beyond that, in order to explain why *women* mother, they tend to rely on vague notions of a girl's subsequent identification with her mother, which makes her and not her brother a primary parent, or on an unspecified and uninvestigated innate femaleness in girls, or on logical leaps from lactation or early vaginal sensations to caretaking abilities and commitments.

The psychoanalytic account of male and female development, when reinterpreted, gives us a developmental theory of the reproduction of women's mothering. Women's mothering reproduces itself through differing object-relational experiences and differing psychic outcomes in women and men. As a result of having been parented by a woman, women are more likely than men to seek to be mothers, that is, to relocate themselves in a primary mother-child relationship, to get gratification from the mothering relationship, and to have psychological and relational capacities for mothering.

The early relation to a primary caretaker provides in children of both genders both the basic capacity to participate in a relationship with the features of the early parent-child one, and the desire to create this intimacy. However, because women mother, the early experience and preoedipal relationship differ for boys and girls. Girls retain more concern with early childhood issues in relation to their mother, and a sense of self involved with these issues. Their attachments therefore retain more preoedipal aspects. The greater length and different nature of their preoedipal experience, and their continuing preoccupation with the issues of this period, mean that women's sense of self is continuous with others and that they retain capacities for primary identification, both of which enable them to experience the empathy and lack of reality sense needed by a cared-for infant. In men, these qualities have been curtailed, both because they are early treated as an opposite by their mother and because their later attachment to her must be repressed. The relational basis for mothering is thus extended in women, and inhibited in men, who experience themselves as more separate and distinct from others.

The different structure of the feminine and masculine oedipal triangle and process of oedipal experience that results from women's mothering contributes further to gender personality differentiation and the reproduction of women's mothering. As a result of this experience, women's inner object world, and the affects and issues associated with it, are more actively sustained and more complex than men's. This means that women define and experience themselves relationally. Their heterosexual orientation is always in internal dialogue with both oedipal and preoedipal mother-child relational issues. Thus, women's heterosexuality is triangular and requires a third person—a child—for its structural and emotional completion. For men, by contrast, the heterosexual relationship alone recreates the early bond to their mother; a child interrupts it. Men, moreover, do not define themselves in relationship and have come to suppress relational capacities and repress relational needs. This prepares them to participate in the affect-denying world of alienated work, but not to fulfill women's needs for intimacy and primary relationships.

The oedipus complex, as it emerges from the asymmetrical organization of parenting, secures a psychological taboo on parent-child incest and pushes boys and girls in the direction of extrafamilial heterosexual relationships. This is one step toward the reproduction of parenting. The creation and maintenance of the incest taboo and of heterosexuality in girls and boys are different, however. For boys, superego formation and identification with their father, rewarded by the superiority of masculinity, maintain the taboo on incest with their mother, while heterosexual orientation continues from their earliest love relation with her. For girls, creating them as heterosexual in the first place maintains the taboo. However, women's heterosexuality is not so exclusive as men's. This makes it easier for them to accept or seek a male substitute for their fathers. At the same time, in a male-dominant society, women's exclusive emotional heterosexuality is not so necessary, nor is her repression of love for her father. Men are more likely to initiate relationships, and women's economic dependence on men pushes them anyway into heterosexual marriage.

Male dominance in heterosexual couples and marriage solves the problem of women's lack of heterosexual commitment and lack of satisfaction by making women more reactive in the sexual bonding process. At the same time, contradictions in heterosexuality help to perpetuate families and parenting by ensuring that women will seek relations to children and will not find heterosexual relationships alone satisfactory. Thus, men's lack of emotional availability and women's less exclusive heterosexual commitment help ensure women's mothering.

Women's mothering, then, produces psychological self-definition and capacities appropriate to mothering in women, and curtails and inhibits these capacities and this self-definition in men. The early experience of being cared for by a woman produces a fundamental structure of expectations in women and men concerning mothers' lack of separate interests from their infants and total concern for their infants' welfare. Daughters grow up identifying with these mothers, about whom they have such expectations. This set of expectations is generalized to the assumption that women naturally take care of children of all ages and the belief that women's "maternal" qualities can and should be extended to the nonmothering work that they do. All these results of women's mothering have ensured that women will mother infants and will take continuing responsibility for children.

The reproduction of women's mothering is the basis for the reproduction of women's location and responsibilities in the domestic sphere. This mothering, and its generalization to women's structural location in the domestic sphere, links the contemporary social organization of gender and social organization of production and contributes to the reproduction of each. That women mother is a fundamental organizational feature of the sex-gender system: It is basic to the sexual division of labor and generates a psychology and ideology of male dominance as well as an ideology about women's capacities and nature. Women, as wives and mothers, contribute as well to the daily and generational reproduction, both physical and psychological, of male workers and thus to the reproduction of capitalist production.

Women's mothering also reproduces the family as it is constituted in male-dominant society. The sexual and familial division of labor in which women mother creates a sexual division of psychic organization and orientation. It produces socially gendered women and men who enter into asymmetrical heterosexual relationships; it produces men who react to, fear, and act superior to women, and who put most of their energies into the nonfamilial work world and do not parent. Finally, it produces women who turn their energies toward nurturing and caring for children—in turn reproducing the sexual and familial division of labor in which women mother.

Social reproduction is thus asymmetrical. Women in their domestic role reproduce men and children physically, psychologically, and emotionally. Women in their domestic role as houseworkers reconstitute themselves physically on a daily basis and reproduce themselves as mothers, emotionally and psychologically, in the next generation. They thus contribute to the perpetuation of their own social roles and position in the hierarchy of gender.

Institutionalized features of family structure and the social relations of reproduction reproduce themselves. A psychoanalytic investigation shows that women's mothering capacities and commitments, and the general psychological capacities and wants which are the basis of women's emotion work, are built developmentally into feminine personality. Because women are themselves mothered by women, they grow up with the relational capacities and needs, and psychological definition of self-in-relationship, which commits them to mothering. Men, because they are mothered by women, do not. Women mother daughters who, when they become women, mother.

Afterword:
Women's Mothering and
Women's Liberation

Women's mothering perpetuates itself through social-structurally induced psychological mechanisms. It is not an unmediated product of physiology. Women come to mother because they have been mothered by women. By contrast, that men are mothered by women reduces their parenting capacities.

My account explains the reproduction of mothering. But it is not intended to demonstrate that this process is unproblematic or without contradictions. Women's mothering has created daughters as maternal, and this has ensured that parenting gets done. Yet the processes through which mothering is reproduced generate tensions and strains that undermine the sex-gender system even while reproducing it. The forms that these tensions and strains take depend in part on the internal development of the sex-gender system, in part on external historical conditions. In specific historical periods, such as the present, contradictions within the sex-gender system fuse with forces outside it, and lead to a situation in which resistance is widespread and often explicitly political.

Those very capacities and needs which create women as mothers create potential contradictions in mothering. A mother's sense of continuity with her infant may shade into too much connection and not enough separateness. Empathy and primary identification, enabling anticipation of an infant's or child's needs, may become an unconscious labeling of what her child ought to need, or what she thinks it needs. The development of a sense of autonomous self becomes difficult for children and leads to a mother's loss of sense of self as well. That women turn to children to complete a relational triangle, or to recreate a mother-child unity, means that mothering is invested with a mother's often conflictual, ambivalent, yet powerful need for her own mother. That women turn to children to fulfill emotional and even erotic desires unmet by men or other women means that a mother expects from infants what only another adult should be expected to give.

These tendencies take different forms with sons and daughters. Sons may become substitutes for husbands, and must engage in defensive assertion of ego boundaries and repression of emotional needs. Daughters may become substitutes for mothers, and develop insufficiently individuated senses of self.

Although these outcomes are potential in those personality characteristics which go into parenting and the psychological outcomes that women's mothering produces in children, their manifestation depends on how the family and women's mothering are situated socially. In a society where women do meaningful productive work, have ongoing adult companionship while they are parenting, and have satisfying emotional relationships with other adults, they are less likely to overinvest in children. But these are precisely the conditions that capitalist industrial development has limited.

Beginning in the 1940s, studies began to claim that mothers in American society were "overprotecting" their children and not allowing them to separate. The mothers these studies describe are mothers of the 1920s. These mothers were rearing children when the new psychology was emphasizing maternal responsibility for children's development, when women were putting more time into child care even as there were fewer children to care for, when family mobility and the beginnings of suburbanization were removing women from daily contact with female kin. Women were expected to mother under precisely those conditions which, according to cross-cultural research, make it hardest to care for children and feel unambivalently affectionate toward them: as full-time mothers, with exclusive responsibility for children, in isolated homes.[1] Most of the studies were not concerned with the lives of the mothers, but only with how their children were affected.

As women have turned for psychological sustenance to children, their overinvestment has perpetuated itself. Girls who grow up in family settings which include neither other women besides their mother nor an actively present father tend to have problems establishing a sufficiently individuated and autonomous sense of self. They in turn have difficulties in experiencing themselves as separate from their own children.

The exclusive responsibility of women for children exacerbates conflicts about masculinity in men. As long as women mother, a stable sense of masculine self is always more problematic than a stable sense of feminine self. Yet cross-culturally, the more father-absence (or absence of adult men) in the family, the more severe are conflicts about masculinity and fear of women.

When people have extreme needs for emotional support, and a few very intense relationships (whose sole basis is emotional connection, ungrounded in cooperative activity or institutionalized nonemotional roles) to provide for these needs, these relationships are liable to be full of conflict. For instance, heterosexual relationships based on idealized expectations of romantic love and total emotional sustenance, without the economic and political basis that marriage once had, often founder, as the present divorce rate testifies. Mother-son relationships in which the mother is looking for a husband create problems and resentments in both. Mother-daughter relationships in which the mother is supported by a network of women kin and friends, and has meaningful work and self-esteem, produce daughters with capacities for nurturance and a strong sense of self. Mother-daughter relationships in which the mother has no other adult support or meaningful work and remains ambivalently attached to her own mother produce ambivalent attachment and inability to separate in daughters. Those aspects of feminine personality which reproduce mothering become distorted.

Contemporary problems in mothering emerge from potential internal contradictions in the family and the social organization of gender—between women's mothering and heterosexual commitment, between women's mothering and individuation in daughters, between emotional connection and a sense of masculinity in sons. Changes generated from outside the family, particularly in the economy, have sharpened these contradictions.

At present, new strains emerge as women enter the paid labor force while continuing to mother. Women today are expected to be full-time mothers and to work in the paid labor force, are considered unmotherly if they demand day-care centers, greedy and unreasonable if they expect help from husbands, and lazy if they are single mothers who want to receive adequate welfare payments in order to be able to stay home for their children.

Women's mothering also affects men. In response to alienation and domination in the paid work world, many men are coming to regret their lack of extended connection with children. They feel that they are missing what remains one of the few deep personal experiences our society leaves us.

Until the contemporary feminist movement, social and psychological commentators put the burden of solution for these problems onto
the individual and did not recognize that anything was systematically
wrong. They described both the potential contradictions in mothering and their actual expression—mothers on a balancing wire of separation and connection, merging and loss of ego while maintaining
a firm sense of autonomous self, drawing from and using the relation
to their own mother while not letting this relationship overwhelm the
relation to their child. They described the production of heterosexual
contradictions and problems of masculinity as a routine product of
women's mothering. To overcome these difficulties, mothers were to
learn their balancing act better, and fathers were to be more seductive
toward daughters and more of a model to sons.

Psychoanalytically oriented psychologists and social psychologists
with whom I have talked about this book have argued that there is
nothing inherently *wrong* with a sexual division of functions or roles
—with the sexual division of labor. They argue that only inequality
and differential valuation are wrong. But historically and cross-culturally we cannot separate the sexual division of labor from sexual
inequality. The sexual division of labor and women's responsibility
for child care are linked to and generate male dominance. Psychologists have demonstrated unequivocally that the very fact of being
mothered by a woman generates in men conflicts over masculinity,
a psychology of male dominance, and a need to be superior to
women. Anthropologists argue that women's child-care responsibilities required that the earliest men hunt, giving them, and not women,
access to the prestige and power that come from control over extradomestic distribution networks.[2] They show that women's continued
relegation to the domestic, "natural" sphere, as an extension of their
mothering functions, has ensured that they remain less social, less
cultural, and also less powerful than men.[3]

Thus the social organization of parenting produces sexual inequality, not simply role differentiation. It is politically and socially
important to confront this organization of parenting. Even though
it is an arrangement that seems universal, directly rooted in biology,
and inevitable, it can be changed. The possibility of change is indicated not only by a theoretical critique of biological determinism, but
by the contradictory aspects of the present organization of parenting.
Even as the present forms reproduce mothering, they help to produce a widespread dissatisfaction with their own limitations among
women (and sometimes men).

If our goal is to overcome the sexual division of labor in which
women mother, we need to understand the mechanisms which re-

produce it in the first place. My account points precisely to where intervention should take place. Any strategy for change whose goal includes liberation from the constraints of an unequal social organization of gender must take account of the need for a fundamental reorganization of parenting, so that primary parenting is shared between men and women.

Some friends and colleagues have said that my account is too unqualified. In fact, *all* women *do not* mother or want to mother, and *all* women are not "maternal" or nurturant. *Some* women are far more nurturant than others, and want children far more. Some *men* are more nurturant than some women. I agree that all claims about gender differences gloss over important differences within genders and similarities between genders. I hope that this book leads people to raise questions about such variations, and to engage in the research that will begin to answer them.

Still, I believe that the intergender differences are socially and politically most significant. It is important to explore intragender differences and intergender similarities in order to argue against views of natural or biological gender differences, but it is crucial to take full account of structural and statistical truths about male-female differences. What is important is not to confuse these truths with prescription.

Some have suggested that I imply that there has been no change in the organization of parenting—that my account is "ahistorical." This criticism strikes at the heart of a problem. The sex-gender system is continually changing, as it responds to and affects other aspects of social and economic organization. Yet it stays the same in fundamental ways. It does not help us to deny the social and psychological rootedness of women's mothering nor the extent to which we participate, often in spite of our conscious intentions, in contemporary sex-gender arrangements. We know almost nothing about historical changes in parenting practices, and little about differences within contemporary society either—about the effects of class differences and of whether a mother works in the paid labor force or not. We know little about the effects of variations in family structure, such as whether a single mother lives with small children or with older ones as well, or if children grow up in a large or small household. We certainly need to know more about the effects of these differences and about historical changes in parenting.

Nor can we assume that the processes I discuss are unchanging. My account relies on psychoanalytic findings that, if we start from the childhood of Freud's first patients, span at least the past hundred years. But even during this period, parenting practices and the organization of parenting have changed. In the past hundred years there have been enormous changes in the availability of contraception and a growth of smaller, more isolated families. Child-rearing activities have become more and more isolated as well. Women spend much less of their lives bearing and rearing children. In the last twenty years, women with children have entered the paid labor force in great numbers, so that, as of 1974, about 46 percent of mothers with children under eighteen were in the labor force—over half of the mothers with school-age children and over a third of those with children under six.[4] These changes have doubtless affected mother-child relationships and the content of mothering, but we do not know how. We do not know when cumulative slight shifts in parenting practices become qualitative, and indicate that we are no longer talking about the same system.

At the same time, women continue to be primary parents, both within the family and in alternate child-care settings. Even when we look at contemporary societies where nonfamilial child care is widespread—Israel, China, the Soviet Union, Cuba—women still perform this care.

My account does not concern the reproduction of mothering for all time. But it is probable that the issues I discuss are relevant in all societies. Many factors have gone into the reproduction of mothering in different societies and different historical periods. The factors I discuss are central to the reproduction of mothering today. If they were less significant in other times and places, this does not take away from my conclusions but points to more we need to know.

Those who suggest that my view does not allow for change often also suggest that I am pessimistic and make the current situation seem inevitable. A seeming inevitability comes first from language which refers to primary parenting activities as "mothering." It is hard for us to separate women from the parenting functions they perform, and to separate the care children need from the question of who performs it. We can and should separate these things, however.

My account also seems to make the processes it explains appear inevitable because I, like others who rely on psychoanalytic modes of explanation, describe things which happen to people by the time they are five. Psychoanalysis does show that we are formed in crucial ways by the time we are five, but it allows for change, either from life experiences or through the analytic process itself. In fact, psychoanalysis was developed not only to explain our early psychic formation but to show us how to overcome its limitations. Psychoanalysis, moreover, argues against a unilateral model of social determination, and for the variation and creativity in what people make of their early childhood experiences and their later experiences as well. In the present case, I show how parenting qualities are created in women through specific social and psychological processes. By implication, I show how these qualities could be created in men, if men and women parented equally.

We can draw on recent psychological theory and research to demonstrate the possibility of change. The earliest psychoanalytic theory stressed the importance of the biological feeding relationship in personality formation. Much recent theory, by contrast, suggests that infants require the whole parenting relationship of warmth, contact, and reliable care, and not the specific feeding relationship itself. This theory has been used to keep mothers in the home, now that biological imperatives are less persuasive. But it also indicates that people other than biological mothers can provide adequate care. Similarly, traditional child development theory has often held that children need parenting from one person only. But recent research suggests that children need consistency of care and the ability to relate to a small number of people stably over time. They do not require an exclusive relationship to one person. Historically, children have rarely been cared for exclusively by a biological mother, and recent studies of day care suggest that what is important is the quality of the day care and of the time spent with parents.

It is true that children grow up differently without exclusive mothering, but not necessarily in ways that are undesirable. Studies of more collective childrearing situations (the kibbutzim, China, Cuba) suggest that children develop more sense of solidarity and commitment to the group, less individualism and competitiveness, are less liable to form intense, exclusive adult relationships, than children reared in Western nuclear families. My view is that exclusive single parenting is bad for mother and child alike. As I point out earlier, mothers in such a setting are liable to overinvest in and overwhelm the relationship. Similarly, I think, children are better off in situations where love and relationship are not a scarce resource controlled and manipulated by one person only.

The current organization of parenting separates children and men. Most commentators claim that children should spend some time with men, but most are hesitant to suggest that this time should be of equivalent emotional quality to time spent with women. Because they are concerned with children's adoption of appropriate gender roles, they assume a different role for the father. Fathers must be primarily masculine role models for boys, and heterosexual objects for girls, because traditional gender roles and heterosexual orientation are necessary and desirable. These roles have been functional, but for a sex-gender system founded on sexual inequality, and not for social survival or free human activity. Fathers are supposed to help children to individuate and break their dependence on their mothers. But this dependence on her, and this primary identification, would not be created in the first place if men took primary parenting responsibilities.

Children could be dependent from the outset on people of both genders and establish an individuated sense of self in relation to both. In this way, masculinity would not become tied to denial of dependence and devaluation of women. Feminine personality would be less preoccupied with individuation, and children would not develop fears of *maternal* omnipotence and expectations of *women's* unique self-sacrificing qualities. This would reduce men's needs to guard their masculinity and their control of social and cultural spheres which treat and define women as secondary and powerless, and would help women to develop the autonomy which too much embeddedness in relationship has often taken from them.

Equal parenting would not threaten anyone's primary sense of gendered self (nor do we know what this self would look like in a nonsexist society). As Stoller has pointed out, men's primary sense of gendered self may be threatened with things as they are anyway. But this sense of self does not best come from role adoption. When it does, it is reactive and defensive rather than secure and flexible. Personal connection to and identification with both parents would enable a person to choose those activities she or he desired, without feeling that such choices jeopardized their gender identity.

My expectation is that equal parenting would leave people of both genders with the positive capacities each has, but without the destructive extremes these currently tend toward. Anyone who has good primary relationships has the foundation for nurturance and love, and women would retain these even as men would gain them. Men would be able to retain the autonomy which comes from differentiation without that differentiation being rigid and reactive, and women would have more opportunity to gain it. People's sexual choices might become more flexible, less desperate.

I would like to think we could simply initiate these transformations on a societywide scale. However, women's mothering is tied to many other aspects of our society, is fundamental to our ideology of gender, and benefits many people. It is a major feature of the sex-gender system. It creates heterosexual asymmetries which reproduce the family and marriage, but leave women with needs that lead them to care for children, and men with capacities for participation in the alienated work world. It creates a psychology of male dominance and fear of women in men. It forms a basis for the division of the social world into unequally valued domestic and public spheres, each the province of people of a different gender.

Women's mothering is also a crucial link between the contemporary organization of gender and organization of production. It produces men with personality characteristics and psychic structure appropriate to participation in the capitalist work world. An ideology of women as mothers extends to women's responsibilities as maternal wives for emotional reconstitution and support of their working husbands. Assumptions that the social organization of parenting is natural and proper (that women's child *care* is indistinguishable from their child*bearing*, that women are for biological reasons better parents than men, moral arguments that women ought to mother) have continued to serve as grounds for arguments against most changes in the social organization of gender. Certainly resistance to changes in the sex-gender system is often strongest around women's maternal functions.

We live in a period when the demands of the roles defined by the sex-gender system have created widespread discomfort and resistance. Aspects of this system are in crisis internally and conflict with economic tendencies. Change will certainly occur, but the outcome is far from certain. The elimination of the present organization of parenting in favor of a system of parenting in which both men and women are responsible would be a tremendous social advance. This outcome is historically possible, but far from inevitable. Such advances do not occur simply because they are better for "society," and certainly not simply because they are better for some (usually less powerful) people. They depend on the conscious organization and activity of all women and men who recognize that their interests lie in transforming the social organization of gender and eliminating sexual inequality.

Notes

CHAPTER 1

1. See Robert V. Wells, 1971, "Demographic Change and the Life Cycle of American Families," *Journal of Interdisciplinary History*, 2, #2, pp. 273–282.

2. See, for example, Alice Clark, 1919, *The Working Life of Women in the Seventeenth Century*, and Robert S. Lynd and Helen Merrell Lynd, 1929, *Middletown*.

3. See, for example, Talcott Parsons, 1942, "Age and Sex in the Social Structure of the United States," and 1943, "The Kinship System of the Contemporary United States," both in *Essays in Sociological Theory*, and 1964, *Social Structure and Personality;* Talcott Parsons and Robert F. Bales, 1955, *Family, Socialization and Interaction Process;* Eli Zaretsky, 1976, *Capitalism, the Family and Personal Life;* Peter L. Berger and Hansfried Kellner, 1974, "Marriage and the Construction of Reality," in Rose Laub Coser, ed., *The Family: Its Structures and Functions.*

4. This phrase is Ruth Bloch's, 1972, "Sex and the Sexes in Eighteenth-Century Magazines."

5. See Philippe Aries, 1960, *Centuries of Childhood: A Social History of Family Life;* William Goode, 1963, *World Revolution and Family Patterns;* Barbara Laslett, 1973, "The Family as a Public and Private Institution: An Historical Perspective," *Journal of Marriage and the Family*, 35, pp. 480–492; Peter Laslett, ed., 1972, *Household and Family in Past Time.*

6. Joann Vanek, 1973, *Keeping Busy: Time Spent in Housework, United States, 1920–1970.*

7. Gayle Rubin, 1975, "The Traffic in Women: Notes on the 'Political Economy' of Sex," in Reyna Reiter, ed., *Toward an Anthropology of Women*, p. 168.

8. Ibid., pp. 165–166.

9. See Michelle Z. Rosaldo, 1974, "Woman, Culture and Society: A Theoretical Overview," in Michelle Z. Rosaldo and Louise Lamphere, eds., *Woman, Culture and Society;* Sherry Ortner, 1974, "Is Female to Male as Nature Is to Culture?" in Rosaldo and Lamphere, eds., *Woman, Culture and Society,* and Nancy Chodorow, 1974, "Family Structure and Feminine Personality," in Rosaldo and Lamphere, eds., *Woman, Culture and Society.*

10. On this, see also Gayle Rubin, 1974, "The Traffic," and Claude Lévi-Strauss, 1956, "The Family," in Harry Shapiro, ed., *Man, Culture and Society.*

11. Ernestine Friedl, 1975, *Women and Men.*

12. See Jane Fishburne Collier and Michelle Zimbalist Rosaldo, 1975, "Marriage, Motherhood and Direct Exchange: Expressions of Male Dominance in 'Egalitarian' Societies."

CHAPTER 2

1. See Frederick Engels, 1884, *The Origin of the Family, Private Property, and the State*.
2. For some empirical elucidation of Engels's theory according to this reading, see Heidi Hartmann, 1976, "Capitalism, Patriarchy, and Job Segregation by Sex," *Signs*, 1, #3, part 2, pp. 137–169; and Reiter, ed., 1975, *Toward an Anthropology of Women*.
3. Parsons, 1942, "Age and Sex"; 1943, "The Kinship System"; 1964, *Social Structure and Personality*; Parsons and Bales, 1955, *Family, Socialization and Interaction Process*; Horkheimer, 1936, "Authority and the Family"; Frankfurt Institute for Social Research, 1972, *Aspects of Sociology*; Mitscherlich, 1963, *Society Without the Father*.
4. Charlotte Perkins Gilman, 1899, *Women and Economics*.
5. On family theory influenced by anthropology, see Coser, ed., 1974*b, The Family*. On feminist theory influenced by anthropology, see Juliet Mitchell, 1974, *Psychoanalysis and Feminism*; and Heidi Hartmann, 1976, "Capitalism, Patriarchy." On feminist theory within anthropology, see Rosaldo and Lamphere, eds., 1974, *Woman, Culture and Society*, and Reiter, ed., 1975, *Toward an Anthropology*.
6. On genital and chromosomal abnormalities in relation to gender labeling, see John Money and Anke A. Ehrhardt, 1972, *Man and Woman, Boy and Girl*. On the issue of statistics and physiological sex differences, see Ruth Hershberger, 1948, *Adam's Rib*. For a study of the way sex and gender become moral as well as natural categories, see Harold Garfinkel, 1967, *Studies in Ethnomethodology*.
7. For (very different) readings of the psychological and psychosocial significance of pregnancy and childbirth, see for example Grete L. Bibring, 1959, "Some Considerations of the Psychological Processes in Pregnancy," *Psychoanalytic Study of the Child*, 14, pp. 113–121; Bibring, Thomas F. Dwyer, Dorothy S. Huntington, and Arthur Valenstein, 1961, "A Study of the Psychological Processes in Pregnancy and of the Earliest Mother-Child Relationship," *Psychoanalytic Study of the Child*, 16, pp. 9–72; and four contributions by Therese Benedek: 1949, "Psychosomatic Implications of the Primary Unit, Mother-Child," *American Journal of Orthopsychiatry*, 19, #4, pp. 642–654; 1952, *Psychosexual Functions in Women;* 1956, "Psychobiological Aspects of Mothering," *American Journal of Orthopsychiatry*, 26, pp. 272–278; 1959, "Parenthood as a Developmental Phase: A Contribution to the Libido Theory," *Journal of the American Psychoanalytic Association*, 7, #3, pp. 389–417.
8. Niles Newton and Michael Newton, 1972, "Psychologic Aspects of Lactation," in Judith M. Bardwick, ed., *Readings on the Psychology of Women*, pp. 277–284.
9. D. W. Winnicott, 1965*b, The Maturational Processes and the Facilitating Environment*.
10. Richard Lee and Irven DeVore, eds., 1968, *Man the Hunter*; Lionel Tiger, 1969, *Men in Groups*; and Alice Rossi, 1977, "A Biosocial Perspective on Parenting," *Daedalus*, 106, #2, pp. 1–31.
11. See Herbert Barry III, Margaret K. Bacon, and Irvin L. Child, 1957, "A Cross-Cultural Survey of Some Sex Differences in Socialization," *Journal of Abnormal and Social Psychology*, 55, #3, pp. 327–332; Roy D'Andrade, 1966, "Sex Differences and Cultural Institutions," in Eleanor E. Maccoby, ed., *The Development of Sex Differences*, pp. 173–204; Friedl, 1975, *Women and Men*; Judith K. Brown, 1971, "A Note on the Division of Labor by Sex," *American Anthropologist*, 72, pp. 1073–1078; and Jane Beckman Lancaster, 1976, "Sex Roles in Primate Societies," in Michael S. Teitelbaum, ed., *Sex Differences*, pp. 22–61.
12. My argument, in what follows, relies on Friedl and Lancaster.
13. Lancaster, 1976, "Sex Roles," p. 47.
14. Rossi, 1977, "Biosocial Perspective," p. 3.
15. Ibid., p. 6.
16. Ibid., p. 24. See, for the anthropological counterevidence to Rossi's claim, bibliographic listings under Margaret Mead, Beatrice B. Whiting, and John W. M. Whiting.
17. Eileen van Tassell (personal communication); B. L. Conner, 1972, "Hormones, Biogenic Amines and Aggression," in Cymour Levine, ed., *Hormones and Behavior*.
18. D'Andrade, 1966, "Sex Differences," p. 176.
19. Barry, Bacon, and Child, 1957, "A Cross-Cultural Survey," p. 329.

20. Brown, 1970, "A Note," p. 1076.

21. Friedl, 1975, *Women and Men*, p. 8.

22. Alice Balint, 1939, "Love for the Mother and Mother-Love," in Michael Balint, ed., *Primary Love and Psycho-analytic Technique*, p. 100.

23. Ibid., p. 101.

24. Michael Balint, 1961, "Contribution to the Symposium on the Theory of the Parent-Infant Relationship," in *Primary Love and Psycho-Analytic Technique*, p. 147.

25. Benedek, 1959, "Parenthood as a Developmental Phase," p. 394.

26. Benedek, 1949, "Psychosomatic Implications," p. 648.

27. D. W. Winnicott, 1960, "The Theory of the Parent-Infant Relationship," *International Journal of Psycho-Analysis*, 41, pp. 593–594.

28. Judith S. Kestenberg, 1956a, "On the Development of Maternal Feelings in Early Childhood: Observations and Reflections," *Psychoanalytic Study of the Child*, 11, p. 289.

29. Ibid., p. 260.

30. Ibid., p. 261.

31. Niles Newton, 1973, "Interrelationships between Sexual Responsiveness, Birth, and Breast Feeding," in Joseph Zubin and John Money, eds., *Contemporary Sexual Behavior: Critical Issues in the 1970's*, p. 96.

32. Benedek, 1959, "Parenthood," p. 390.

33. Winnicott, 1960, "The Theory," p. 593.

34. The following discussion comes from my reading and interpretation of Money and Ehrhardt, 1972, *Man and Woman*; Anke Ehrhardt, 1973, "Maternalism in Fetal Hormonal and Related Syndromes," in Zubin and Money, eds., *Contemporary Sexual Behavior*; Eleanor Maccoby and Carol Jacklin, 1974, *The Psychology of Sex Differences*; M. Kay Martin and Barbara Voorhies, 1975, *Female of the Species*; H. F. Harlow, M. K. Harlow, R. O. Dodsworth, and G. L. Arling, 1970, "Maternal Behavior of Rhesus Monkeys Deprived of Mothering and Peer Associations in Infants," in Freda Rebelsky, ed., *Child Development and Behavior*, pp. 88–98; Niles Newton, 1955, "Maternal Emotions: A Study of Women's Feelings toward Menstruation, Pregnancy, Childbirth, Breast Feeding, Infant Care, and Other Aspects of Their Femininity," *Psychosomatic Medicine Monograph*, and 1973, "Interrelationships"; Rossi, 1977, "A Biosocial Perspective"; Teitelbaum, ed., 1976, *Sex Differences*; and my review of Clellan S. Ford and Frank A. Beach, 1951, *Patterns of Sexual Behavior;* Frank A. Beach, 1965, *Sex and Behavior;* Irenaus Eibl-Eibesfeldt, 1970, *Ethology: The Biology of Behavior;* and Jessie Bernard, 1974, *The Future of Motherhood*.

35. All the evidence I point to on hormonal and chromosomal abnormalities comes from Money and Ehrhardt, 1972, *Man and Woman*, and Ehrhardt, 1973, "Maternalism."

36. Beatrice Whiting, ed., 1963, *Six Cultures: Studies of Child-Rearing*; Beatrice B. Whiting and John W. M. Whiting, 1975, *Children of Six Cultures*; Margaret Mead, 1935, *Sex and Temperament in Three Primitive Societies*, and 1949, *Male and Female*; Nancy Chodorow, 1971, "Being and Doing: A Cross-Cultural Examination of the Socialization of Males and Females," in Vivian Gornick and Barbara K. Moran, *Woman in Sexist Society*.

37. Maccoby and Jacklin, 1974, *Psychology of Sex Differences*, p. 216.

38. Eileen van Tassell (personal communication).

39. Hess and Beck, as reported in Eibl-Eibesfeldt, 1970, *Ethology*, p. 438.

40. Ehrhardt, 1973, "Maternalism," p. 100.

41. See A. D. Leifer, P. H. Leiderman, C. R. Barnett, and J. A. Williams, 1973, "Effects of Mother-Infant Separation on Maternal Attachment Behavior," in F. Rebelsky and L. Dormon, eds., *Child Development and Behavior*.

42. Maccoby and Jacklin, 1974, *Psychology*, p. 220.

43. Harlow et al., 1970, "Maternal Behavior."

44. Winnicott, 1960, "The Theory," p. 594.

45. For good examples of the tendency to explain the reproduction and maintenance of gender-role differentiation through consciously intended socialization and training, see Lenore J. Weitzman, 1975, "Sex-Role Socialization," in Jo Freeman, ed., *Women: A Feminist Perspective*, pp. 105–144; Jo Freeman, 1971, "The Social Construc-

tion of the Second Sex," in Michelle Garskof, ed., *Roles Women Play*; and the journal *Sex Roles*. For investigations of propulsion (and seduction) into motherhood by media and ideology, see Jessie Bernard, 1974, *The Future of Motherhood*; and Ellen Peck and Judith Senderowitz, eds., 1974, *Pronatalism: The Myth of Mom and Apple Pie*. For an account of gender-role socialization as a product of a child's learning it is a girl or boy, see Lawrence Kohlberg, 1966, "A Cognitive Developmental Analysis of Sex-Role Concepts and Attitudes," in E. Maccoby, ed., *The Development of Sex Differences*. For discussions of identification and gender-role learning, see David B. Lynn, 1959, "A Note on Sex Differences in the Development of Masculine and Feminine Identification," *Psychological Review*, 66, pp. 126–135, and 1962, "Sex Role and Parent Identification," *Child Development*, 33, pp. 555–564; Parsons and Bales, 1955, *Family*; Parsons, 1942, "Age and Sex"; Robert F. Winch, 1962, *Identification and Its Familial Determinants*; Walter Mischel, 1966, "A Social-Learning View of Sex Differences in Behavior," in Maccoby, ed., *The Development of Sex Differences*; and Walter Mischel, 1970, "Sex Typing and Socialization," in Paul Mussen, ed., *Carmichael's Manual of Child Psychology*, vol. 2, 3rd ed., pp. 3–72.

46. Margaret Polatnick, 1973, "Why Men Don't Rear Children: A Power Analysis," *Berkeley Journal of Sociology*, 18, p. 60.

47. See Parsons with Winston White, 1961, "The Link Between Character and Society," in *Social Structure and Personality*; Parsons and Bales, 1955, *Family, Socialization*; Frankfurt Institute, 1972, *Aspects*; Wilhelm Reich, 1966, *Sex-Pol*; Philip E. Slater, 1970, *The Pursuit of Loneliness*, and 1974, *Earthwalk*; and Warren G. Bennis and Philip Slater, 1968, *The Temporary Society*; Samuel Bowles and Herbert Gintis, 1976, *Schooling in Capitalist America*; Richard C. Edwards, 1975, "The Social Relations of Production in the Firm and Labor Market Structure," in Edwards, Michael Reich, and David M. Gordon, eds., *Labor Market Segmentation*.

48. See John Bowlby, 1951, *Maternal Care and Mental Health*; Margaret S. Mahler, 1968, *On Human Symbiosis and the Vicissitudes of Individuation. Volume 1: Infantile Psychosis*; Rene Spitz, 1965, *The First Year of Life: A Psychoanalytic Study of Normal and Deviant Development of Object Relations*; Winnicott, 1965b, *Maturational Processes*.

49. Rudolph Schaffer, 1977, *Mothering*, p. 103.

50. Ibid., p. 105. For another attempt to review research which separates out the various factors involved in "maternal deprivation," see Michael Rutter, 1972, *Maternal Deprivation Reassessed*.

51. Joel Kovel, 1970, *White Racism*.

52. See Chapters 11 and 12 for more extended discussion.

53. Karl Marx, 1867, *Capital*, vol. 1, p. 577.

54. Claude Lévi-Strauss, 1956, "The Family," p. 269.

55. Ibid., p. 277.

56. See, for example, Carol B. Stack, 1975, *All Our Kin*; Michael Young and Peter Willmott, 1957, *Family and Kinship in East London*.

57. See Lillian Breslow Rubin, 1976, *Worlds of Pain: Life in the Working-Class Family*, for discussion of women and men in the contemporary isolated working-class family.

58. Horkheimer, 1936, "Authority," p. 67.

59. Talcott Parsons, 1951, *The Social System*, p. 42.

69. Frankfurt Institute, 1972, *Aspects*, p. 133.

61. For example, David Bakan, 1966, *The Duality of Human Existence: Isolation and Communion in Western Man*; Mitscherlich, 1963, *Society Without the Father*; Slater, 1970, *Pursuit*, and 1974, *Earthwalk*.

62. Especially Peggy Morton, 1970, "A Woman's Work is Never Done," *Leviathan*, 2, #1, pp. 32–37. Other Marxist feminist theorists also talk implicitly about the reproduction of male workers, but Morton is the only one to speak to the psychological dynamics I am currently discussing, rather than to physical reproduction.

63. See, for example, Roger V. Burton and John W. M. Whiting, 1961, "The Absent Father and Cross-Sex Identity," *Merrill-Palmer Quarterly of Behavior and Development*, 7, #2, pp. 85–95; John W. M. Whiting, Richard Kluckhohn, and Albert Anthony, 1958, "The Function of Male Initiation Rites at Puberty," in E. E. Maccoby, T. M. Newcomb,

and E. L. Hartley, eds., *Readings in Social Psychology*; David Levy, 1943, *Maternal Overprotection*; Philip E. Slater, 1968, *The Glory of Hera: Greek Mythology and the Greek Family*, and 1970, *Pursuit*, and 1974, *Earthwalk;* William N. Stephens, 1963, *The Family in Cross-Cultural Perspective*. For exceptions, see E. M. Hetherington, 1972, "Effects of Father Absence on Personality Development in Adolescent Daughters," *Developmental Psychology*, 7, pp. 313–326, and 1973, "Girls Without Fathers," *Psychology Today*, 6, pp. 46–52; Lynn, 1959, "A Note on Sex Differences," and 1962, "Sex Role and Parent Identification"; Lynn and W. L. Sawrey, 1959, "The Effects of Father-Absence on Norwegian Boys and Girls," *Journal of Abnormal and Social Psychology*, 59, pp. 258–262; and Biller's review (1971) of the literature on "fathering and female personality development"—one short chapter of an entire book on *Father, Child and Sex Role*.

CHAPTER 3

1. See David Rapaport, 1960, "The Structure of Psychoanalytic Theory," *Psychological Issues*, monograph 6, vol. 2, no. 2.

2. See Josef Breuer and Sigmund Freud, 1895, *Studies on Hysteria, SE*, vol. 2, pp. 1–319.

3. Sigmund Freud, 1901, "The Interpretation of Dreams," *SE*, vols, 4 and 5, pp. 1–713.

4. Sigmund Freud, 1933, *New Introductory Lectures on Psychoanalysis, SE*, vol. 22, pp. 3–182.

5. The best summary of Freud's conception of mental activity is found in Sigmund Freud, 1917, *Introductory Lectures on Psycho-Analysis, SE*, vols. 15 and 16, pp. 3–476.

6. Rapaport, 1960, "The Structure," p. 46.

7. On introjection, see, for example, Roy Schafer, 1968, *Aspects of Internalization*; W. R. D. Fairbairn, 1952, *An Object-Relations Theory of the Personality*; Hans W. Loewald, 1962, "Internalization, Separation, Mourning, and the Superego," *Psychoanalytic Quarterly*, 31, pp. 483–504, and 1973, "On Internalization," *International Journal of Psychoanalysis*, 54, pp. 9–17.

8. On identification, see, for example, Edith Jacobson, 1964, *The Self and the Object World*.

9. Schafer, 1968, *Aspects*, p. 9.

10. See Anna Freud, 1936, *The Ego and the Mechanisms of Defense*.

11. See Heinz Hartmann, 1939, *Ego Psychology and the Problem of Adaptation*, and Heinz Hartmann, E. Kris, and R. M. Loewenstein, 1964, "Papers on Psychoanalytic Psychology," *Psychological Issues*, monograph 14, vol. 4, no. 2.

12. Jacobson, 1964, *The Self and the Object World*.

13. Fairbairn, 1952, *An Object-Relations Theory*.

14. Winnicott, 1965*b*, *The Maturational Processes*.

15. Freud, 1933, *New Introductory Lectures*, pp. 57–80.

16. See for an argument along these lines, Fairbairn, 1952, *An Object-Relations Theory*.

17. See Loewald, 1962, "Internalization, Separation."

18. See for example translator's note in Jurgen Habermas, 1971, *Knowledge and Human Interests*, p. 344.

19. Fairbairn, 1952, *An Object-Relations Theory*; Harry Guntrip, 1961, *Personality Structure and Human Interaction: The Developing Synthesis of Psycho-Dynamic Theory*, and 1971, *Psychoanalytic Theory, Therapy, and the Self*.

20. For classic formulations of the ego psychological position, see Heinz Hartmann, 1939, *Ego Psychology*; Hartmann, Kris, and Loewenstein, 1964, "Papers"; and Rapaport, 1960, "Structure."

21. Rapaport, 1960, "Structure," p. 53.

22. See John D. Benjamin, 1961, "The Innate and the Experiential in Child Development," in Henry W. Brosin, ed., *Lectures on Experimental Psychiatry*, p. 22.

23. S. Freud, 1905, "Three Essays on the Theory of Sexuality," *SE*, vol. 7, pp. 125–245. See also Karl Abraham, 1966, *On Character and Libido Development*.

24. See Melanie Klein, 1932, *The Psychoanalysis of Children,* and 1948, *Contributions to Psycho-analysis, 1921–1945*; and Klein, Paula Heimann, Susan Isaacs, and Joan Riviere, 1952, *Developments in Psycho-analysis.*

25. Karen Horney, 1967, *Feminine Psychology*; Clara M. Thompson, 1964, *On Women.*

26. Especially as it has been developed by Alice Balint, 1939, "Love for the Mother," and 1954, *The Early Years of Life: A Psychoanalytic Study*; Michael Balint, 1965, *Primary Love and Psychoanalytic Technique,* and 1968, *The Basic Fault: Therapeutic Aspects of Regression*; Fairbairn, 1952, *An Object-Relations Theory*; Guntrip, 1961, *Personality Structure,* and 1971, *Psychoanalytic Theory, Therapy, and the Self*; Winnicott, 1958*b*, *Collected Papers: Through Paediatrics to Psycho-Analysis,* 1965*b*, *The Maturational Processes,* and 1971, *Playing and Reality.* Roy Schafer, 1968, *Aspects of Internalization,* and Hans Loewald, 1962, "Internalization, Separation," and 1973, "On Internalization," also argue in object-relational directions that have influenced me.

27. Jacobson, 1964, *The Self,* pp. 35–36.

28. Fairbairn, 1954, "Observations of the Nature of Hysterical States," *British Journal of Medical Psychology,* 27, #3, p. 125.

29. See Michael Balint, 1956*b*, "Pleasure, Object, and Libido. Some Reflections on Fairbairn's Modifications on Psychoanalytic Theory," *British Journal of Medical Psychology,* 29, #2, pp. 162–167.

30. See Guntrip, 1971, *Psychoanalytic Theory.*

31. Ibid., p. 41.

32. See Benjamin, 1961, "The Innate and the Experiential."

33. Schafer, 1968, *Aspects of Internalization,* p. 11.

34. Freud, 1923*a*, "The Ego and the Id," *SE,* vol. 19, p. 29.

35. See Reich, 1926, *Character Analysis,* and 1966, *Sex-Pol*; Parsons, 1964, *Social Structure and Personality*; Parsons and Bales, 1955, *Family, Socialization*; Fairbairn, 1952, *An Object-Relations Theory*; and Guntrip, 1961, *Personality Structure.*

36. See Michael Balint, 1968, *The Basic Fault.*

37. Freud, 1913, *Totem and Taboo, SE,* vol. 13, pp. 1–162; 1921, *Group Psychology and the Analysis of the Ego, SE,* vol. 18, pp. 67–143; 1927, *Future of an Illusion, SE,* vol. 21, pp. 3–56; 1930, *Civilization and Its Discontents, SE,* vol. 21, pp. 59–145; 1939, *Moses and Monotheism: Three Essays, SE,* vol. 23, pp. 3–137.

38. Michael Balint, 1961, "Contribution to the Symposium," p. 145.

CHAPTER 4

1. See Gordon, ed., 1973, *The American Family*; Barbara Laslett, 1973, "The Family as a Public and Private Institution"; Peter Laslett, 1972, *Household and Family.*

2. Michael Balint, 1937, "Early Developmental States of the Ego, Primary Object-Love," in *Primary Love,* p. 82.

3. Mahler, 1968, *On Human Symbiosis,* p. 16.

4. Sylvia Brody and Sidney Axelrad, 1970, *Anxiety and Ego Formation in Infancy,* p. 9.

5. Anna Freud, 1962, "Contribution to Discussion, 'The Theory of the Parent-Infant Relationship,' " *International Journal of Psycho-Analysis,* 43, p. 241.

6. Benedek, 1949, "Psychosomatic Implications," and 1959, "Parenthood as a Developmental Phase."

7. Erik Erikson, 1950, *Childhood and Society.*

8. Michael Balint, 1968, *The Basic Fault,* p. 22.

9. Winnicott, 1960, "The Theory of the Parent," p. 588.

10. Ibid., p. 590.

11. Ibid.

12. Guntrip, 1971, *Psychoanalytic Theory,* p. 104.

13. See, for example, Laing, 1959, *The Divided Self*; Harry Stack Sullivan, 1953, *The Interpersonal Theory of Psychiatry.*

14. Heinz Hartmann, 1939, *Ego Psychology.*

15. Anna Freud, 1936, *The Ego and the Mechanisms*; Jacobson, 1964, *The Self and the Object World*.

16. See, for example, the accounts of Bowlby, 1951, *Maternal Care*, and Spitz, 1965, *The First Year of Life*.

17. Freud, 1923a, "The Ego and the Id," *SE*, vol. 19, p. 31.

18. Henri Parens, 1971, "A Contribution of Separation-Individuation to the Development of Psychic Structure," in McDevitt and Settlage, eds., *Separation-Individuation: Essays in Honor of Margaret S. Mahler*, p. 108.

19. Mahler, 1968, *On Human Symbiosis*, p. 3.

20. Ibid., pp. 7–8.

21. Ibid., p. 10.

22. Sigmund Freud, 1914, "On Narcissism: An Introduction," *SE*, vol. 14, pp. 69–102.

23. Alice Balint, 1939, "Love for the Mother," p. 95.

24. See Klaus Angel, 1972, "The Role of the Internal Object and External Object in Object Relationships, Separation Anxiety, Object Constancy, and Symbiosis," *International Journal of Psycho-Analysis*, 53, pp. 541–546, for further elaboration of this point.

25. See, in addition to Michael Balint's extended refutation of Freud's hypothesis of primary narcissism (1935, "Critical Notes on the Theory of the Pregenital Organizations of the Libido," in *Primary Love*, pp. 37–58; 1937, "Early Developmental States"; and 1968, *The Basic Fault*), Fairbairn's account of autoeroticism, and his more general arguments that people seek object-connection for itself and use libidinal channels as a vehicle toward this goal (1952, *An Object-Relations Theory*, and 1954, "Observations of the Nature"), as well as Winnicott's analysis of the importance of basic relatedness in the facilitating environment (1965b, *The Maturational Processes*). See, for summary comparisons of the positions of object-relations theory and ego psychology on the earliest state of the infant, John Bowlby, 1969, *Attachment and Loss, Volume 1: Attachment*, appendix; and Mary Salter Ainsworth, 1969, "Object Relations, Dependency, and Attachment: A Theoretical Review of the Infant-Mother Relationship," *Child Development*, 40, #4, pp. 969–1025.

26. Freud, 1914, "On Narcissism," *SE*, vol. 14, p. 88.

27. Bowlby, 1969, *Attachment and Loss*, p. 222.

28. See editor's footnote to Freud, "On Narcissism," *SE*, vol. 14, p. 87.

29. Michael Balint, 1965, *Primary Love*, and 1968, *The Basic Fault*.

30. M. Balint, 1937, "Early Developmental States," p. 82.

31. See, for example, H. F. Harlow and M. K. Zimmerman, 1959, "Affectional Responses in the Infant Monkey," *Science*, 130, pp. 421–432.

32. Bowlby, 1969, *Attachment and Loss*, p. 222.

33. Jacobson, 1964, *The Self and the Object World*, pp. 35–36.

34. Bowlby, 1969, *Attachment and Loss*, p. 222.

35. Benedek, 1956, "Psychobiological Aspects."

36. Fairbairn, 1941, "A Revised Psychopathology of the Psychoses and Psychoneuroses," in *An Object-Relations Theory of the Personality*, pp. 28–58.

37. A. Balint, 1939, "Love for the Mother," p. 95.

38. Mahler, 1968, *On Human Symbiosis*, p. 12.

39. Ibid., p. 11.

40. Winnicott, 1960, "The Theory of the Parent," p. 590.

41. For an analysis of the twofold development of the self which emphasizes the development of a body self, or body ego, see Phyllis Greenacre, 1958, "Early Physical Determinants in the Development of the Sense of Identity," *Journal of the American Psychoanalytic Association*, 6, #4, pp. 612–627.

42. Winnicott, 1958a, "The Capacity to Be Alone," in *The Maturational Processes*, pp. 29–36.

43. Winnicott, 1960, "The Theory of the Parent," p. 589.

44. Benedek, 1959, "Parenthood as a Developmental Phase," p. 390.

45. A. Balint, 1939, "Love for the Mother," p. 390.

46. Ibid., p. 103.

47. Balint points this out, ibid.

48. Fairbairn, 1952, *An Object-Relations Theory*.

49. Freud, 1926, "Inhibitions, Symptoms and Anxiety," *SE*, vol. 20, pp. 77–174.

50. Anna Freud, 1936, *The Ego and the Mechanisms*; Brody and Axelrad, 1970, *Anxiety and Ego Formation*.

51. Brody and Axelrad, 1970, *Anxiety and Ego Formation*, p. 8.

52. Fairbairn is the major theorist of these processes. See also Parens, 1971, "A Contribution of Separation-Individuation." For an interesting clinical account, see Herman Roiphe and Eleanor Galenson, 1973, "Object Loss and Early Sexual Development," *Psychoanalytic Quarterly*, 52, pp. 73–90.

53. For further discussion of the role of the father and other rivals in individuation, see Jacobson, 1964, *The Self and the Object World*; Mitchell, 1974, *Psychoanalysis and Feminism*; and Ernest L. Abelin, 1971, "The Role of the Father in the Separation-Individuation Phase," in McDevitt and Settlage, eds., *Separation-Individuation*, pp. 229–252.

54. See on this Abelin, 1971, "The Role of the Father."

55. Bowlby, 1969, *Attachment and Loss*.

56. See especially H. Rudolph Schaffer and Peggy Emerson, 1964, "The Development of Social Attachments in Infancy," *Monographs of the Society for Research in Child Development*, 29, #3, and H. R. Schaffer, 1971, *The Growth of Sociability*. See also Milton Kotelchuck, 1972, *The Nature of the Child's Tie to His Father*.

57. Winnicott, 1960, "The Theory of the Parent," p. 589.

58. Fairbairn, 1952, *An Object-Relations Theory*.

59. Jacobson, 1964, *The Self and the Object World*.

60. Alice Balint, 1939, "Love for the Mother," p. 107.

61. My account here derives mainly from Jacobson, 1964, *The Self and the Object World*.

62. See, for example, Bowlby, 1951, *Maternal Care*; Mahler, 1968, *On Human Symbiosis*; Spitz, 1965, *The First Year*.

63. Rose Coser reminded me of this (personal communication).

64. The only exception I have found is a study by Cambor (C. Glenn Cambor, 1969, "Preoedipal Factors in Superego Development: The Influence of Multiple Mothers," *Psychoanalytic Quarterly*, 38, #1, pp. 81–96), who reports a clinical case demonstrating the effect on superego formation of dual parenting by a rejecting, white biological mother and a nurturant black nurse.

65. Bowlby, 1969, *Attachment and Loss*, p. 367.

66. Bettye Caldwell et al., 1963, "Mother-Infant Interaction in Monomatric and Polymatric Families," *American Journal of Orthopsychiatry*, 33, p. 663.

67. Bettye Caldwell, Charlene Wright, Alice Honig, and Jordan Tannenbaum, 1970, "Infant Day Care and Attachment," *American Journal of Orthopsychiatry*, 40, #3, pp. 397–412.

68. Rutter, 1972, *Maternal Deprivation Reassessed*; Schaffer, 1977, *Mothering*.

69. Yudkin and Holme, 1963, cited in Rutter, 1972, *Maternal Deprivation*, p. 61, and Schaffer, 1977, *Mothering*, p. 105.

70. Irvine, 1966, and Miller, 1969, cited in Rutter, 1972, *Maternal Deprivation*, p. 62.

71. Margaret Mead, 1954, "Some Theoretical Considerations on the Problem of Mother-Child Separation," *American Journal of Orthopsychiatry*, 24, pp. 471–483, and 1962, "A Cultural Anthropologist's Approach to Maternal Deprivation," *Maternal Care and Mental Health/Deprivation of Maternal Care*, pp. 237–254.

72. Schaffer, 1977, *Mothering*, p. 100. See also for an equivalent conclusion, Rutter, 1972, *Maternal Deprivation Reassessed*, p. 125.

73. Parsons, 1942, "Age and Sex," and 1943, "The Kinship System"; and Goode, 1963, *World Revolution*.

74. An exception here is Muensterberger (Warner Muensterberger, 1969, "Psyche and Environment: Sociocultural Variations in Separation and Individuation," *Psychoanalytic Quarterly*, 38, pp. 191–216), whose discussion, though marred by Western ethnocentrism, nevertheless makes a persuasive case that psychoanalytic theory derives

from dealing with a specific developmental situation. See also George W. Goethals, 1974, "Mother-Infant Attachment and Premarital Behavior: The Contact Hypothesis," for further cross-cultural comparison of the effects of these differences, as well as Margaret Mead, 1954, "Some Theoretical Considerations," and John W. M. Whiting, "Causes and Consequences of the Amount of Body Contact between Mother and Infant."

CHAPTER 5

1. See Benedek, 1959, "Parenthood as Developmental Phase," and Fairbairn, 1952, *An Object-Relations Theory,* for descriptions of this process.

2. Freud, 1930, *Civilization and Its Discontents.*

3. Michael Balint, 1935, "Critical Notes on the Theory," p. 50.

4. Mead, 1954, "Some Theoretical Considerations," and 1962, "A Cultural Anthropologist's Approach"; Slater, 1970, *Pursuit,* and 1974, *Earthwalk;* and George W. Goethals, 1974, "Mother-Infant Attachment," discuss the two-person relationship (intensely monogamous, potentially jealous, fearful of loss or, alternately, entirely denying of need by extreme fickleness and refusal to commit oneself) that our culture's exclusive mothering produces.

5. Benedek, 1959, "Parenthood as Developmental Phase," p. 400.

6. Fairbairn, 1940, "Schizoid Factors in the Personality," in *An Object-Relations Theory,* p. 24.

7. See chapter epigraph, from *Introductory Lectures, SE,* vol. 26, p. 314.

8. Alice Balint, 1939, "Love for the Mother."

9. Ibid., p. 98.

10. Ibid.

11. Ibid., p. 100.

12. Janine Chasseguet-Smirgel, 1964, "Feminine Guilt and the Oedipus Complex," in *Female Sexuality,* pp. 94–134, and Dorothy Burlingham, 1973, "The Pre-Oedipal Infant-Father Relationship," *Psychoanalytic Study of the Child,* 28, pp. 23–47, discuss this side of the relation to the father.

13. See Kotelchuck, 1972, *The Nature of the Child's Tie.*

14. Burlingham, 1973, "The Pre-Oedipal Infant-Father Relationship."

15. Mitchell, 1974, *Psychoanalysis and Feminism.*

16. A. Balint, 1939, "Love for the Mother," p. 97.

17. Quoted in Henriette Glatzer, 1959, "Notes on the Preoedipal Fantasy," *American Journal of Orthopsychiatry,* 24, pp. 383–390.

18. Joan Riviere, 1937, "Hate, Greed, and Aggression," in Melanie Klein and Joan Riviere, *Love, Hate and Reparation.* See also Helene Deutsch, 1944, *Psychology of Women,* vols. 1 and 2; Parsons, 1964, *Social Structure and Personality;* Parsons and Bales, 1955, *Family, Socialization.* Erik Erikson, 1964a, *Insight and Responsibility,* discusses a dream of Freud's (the dream of the Three Fates) in a way that exhibits the same associative complex around women and mothers. (What is relevant here is not the accuracy or completeness of his interpretation, but his unquestioning formulation of the symbolic associations). He talks of Freud's "successful" and "forward-looking" reexperiencing of oral issues in which Freud "turns resolutely away from the mother" (p. 184), and approvingly shows how Freud associates women and death; makes autonomy from women synonymous with participation in the intellectual world; and, finally, draws parallels among the turn "from dependence to self-help, from women to men, [and] from perishable to eternal substances" (p. 184).

19. See Brody and Axelrad, 1970, *Anxiety and Ego Formation;* Mahler, 1968, *On Human Symbiosis;* and Winnicott, 1965b, *The Maturational Processes.*

20. For a clinical description of the development of a false sense of self in a little girl as a defensive reaction to both overwhelming environmental intrusion and nonempathic, while overcontrolling, maternal behavior, see Samuel Ritvo and Albert J.

Solnit, 1958, "Influences of Early Mother-Child Interaction on Identification Processes," *Psychoanalytic Study of the Child*, 13, pp. 64–85.

21. What David Levy (1943, *Maternal Overprotection*) bemoans.

22. What Bowlby (1951, *Maternal Care*), Spitz (1965, *The First Year of Life*), and Mahler (1968, *On Human Symbiosis*) fear. See also Winnicott, 1960, "The Theory of the Parent-Infant Relationship." For an account of the continuance of this double-bind in later mother-child relationships, see Rose Laub Coser, 1974a, "Authority and Structural Ambivalence in the Middle-Class Family," in *The Family: Its Structures and Functions*.

23. Winnicott, 1960, "The Theory," p. 592.

24. Ibid., p. 591.

25. Bowlby, 1969, *Attachment and Loss*, p. 286.

26. Winnicott, 1965a, *The Family and Individual Development*, p. 15.

27. Benedek, 1956, "Psychobiological Aspects of Mothering."

28. Michael Balint, 1937, "Early Developmental States," p. 83, citing Alice Balint.

29. Alice Balint, 1939, "Love for the Mother," p. 101.

30. Ibid.

31. Ibid. See also Robert Fliess, 1961, *Ego and Body Ego: Contributions to Their Psychoanalytic Psychology*, who suggests that the baby is a "regressively erotogenic zone" of the mother in addition to being an object of her affection, and that mothers get narcissistic (as well as, or as opposed to, object-libidinal) gratification from fondling, rocking, and caring for their babies. He and medical researcher Niles Newton, 1973, "Interrelationships between Sexual Responsiveness," point also to the sexual sensations that nursing may evoke in a mother.

32. Winnicott, 1960, "The Theory," p. 594.

33. Christine Olden, 1958, "Notes on the Development of Empathy," *Psychoanalytic Study of the Child*, 13, p. 513.

34. Ibid., p. 514.

35. Parsons and Bales, 1955, *Family, Socialization*.

36. Alice S. Rossi, 1968, "Transition to Parenthood," *Journal of Marriage and the Family*, 30, pp. 26–39.

37. Therese Benedek, 1960, "The Organization of the Reproductive Drive," *International Journal of Psycho-Analysis*, 41, p. 10.

38. Ibid., p. 13.

39. See Benedek, 1956, "Psychobiological Aspects of Mothering," and 1959, "Parenthood as Developmental Phase."

40. See Winnicott, 1965b, *The Maturational Processes*.

41. See Benedek, 1956, "Psychobiological Aspects," and 1960, "The Organization."

42. Kestenberg, 1956a, "On the Development of Maternal Feelings."

43. See Freud, 1925, "Some Psychical Consequences of the Anatomical Distinction Between the Sexes," *SE*, vol. 29, pp. 248–258. I discuss this theory more fully in a later chapter.

44. See, for example, Benedek, 1949, "Psychosomatic Implications," 1952, *Psychosexual Functions*, and 1960, "Organization," and Ruth Mack Brunswick, 1940, "The Preoedipal Phase of the Libido Development," in Robert Fliess, ed., *The Psychoanalytic Reader: An Anthology of Essential Papers with Critical Introductions*, pp. 231–253.

45. See, for example, Kohlberg, 1966, "A Cognitive-Developmental Analysis."

46. Edith Jacobson, 1968, "On the Development of the Girl's Wish for a Child," *Psychoanalytic Quarterly*, 37, pp. 523–538.

47. Burton Lerner, Raymond Raskin, and Elizabeth Davis, 1967, "On the Need to Be Pregnant," *International Journal of Psycho-Analysis*, 48, pp. 288–297. Jacobson focuses on libidinal issues and body fantasies; Lerner et al. focus on ego issues.

48. Melanie Klein, 1937, "Love, Guilt and Reparation," in Klein and Riviere, eds., *Love, Hate and Reparation*.

49. See also R. W. Coleman, E. Kris, and S. Provence, 1953, "Study of Variations in Early Parental Attitudes," *Psychoanalytic Study of the Child*, 8, pp. 20–47, and Benedek, 1959, "Parenthood as Developmental Phase."

50. Edith Jacobson, 1950, "Development of the Wish for a Child in Boys," *Psychoan-*

alytic Study of the Child, 5, pp. 139–152, and 1968, "On the Development of the Girl's Wish for a Child."

CHAPTER 6

1. See, for example, Roy Schafer, 1974, "Problems in Freud's Psychology of Women," *Journal of the American Psychoanalytic Association*, 22, #3, pp. 459–485; William H. Masters and Virginia E. Johnson, 1966, *Human Sexual Response*; Mary Jane Sherfey, 1966, "The Evolution and Nature of Female Sexuality in Relation to Psychoanalytic Theory," *Journal of the American Psychoanalytic Association*, 14, #1, pp. 28–128.

2. Freud, 1924, "The Dissolution of the Oedipus Complex," *SE*, vol. 19, pp. 172–179; Freud, 1933, *New Introductory Lectures on Psychoanalysis*.

3. Freud, 1925, "Some Psychical Consequences."

4. Ibid., p. 252.

5. Jeanne Lampl-de Groot, 1927, "The Evolution of the Oedipus Complex in Women," in Fliess, ed., *The Psychoanalytic Reader*, pp. 180–194.

6. Freud, 1931, "Female Sexuality," *SE*, vol. 21, pp. 223–243; see also Freud, 1933, *New Introductory Lectures*.

7. Freud, 1933, *New Introductory Lectures*, and Brunswick, 1940, "The Preoedipal Phase."

8. Helene Deutsch, 1944, *Psychology of Women*.

9. Freud, 1933, *New Introductory Lectures*, p. 237.

10. Maccoby and Jacklin, 1974, *The Psychology of Sex Differences*.

11. Eleanor Galenson, 1976, "Scientific Proceedings—Panel Reports," Panels on the Psychology of Women, Annual Meeting of the American Psychoanalytic Association, 1974. *Journal of the American Psychoanalytic Association*, 24, #1, p. 159.

12. Jerome Kagan and Marion Freeman, 1963, "Relation of Childhood Intelligence, Maternal Behaviors and Social Class to Behavior During Adolescence," *Child Development*, 36, pp. 899–911, and Virginia C. Crandall, 1972, "The Fels Study; Some Contributions to Personality Development and Achievement in Childhood and Adulthood," *Seminars in Psychiatry*, 4, #4, pp. 383–397.

13. Robert Fliess, 1961, *Ego and Body Ego*; Klaus Angel, 1967, "On Symbiosis and Pseudosymbiosis," *Journal of the American Psychoanalytic Association*, 15, #2, pp. 294–316; Enid Balint, 1963, "On Being Empty of Oneself," *International Journal of Psycho-Analysis*, 44, #4, pp. 470–480; Melitta Sperling, 1950, "Children's Interpretation and Reaction to the Unconscious of Their Mothers," *International Journal of Psycho-Analysis*, 31, pp. 36–41; C. Olden, 1958, "Notes on Empathy"; and Dorothy Burlingham, 1967, "Empathy Between Infant and Mother," *Journal of the American Psychoanalytic Association*, 15, pp. 764–780.

14. Robert Fliess, 1961, *Ego and Body Ego*.

15. Ibid., p. 49.

16. Ibid., p. 48.

17. For a more accessible example of what Fliess describes—again, a mother-daughter case—see Flora Schreiber, 1973, *Sybil*.

18. Enid Balint, 1963, "On Being Empty."

19. Ibid., p. 478.

20. Ibid., p. 476.

21. Christine Olden, 1958, "Notes on Empathy."

22. Ibid., p. 505.

23. Ibid.

24. Ibid., p. 512.

25. Klaus Angel, 1967, "On Symbiosis."

26. Ibid., p. 315.

27. Dorothy Burlingham, 1967, "Empathy Between Infant."

28. Melitta Sperling, 1950, "Children's Interpretation."

29. Dorothy Burlingham, 1967, "Empathy Between Infant," p. 779.

30. Grete Bibring, 1953, "On the 'Passing of the Oedipus Complex' in a Matriarchal Family Setting," in R. M. Loewenstein, ed., *Drives, Affects, and Behavior: Essays in Honor of Marie Bonaparte*, pp. 278–284; Philip E. Slater, 1968, *The Glory of Hera*; John W. M. Whiting, 1959, "Sorcery, Sin and the Superego: A Cross-Cultural Study of Some Mechanisms of Social Control," in Clellan S. Ford, ed., *Cross-Cultural Approaches: Readings in Comparative Research*, pp. 147–168; 1960, "Totem and Taboo—A Re-evaluation," in Jules H. Masserman, ed., *Psychoanalysis and Human Values*; Whiting et al., 1958, "The Function of Male Initiation"; Roger V. Burton and Whiting, 1961, "The Absent Father"; and Phyllis Greenacre, 1968, "Perversions: General Considerations Regarding Their Genetic and Dynamic Background," *Psychoanalytic Study of the Child*, 23, pp. 47–62.

31. Grete Bibring, 1953, "On the 'Passing of the Oedipus Complex,' " p. 281.

32. Philip E. Slater, 1968, *The Glory of Hera*, 1970, *The Pursuit of Loneliness*, 1974, *Earthwalk*.

33. Theodore Lidz, Stephen Fleck, and Alice R. Cornelison, 1965, *Schizophrenia and the Family*.

34. Philip E. Slater, 1968, *The Glory of Hera*.

35. See John Whiting, 1959, "Sorcery, Sin," and 1960, "Totem and Taboo"; Whiting et al., 1958, "The Function of Male Initiation"; and Burton and Whiting, 1961, "The Absent Father."

36. For example, Whiting et al., 1958, "The Function of Male Initiation."

37. Ibid., p. 362.

38. John Whiting, 1959, "Sorcery, Sin," p. 150.

39. Phyllis Greenacre, 1968, "Perversions."

40. Ibid., p. 47.

41. Ibid., and Herman Roiphe, 1968, "On an Early Genital Phase: With an Addendum on Genesis," *Psychoanalytic Study of the Child*, 23, pp. 348–365.

42. Signe Hammer, 1975, *Daughters and Mothers: Mothers and Daughters*.

43. See Peter Blos, 1957, *On Adolescence: A Psychoanalytic Interpretation*; Deutsch, 1944, *Psychology of Women*; Kata Levy, 1960, "Simultaneous Analysis of a Mother and Her Adolescent Daughter: The Mother's Contribution to the Loosening of the Infantile Object Tie," *Psychoanalytic Study of the Child*, 15, pp. 378–391; Marjorie P. Sprince, 1962, "The Development of a Preoedipal Partnership Between an Adolescent Girl and Her Mother," *Psychoanalytic Study of the Child*, 17, pp. 418–450.

CHAPTER 7

1. See Freud, 1925, "Some Psychical Consequences," 1931, "Female Sexuality," 1933, *New Introductory Lectures*.

2. Schafer, 1974, "Problems in Freud's Psychology," p. 482.

3. Karen Horney, 1926, "The Flight from Womanhood: The Masculinity Complex in Women as Viewed by Men and by Women," *Feminine Psychology*, pp. 54–70; 1932, "The Dread of Women," *International Journal of Psycho-Analysis*, 13, pp. 348–360; and 1933, "The Denial of the Vagina: A Contribution to the Problem of the Genital Anxieties Specific to Women," *Feminine Psychology*, pp. 147–161; Melanie Klein, 1928, "Early Stages of the Oedipus Conflict," *International Journal of Psycho-Analysis*, 9, pp. 167–180; Judith S. Kestenberg, 1956a, "On the Development of Maternal Feelings," and 1968, "Outside and Inside, Male and Female," *Journal of the American Psychoanalytic Association*, 16, #3, pp. 457–520.

4. Sherfey, 1966, "The Evolution and Nature"; Therese Benedek, 1968, "Discussion of Mary Jane Sherfey: The Evolution and Nature of Female Sexuality in Relation to Psychoanalytic Theory," *Journal of the American Psychoanalytic Association*, 16, pp. 424–448; Marcel Heiman, 1968, "Discussion of Sherfey's Paper on Female Sexuality," *Journal of the American-Psychoanalytic Association*, 16, pp. 406–416; Sylvan Keiser, 1968, "Discussion of Sherfey's Paper on Female Sexuality," *Journal of the American Psychoanalytic Association*, 16, pp. 440–456; Kestenberg, 1968, "Outside and Inside."

5. Masters and Johnson, 1966, *Human Sexual Response*.

6. Schafer, 1974, "Problems in Freud's Psychology," p. 482.

7. Ibid., p. 469.

8. Ibid., p. 471.

9. See, for example, Freud, 1908, " 'Civilized' Sexual Morality and Modern Nervousness," *SE*, vol. 9, pp. 179–204; 1905a, "Fragment of an Analysis of a Case of Hysteria," *SE*, vol. 7, pp. 3–122; 1909, "Analysis of a Phobia in a Five-Year-Old Boy," *SE*, vol. 10, pp. 3–149. For fuller discussions of these tendencies, see especially Schafer, 1974, "Problems in Freud's Psychology," and Gayle Rubin, 1975, "The Traffic in Women."

10. Brunswick, 1940, "The Preoedipal Phase," p. 246.

11. Jeanne Lampl-de Groot, 1952, "Re-evaluation of the Role of the Oedipus Complex," *International Journal of Psycho-Analysis*, 33, pp. 335–342; Ruth Mack Brunswick, 1940, "The Preoedipal Phase."

12. See Kohlberg, 1966, "A Cognitive-Developmental Analysis."

13. Freud, 1925, "Some Psychical Consequences," p. 256.

14. Brunswick, 1940, "The Preoedipal Phase," p. 238. See also Jeanne Lampl-de Groot, 1933, "Problems of Femininity," *Psychoanalytic Quarterly*, 2, pp. 489–518, for an interpretation of the feminine oedipus complex stressing complete rejection of the mother.

15. See, for example, Freud, 1905a, "Fragment of an Analysis."

16. For helpful discussions of the development of these explanations, see Janine Chasseguet-Smirgel, 1964, Introduction to *Female Sexuality*; Zenia Odes Fliegel, 1973, "Feminine Psychosexual Development in Freudian Theory: A Historical Reconstruction," *Psychoanalytic Quarterly*, 42, pp. 385–408; and Roy C. Calogeras and Fabian X. Schupper, 1972, "Origins and Early Formulations of the Oedipus Complex," *Journal of the American Psychoanalytic Association*, 20, #4, pp. 751–775.

17. Horney, 1926, "The Flight from Womanhood"; Ernest Jones, 1927, "The Early Development of Female Sexuality," *International Journal of Psycho-Analysis*, 8, pp. 459–472, 1931, "The Phallic Phase," *International Journal of Psycho-Analysis*, 14, pp. 1–33, and 1935, "Early Female Sexuality," *International Journal of Psycho-Analysis*, 16, pp. 263–273; Melanie Klein, 1928, "Early Stages," and 1932, *The Psychoanalysis of Children*; Chasseguet-Smirgel, 1964, "Outline for a Study of Narcissism in Female Sexuality," in Chasseguet-Smirgel, ed., *Female Sexuality*, pp. 68–83.

18. Horney, 1926, "The Flight from Womanhood," p. 68.

19. Jones, 1935, "Early Female Sexuality," p. 273.

20. Mitchell, 1974, *Psychoanalysis and Feminism*.

21. Jones, 1935, "Early Female Sexuality," p. 273.

22. Marjorie R. Leonard, 1966, "Fathers and Daughters: The Significance of 'Fathering' in the Psychosexual Development of the Girl," *International Journal of Psycho-Analysis*, 47, pp. 325–334.

23. For psychoanalytic reports, see Freud's cases of "Dora" (1905a, "Fragment of an Analysis") and "Little Hans" (1909, "Analysis of a Phobia"). For reviews of the social psychological literature that demonstrates this, see Miriam Johnson, 1963, "Sex Role Learning in the Nuclear Family," *Child Development*, 34, pp. 319–334, and 1975, "Fathers, Mothers and Sex-Typing," *Sociological Inquiry*, 45, #1, pp. 15–26; Maccoby and Jacklin, 1974, *The Psychology of Sex Differences*.

24. From Goodenough, 1957, cited in Maccoby and Jacklin, p. 329.

25. Ibid.

26. Ibid. See also Johnson, 1963, "Sex Role Learning," and 1975, "Fathers, Mothers," and Henry B. Biller, 1971, *Father, Child, and Sex Role*.

27. See, for example, Freud, 1925, "Some Psychical Consequences," 1931, "Female Sexuality," and 1933, *New Introductory Lectures*; Lampl-de Groot, 1933, "Problems of Femininity"; and Brunswick, 1940, "The Preoedipal Phase."

28. Lampl-de Groot, 1933, "Problems of Femininity," p. 497.

29. Freud, 1933, *New Introductory Lectures*, pp. 126–127.

30. Schafer, 1974, "Problems in Freud's Psychology," p. 473.

31. Ibid., pp. 474–475.

32. Freud, 1933, *New Introductory Lectures,* p. 124.

33. Brunswick, 1940, "The Preoedipal Phase," p. 247.

34. Chasseguet-Smirgel, 1964, "Feminine Guilt."

35. Ibid., p. 112.

36. Ibid., p. 115.

37. Ibid., pp. 115–116.

38. Ibid., p. 118.

39. Alice Balint, 1954, *The Early Years of Life*; Brunswick, 1940, "The Preoedipal Phase"; J. Lampl-de Groot, 1927, "The Evolution of the Oedipus Complex," and 1952, "Re-evaluation of the Role"; Gayle Rubin, 1975, "The Traffic in Women."

40. Alice Balint, 1954, *The Early Years of Life,* p. 85.

41. Lampl-de Groot, 1933, "Problems of Femininity," p. 497.

42. Alice Balint, 1954, *The Early Years of Life,* p. 86.

43. Gayle Rubin, 1975, "The Traffic in Women," p. 187.

44. Fairbairn, 1944, "Endopsychic Structure Considered in Terms of Object-Relationships," in *An Object-Relations Theory,* p. 124.

45. Lampl-de Groot, 1952, "Re-evaluation of the Role," p. 338.

46. Ibid., p. 342.

47. Freud, 1923a, *The Ego and the Id.*

48. Brunswick, 1940, "The Preoedipal Phase," p. 238.

49. Deutsch, 1944, *Psychology of Women,* p. 32.

50. Brunswick, 1940, "The Preoedipal Phase," pp. 250–251.

51. Helene Deutsch, 1932, "On Female Homosexuality," in Fliess, ed., *The Psychoanalytic Reader,* p. 225. See also 1944, *Psychology of Women.*

CHAPTER 8

1. Freud, 1925, "Some Psychical Consequences," and 1933, *New Introductory Lectures.*

2. For an excellent discussion of everything wrong with Freud's reasoning here, see Schafer, 1974, "Problems in Freud's Psychology."

3. Freud, 1924, "The Dissolution."

4. Jones, 1927, "The Early Development."

5. Ibid.; Klein, 1932, *The Psychoanalysis of Children.*

6. See, for example, Freud, 1917, *Introductory Lectures*; 1930, *Civilization and Its Discontents*; and 1923a, *The Ego and the Id.*

7. See Freud, 1924, "The Dissolution"; Deutsch, 1944, *Psychology of Women*; Horney, 1926, "The Flight from Womanhood"; Leonard, 1966, "Fathers and Daughters."

8. Talcott Parsons, 1954, "The Incest Taboo in Relation to Social Structure and the Socialization of the Child," in *Social Structure and Personality*; Johnson, 1975, "Fathers, Mothers."

9. See, for the classic formulation here, Freud, 1910, "A Special Type of Choice of Object Made by Men (Contributions to the Psychology of Love I)," *SE,* vol. 11, pp. 164–175. See also Slater, 1970, *The Pursuit,* and 1974, *Earthwalk.*

10. For example, Freud, 1931, "Female Sexuality"; David Freedman, 1961, "On Women Who Hate Their Husbands," in Hendrik M. Ruitenbeek, ed., *Psychoanalysis and Female Sexuality*; Deutsch, 1944, *Psychology of Women*; Mabel B. Cohen, 1966, "Personal Identity and Sexual Identity," in Jean Baker Miller, ed., *Psychoanalysis and Women,* pp. 156–182.

11. Reported in Julia Sherman, 1971, *On the Psychology of Women.*

12. Peter Blos, 1962, *On Adolescence.*

13. Ibid., p. 75.

14. Ibid., p. 66.

15. Deutsch, 1944, *Psychology of Women*; Alice Balint, 1954, *The Early Years of Life.*

16. Alice Balint, 1954, *The Early Years of Life,* p. 90.

17. For example, Peter Blos, 1957, "Preoedipal Factors in the Etiology of Female

Delinquency," *Psychoanalytic Study of the Child*, 12, pp. 229–249, and 1962, *On Adolescence*; Kata Levy, 1960, "Simultaneous Analysis"; and Sprince, 1962, "The Development of a Preoedipal Partnership."

18. See also Hammer, 1975, *Daughters and Mothers*.

19. Harry Stack Sullivan, 1953, *The Interpersonal Theory of Psychiatry*.

20. For a clinical example of the processes Deutsch discusses, with all these issues writ large, see Kata Levy's (1960, "Simultaneous Analysis") and Sprince's (1962, "The Development") accounts of the simultaneous analysis they did of a mother-daughter pair.

21. Helene Deutsch, 1944, *Psychology of Women*, p. 116.

22. See, for a review of this literature, Biller, 1971, *Father, Child and Sex Role*.

23. See, for discussion of these problems, Miriam M. Johnson, Jean Stockard, Joan Acker, and Claudeen Naffziger, 1975, "Expressiveness Re-evaluated," *School Review*, 88, pp. 617–644; Elizabeth Herzog and Cecelia E. Sudia, 1972, "Families Without Fathers," *Childhood Education*, January, pp. 175–181.

24. Hetherington, 1972, "Effects of Father Absence," and 1973, "Girls Without Fathers"; Johnson, 1975, "Fathers, Mothers."

25. Johnson, 1975, "Fathers, Mothers," p. 16.

26. Freud, 1933, *New Introductory Lectures*, p. 117.

27. Deutsch, 1944, *Psychology of Women*, p. 250.

28. Ibid., pp. 251–252.

29. Ibid., p. 116.

30. Ibid., p. 20.

CHAPTER 9

1. See Mitchell, 1974, *Psychoanalysis and Feminism*. See also Gayle Rubin, 1975, "The Traffic in Women."

2. For example, see Schafer, 1974, "Problems"; First's review of Mitchell, 1974, *New York Times*, May 19, 1974; Chasseguet-Smirgel, 1964, "Feminine Guilt"; recent reports in both the *Journal of the American Psychoanalytic Association* (24, #1, 1976) and the *International Journal of Psycho-Analysis* (57, part 3, 1976). See also neo-Freudian and other critical reformulations such as Jean Baker Miller, ed., 1973, *Psychoanalysis and Women*, and Jean Strouse, ed., 1974, *Women and Analysis*.

3. For an excellent evaluation of this kind, see Susan C. Weisskopf, 1972, "The Psychoanalytic Theory of Female Development: A Review and a Critique". Sherman, 1971, *On the Psychology of Women*, claims to do the same thing (and has the advantage of being published), but her account draws randomly and inappropriately from diverse social psychological experiments and does not really understand the theory it claims to criticize. See also Miller, 1973, *Psychoanalysis and Women*, especially the Stoller articles.

4. Freud, 1923a, *The Ego and the Id*, p. 31.

5. Freud, 1924, "The Dissolution," p. 179.

6. Freud, 1933, *New Introductory Lectures*, p. 135.

7. Freud, 1925, "Some Psychical Consequences," p. 257.

8. Freud, 1933, *New Introductory Lectures*.

9. Freud, 1925, "Some Psychical Consequences," p. 257.

10. Freud, 1933, *New Introductory Lectures*, p. 135.

11. Freud, 1924, "The Dissolution," p. 178.

12. Freud, 1925, "Some Psychical Consequences," p. 258.

13. Freud, 1933, *New Introductory Lectures*, p. 129.

14. Freud, 1931, "Female Sexuality."

15. Freud, 1933, *New Introductory Lectures*, p. 117.

16. Brunswick, 1940, "The Preoedipal Phase," p. 246.

17. Horney, 1926, "The Flight from Womanhood."

18. Freud, 1933, *New Introductory Lectures*, p. 126 (my italics).

19. Freud, 1925, "Some Psychical Consequences," p. 253 (my italics).

20. Freud, 1933, *New Introductory Lectures*, p. 132.

21. Brunswick, 1940, "The Preoedipal Phase," p. 239 (my italics).

22. Karl Abraham, 1920, "Manifestations of the Female Castration Complex," p. 132 (my italics).

23. Ibid., p. 129.

24. Freud, 1925, "Some Psychical Consequences," p. 253.

25. Schafer, 1974, "Problems," p. 463.

26. Ibid., pp. 267–268.

27. Freud, 1923*b*, "The Infantile Genital Organization (An Interpolation into the Theory of Sexuality)," *SE*, vol. 19, p. 142.

28. Freud, 1933, *New Introductory Lectures*, p. 65.

29. Helene Deutsch, 1925, "The Psychology of Woman in Relation to the Functions of Reproduction," in Fliess, ed., *The Psychoanalytic Reader*, p. 168.

30. Freud, 1933, *New Introductory Lectures*, p. 118.

31. Brunswick, 1940, "The Preoedipal Phase," p. 233.

32. Freud, 1931, "Female Sexuality," p. 228.

33. Freud, 1923*b*, "The Infantile Genital," p. 145.

34. Brunswick, 1940, "The Preoedipal Phase," p. 234.

35. Freud, 1923*b*, "The Infantile Genital," p. 145.

36. Freud, 1933, *New Introductory Lectures*, p. 128–129.

37. Horney, 1926, "The Flight from Womanhood," p. 65.

38. Ibid., p. 60.

39. Horney, 1933, "The Denial of the Vagina," p. 149.

40. See Robert Stoller, 1972, "The Bedrock of Masculinity and Femininity: Bisexuality," *Archives of General Psychiatry*, 26, pp. 207–212, 1973, "Overview: The Impact of New Advances in Sex Research on Psychoanalytic Theory," *American Journal of Psychiatry*, 130, #3, pp. 241–251, and 1974, "Facts and Fancies: An Examination of Freud's Concept of Bisexuality," in Strouse, ed., *Women and Analysis*; and Money and Ehrhardt, 1972, *Man and Woman*.

41. See, for example, Mitchell, 1974, *Psychoanalysis and Feminism*; Burness E. Moore, 1976, "Freud and Female Sexuality: A Current View," *International Journal of Psycho-Analysis*, 57, #3, pp. 287–300.

42. Horney, 1933, "The Denial of the Vagina," p. 160.

43. Freud, 1931, "Female Sexuality," p. 228, cited in Janine Chasseguet-Smirgel, 1976, "Freud and Female Sexuality: The Consideration of Some Blind Spots in the Exploration of the 'Dark Continent,' " *International Journal of Psycho-Analysis*, 57, #3, pp. 275–286. See also Chasseguet-Smirgel, 1964, "Introduction" to *Female Sexuality*.

44. Freud, 1909, "Analysis of a Phobia," p. 95, cited in Chasseguet-Smirgel, 1976, "Freud and Female Sexuality."

45. See, for example, Kestenberg, 1956*a*, "On the Development," 1956*b*, "Vicissitudes of Female Sexuality," *Journal of the American Psychoanalytic Association*, 4, pp. 453–476, and 1968, "Outside and Inside"; Phyllis Greenacre, 1950, "Special Problems of Early Female Sexual Development," *Psychoanalytic Study of the Child*, 5, pp. 122–138; Marjorie C. Barnett, 1968, " 'I Can't' Versus 'He Won't': Further Considerations of the Psychical Consequences of the Anatomic and Physiological Differences Between the Sexes," *Journal of the American Psychoanalytic Association*, 16, pp. 588–600; Chasseguet-Smirgel, 1964, "Feminine Guilt," and 1976, "Freud and Female Sexuality."

46. See Robert Stoller, 1964, "A Contribution to the Study of Gender Identity," *International Journal of Psycho-Analysis*, 45, pp. 220–226, 1965, "The Sense of Maleness," *Psychoanalytic Quarterly*, 34, pp. 207–218, 1972, "The Bedrock," 1973, "Overview," and 1974, "Facts and Fancies"; Money and Ehrhardt, 1972, *Man and Woman*; and Kohlberg, 1966, "A Cognitive-Developmental Analysis."

47. Freud, 1931, "Female Sexuality," p. 230.

48. See Roiphe, 1968, "On an Early Genital Phase"; Eleanor Galenson, 1971, "A Consideration of the Nature of Thought in Childhood Play," in John B. McDevitt and Calvin F. Settlage, eds., *Separation-Individuation: Essays in Honor of Margaret S. Mahler*; Eleanor Galenson and Herman Roiphe, 1971, "The Impact of Early Sexual Discovery

on Mood, Defensive Organization, and Symbolization," *Psychoanalytic Study of the Child*, 27, pp. 195–216; Roiphe and Galenson, 1973, "Object Loss"; Roiphe and Galenson, 1975, "Some Observations on Transitional Object and Infantile Fetish," *Psychoanalytic Quarterly*, 44, #2, pp. 206–231; Greenacre, 1968, "Perversions."

49. For the most extreme statement of this position, see Abraham, 1920, "Manifestations."

50. Freud, 1937, "Analysis Terminable and Interminable," *SE*, vol. 23, p. 252.

51. Ibid., pp. 250–251.

52. Freud, 1933, *New Introductory Lectures*, p. 135.

53. Abraham, 1920, "Manifestations," p. 123.

54. Freud, 1924, "The Dissolution," p. 178.

55. See Schafer, 1974, "Problems."

56. Freud, 1933, *New Introductory Lectures*, p. 117.

57. Ibid., p. 131.

58. Helene Deutsch, 1930, "The Significance of Masochism in the Mental Life of Women," in Fliess, ed., *The Psychoanalytic Reader: An Anthology of Essential Papers with Critical Introductions*, p. 205.

59. Ibid., p. 207.

60. Charles Sarlin, 1963, "Feminine Identity," *Journal of the American Psychoanalytic Association*, 11, #4, p. 813.

61. Freud, 1933, *New Introductory Lectures*, p. 119.

62. Sarlin, 1963, "Feminine Identity," p. 794. On clitoridectomy and other operations against female anatomy in the nineteenth- and early twentieth-century United States, see Bernard Barker-Benfield, 1973, "The Spermatic Economy of the Nineteenth Century," in Michael Gordon, ed., *The American Family in Social-Historical Perspective*, and Barbara Ehrenreich and Deirdre English, 1973, *Complaints and Disorders*.

CHAPTER 10

1. Freud, 1931, "Female Sexuality," p. 238.

2. See Ernest Jones, 1961, *The Life and Work of Sigmund Freud*, and Paul Roazen, 1969, *Brother Animal: The Story of Freud and Tausk*.

3. Freud, 1913, *Totem and Taboo*.

4. Gregory Zilboorg, 1944, "Masculine and Feminine: Some Biological and Cultural Aspects," in Miller, ed., *Psychoanalysis and Women*, pp. 96–131.

5. Benedek, 1959, "Parenthood as Developmental Phase," p. 412.

6. Zilboorg, 1944, "Masculine and Feminine," p. 123.

7. Bakan, 1966, *The Duality of Human Existence*, and 1968, *Disease, Pain and Sacrifice: Toward a Psychology of Suffering*.

8. The importance of the uncertainty of paternity was first brought to my attention by Nancy Jay, n.d., "The Uncertainty of Paternity."

9. See also Meyer Fortes, 1974, "The First Born," *Journal of Child Psychology and Psychiatry*, 15, pp. 81–104.

10. Harry Guntrip, 1961, *Personality Structure*.

11. Bibring, 1959, "Some Considerations," and Bibring et al., 1961, "A Study of the Psychological"; Benedek, 1959, "Parenthood as Developmental Phase."

12. Loewald, 1962, "Internalization, Separation."

13. See Moore, 1976, "Freud and Female Sexuality."

14. The terms are H. V. Dicks's (1967, *Marital Tensions*).

15. See, for example, Deutsch, 1944, *Psychology of Women*.

16. Erik Erikson, 1964*b*, "Womanhood and the Inner Space."

CHAPTER 11

1. For a review of the literature which argues this, see Biller, 1971, *Father, Child*. See also Stoller, 1965, "The Sense of Maleness." For a useful recent formulation, see Johnson, 1975, "Fathers, Mothers."

2. See Mead, 1949, *Male and Female*; Michelle Z. Rosaldo, 1974, "Woman, Culture, and Society"; Nancy Chodorow, 1971, "Being and Doing," and 1974, "Family Structure and Feminine Personality," in Rosaldo and Lamphere, eds., *Woman, Culture and Society*, pp. 43–66; Beatrice Whiting, ed., 1963, *Six Cultures*; Beatrice B. Whiting and John W. M. Whiting, 1975, *Children of Six Cultures*; John Whiting, 1959, "Sorcery, Sin"; Burton and Whiting, 1961, "The Absent Father."

3. See Richard T. Roessler, 1971, "Masculine Differentiation and Feminine Constancy," *Adolescence*, 6, #22, pp. 187–196; E. M. Bennett and L. R. Cohen, 1959, "Men and Women, Personality Patterns and Contrasts," *Genetic Psychology Monographs*, 59, pp. 101–155; Johnson, 1963, "Sex Role Learning," and 1975, "Fathers, Mothers"; Stoller, 1964, "A Contribution to the Study," 1965, "The Sense of Maleness," and 1968, "The Sense of Femaleness," *Psychoanalytic Quarterly*, 37, #1, pp. 42–55.

4. See Biller, 1971, *Father, Child*.

5. Mitscherlich, 1963, *Society Without the Father*; Philip E. Slater, 1961, "Toward a Dualistic Theory of Identification," *Merrill-Palmer Quarterly of Behavior and Development*, 7, #2, pp. 113–126; Robert F. Winch, 1962, *Identification and Its Familial Determinants*; David B. Lynn, 1959, "A Note on Sex Differences," and 1962, "Sex Role and Parent."

6. Johnson, 1975, "Fathers, Mothers," and Maccoby and Jacklin, 1974, *The Psychology of Sex Differences*, point this out.

7. D. B. Lynn, 1959, "A Note on Sex Differences," p. 130.

8. See Slater, 1961, "Toward a Dualistic Theory," and Johnson, 1975, "Fathers, Mothers."

9. This phrase is Arlie Hochschild's. (See Arlie Russell Hochschild, 1975*b*, "The Sociology of Feeling and Emotion: Selected Possibilities," in Marcia Millman and Rosabeth Moss Kanter, eds., *Another Voice*, pp. 280–307.) She uses it to refer to the internal work women do to make their feelings accord with how they think they ought to feel. My usage here extends also to work for and upon other people's emotions.

10. See, for example, Johnson, 1975, "Fathers, Mothers"; Parsons and Bales, 1955, *Family, Socialization*; Deutsch, 1944, *Psychology of Women*.

11. Alice Balint, 1939, "Love for the Mother."

12. Rosaldo, 1974, "Woman, Culture and Society."

13. On these issues, see Lynn, 1959, "A Note on Sex Differences," and 1962, "Sex Role and Parent"; Parsons, 1942, "Age and Sex"; Mitscherlich, 1963, *Society Without the Father*; Slater, 1968, *The Glory of Hera*; Mead, 1949, *Male and Female*.

14. Freud, 1925, "Some Psychical Consequences," p. 253.

15. Brunswick, 1940, "The Preoedipal Phase," p. 246.

16. Ibid.

17. Freud, 1909, "Analysis of a Phobia."

18. Horney, 1932, "The Dread of Women."

19. Ibid., p. 351.

20. Ibid.

21. Ibid., p. 135.

22. Ibid., p. 136.

23. Ibid.

24. Slater (1968, *The Glory of Hera*, p. 19) points this out. For cross-cultural comparisons of the relationship between family structure and men's preoccupation with masculinity, see, in addition to Slater, Whiting et al., 1958, "The Function of Male Initiation Rites"; Whiting, 1959, "Sorcery, Sin"; and Burton and Whiting, 1961, "The Absent Father."

25. On the relation of proletarianization to the decline of the oedipal father, see Horkheimer, 1936, "Authority and the Family," and Mitscherlich, 1963, *Society Without the Father*.

26. Bibring, 1953, "On the 'Passing of the Oedipus Complex.' "

27. Ibid., p. 280.

28. Ibid., p. 281.

29. Ibid.

30. Ibid.

31. Ibid., p. 282.

32. Ibid.

33. But for discussions of ways that this accountability is actively maintained, see Joseph H. Pleck and Jack Sawyer, 1974, *Men and Masculinity*, and Marc F. Fasteau, 1974, *The Male Machine*.

34. My formulation of the personality requirements of the hierarchical firm follows Edwards, 1975, "The Social Relations of Production."

35. See Melvin L. Kohn, 1969, *Class and Conformity*.

36. Frankfurt Institute, 1972, *Aspects*; Horkheimer, 1936, "Authority and the Family"; Mitscherlich, 1963, *Society Without the Father*; Parsons, 1964, *Social Structure and Personality*; Parsons and Bales, 1955, *Family, Socialization*; Slater, 1970, *The Pursuit of Loneliness*, and 1974, *Earthwalk*.

37. Talcott Parsons with Winston White, 1961, "The Link Between Character and Society," in *Social Structure and Personality*, p. 218.

38. Ibid., p. 203.

39. Ibid., p. 233.

40. Slater, 1974, *Earthwalk*, p. 131. See also Slater, 1970, *The Pursuit of Loneliness*.

41. Horkheimer, 1936, "Authority and the Family," p. 108.

CHAPTER 12

1. Some of the material in this section appeared previously in Nancy Chodorow, 1976, "Oedipal Asymmetries and Heterosexual Knots," *Social Problems*, 23, #4, pp. 454–468.

2. Deutsch, 1925, "The Psychology of Woman," p. 165.

3. Ibid.

4. This claim comes from my reading of ethnographic literature and is confirmed by anthropologist Michelle Z. Rosaldo (personal communication).

5. Michael Balint, 1935, "Critical Notes on the Theory," p. 50.

6. Michael Balint, 1956a, "Perversions and Genitality," in *Primary Love and Psycho-Analytic Technique*, p. 141. Balint follows Sandor Ferenczi here (1924, *Thalassa: A Theory of Genitality*).

7. Freud, 1931, "Female Sexuality."

8. See Freedman, 1961, "On Women Who Hate," for an excellent clinical account of this.

9. See Chasseguet-Smirgel, 1964, "Feminine Guilt," and Grunberger, 1964, "Outline for a Study."

10. For sociological confirmation of this, see William M. Kephart, 1967, "Some Correlates of Romantic Love," *Journal of Marriage and the Family*, 29, pp. 470–474, and Zick Rubin, 1970, "Measurement of Romantic Love," *Journal of Personality and Social Psychology*, 6, pp. 265–273.

11. Chasseguet-Smirgel, 1964, "Feminine Guilt," and Grunberger, 1964, "Outline for a Study."

12. Alan Booth (1972, "Sex and Social Participation," *American Sociological Review*, 37, pp. 183–193) reports that women's friendships in our society are affectively richer than men's. Along the same lines, Mirra Komarovsky (1974, "Patterns of Self-Disclosure of Male Undergraduates," *Journal of Marriage and the Family*, 36, #4, pp. 677–686) found that men students confided more in a special woman friend and that they maintained a front of strength with men. Moreover, these men felt at a disadvantage vis-à-vis their woman confidante, because she tended to have a number of other persons in whom she could confide.

13. Grunberger, 1964, "Outline for a Study," p. 74.

14. See Martha Baum, 1971, "Love, Marriage and the Division of Labor," *Sociological Inquiry*, 41, #1, pp. 107–117; Arlie Russell Hochschild, 1975a, "Attending to, Codifying, and Managing Feelings"; Kephart, 1967, "Some Correlates"; Zick Rubin, 1975, "Loving and Leaving."

15. Goethals, 1973, "Symbiosis," p. 96.

16. Zick Rubin, 1975, "Loving and Leaving."

17. Jessie Bernard, 1972, *The Future of Marriage.*

18. Freud, 1933, *New Introductory Lectures*, p. 134.

19. Booth, 1972, "Sex and Social Participation"; this is a finding certainly confirmed by most writing from the men's liberation movement.

20. See, for cross-cultural confirmation, most ethnographies and also Rosaldo and Lamphere, 1974, *Woman, Culture and Society.* For contemporary capitalist society, see Booth, 1972, "Sex and Social Participation," and for concrete illustration, Elizabeth Bott, 1957, *Family and Social Network: Roles, Norms and External Relationships in Ordinary Urban Families*; Herbert Gans, 1967, *The Levittowners*; Mirra Komarovsky, 1962, *Blue-Collar Marriage*; Carol B. Stack, 1974, *All Our Kin*; Young and Willmott, 1957, *Family and Kinship.*

21. See Deutsch, 1944, *Psychology of Women*; Charlotte Wolff, 1971, *Love Between Women*; Adrienne Rich, 1976, *Of Woman Born: Motherhood as Experience and Institution.*

22. For a contemporary account of exactly this transition, see Young and Willmott, 1957, *Family and Kinship.*

23. Deutsch, 1925, "The Psychology of Woman," p. 171.

24. Freud, 1914, "On Narcissism," p. 88.

25. See Heinz Kohut, 1971, *Analysis of Self: A Systematic Approach to the Psychoanalytic Treatment of Narcissistic Personality Disorders. Psychoanalytic Study of the Child*, monograph #4. New York, International Universities Press; Otto Kernberg, 1975, *Borderline Conditions and Pathological Narcissism.*

26. Fliess, 1961, *Ego and Body Ego*; Deutsch, 1944, *Psychology of Women.*

27. Deutsch, 1944, *Psychology of Women.*

28. Benedek, 1949, "Psychosomatic Implications," p. 643.

29. On this, see Alice Balint, 1939, "Love for the Mother"; Fliess, 1961, *Ego and Body Ego*; Whiting et al., 1958, "The Function of Male Initiation Rites"; Newton, 1955, *Maternal Emotions*, and 1973, "Interrelationships between Sexual Responsiveness."

30. Deutsch, 1944, *Psychology of Women*, p. 205.

31. Benedek, 1959, "Parenthood as Developmental Phase."

32. See Klein, 1937, "Love, Guilt and Reparation." Barbara Deck (personal communication) pointed out to me that Klein's interpretation of a woman's participation in mothering is homologous to that described by Ferenczi and Balint in coitus. A woman's gratification in mothering comes from becoming her mother and from identifying with her mothered infant. Similarly, she is both the receiving mother (womb) and identifies with the male penetrating her in coitus.

33. The mothers I describe in Chapter 6 are cases in point.

AFTERWORD

1. Bernard, 1974, *The Future of Motherhood*, citing Minturn and Lambert, 1964.

2. See Friedl, 1975, *Women and Men.*

3. See Ortner, 1974, "Is Female to Male as Nature Is to Culture?"

4. U.S. Department of Labor, Employment Standards Administration, Women's Bureau, *1975 Handbook on Women Workers*, Bulletin 297.

Bibliography

ABELIN, ERNEST L., 1971, "The Role of the Father in the Separation-Individuation Phase," pp. 229–252 in John B. McDevitt and Calvin F. Settlage, eds., *Separation-Individuation: Essays in Honor of Margaret S. Mahler*. New York, International Universities Press.

ABRAHAM, KARL, 1920, "Manifestations of the Female Castration Complex," pp. 109–135 in Jean Strouse, ed., *Women and Analysis*. New York, Grossman Publishers, 1974.

———, 1966, *On Character and Libido Development*. New York, W. W. Norton.

AINSWORTH, MARY SALTER, 1969, "Object Relations, Dependency, and Attachment: A Theoretical Review of the Infant-Mother Relationship," *Child Development*, 40, #4, pp. 969–1025.

ANGEL, KLAUS, 1967, "On Symbiosis and Pseudosymbiosis," *Journal of the American Psychoanalytic Association*, 15, #2, pp. 294–316.

———, 1972, "The Role of the Internal Object and External Object in Object Relationships, Separation Anxiety, Object Constancy, and Symbiosis," *International Journal of Psycho-Analysis*, 53, pp. 541–546.

ARIÈS, PHILIPPE, 1960, *Centuries of Childhood: A Social History of Family Life*. New York, Vintage Books.

BAKAN, DAVID, 1966, *The Duality of Human Existence: Isolation and Communion in Western Man*. Boston, Beacon Press.

———, 1968, *Disease, Pain, and Sacrifice: Toward a Psychology of Suffering*. Boston, Beacon Press.

BALINT, ALICE, 1939, "Love for the Mother and Mother-Love," pp. 91–108 in Michael Balint, ed., *Primary Love and Psycho-Analytic Technique*. New York, Liveright Publishing, 1965.

———, 1954, *The Early Years of Life: A Psychoanalytic Study*. New York, Basic Books.

BALINT, ENID, 1963, "On Being Empty of Oneself," *International Journal of Psycho-Analysis*, 44, #4, pp. 470–480.

BALINT, MICHAEL, 1935, "Critical Notes on the Theory of the Pregenital Organizations of the Libido," pp. 37–58 in *Primary Love and Psycho-Analytic Technique*.

———, 1937, "Early Developmental States of the Ego, Primary Object-Love," pp. 74–90 in *Primary Love and Psycho-Analytic Technique*.

———, 1956a, "Perversions and Genitality," in *Primary Love and Psycho-Analytic Technique*.

———, 1956b, "Pleasure, Object, and Libido. Some Reflections on Fairbairn's Modifications on Psychoanalytic Theory," *British Journal of Medical Psychology*, 29, #2, pp. 162–167.

———, 1961, "Contribution to the Symposium on the Theory of the Parent-Infant Relationship," pp. 145–147 in *Primary Love and Psycho-Analytic Technique*.

———, 1965, *Primary Love and Psycho-Analytic Technique*. London, Tavistock Publications; New York, Liveright Publishing.

———, 1968, *The Basic Fault: Therapeutic Aspects of Regression*. London, Tavistock Publications.

BARKER-BENFIELD, BERNARD, 1973, "The Spermatic Economy: A Nineteenth-Century View of Sexuality," pp. 336–372 in Michael Gordon, ed., *The American Family in Social-Historical Perspective*. New York, St. Martin's Press.

BARNETT, MARJORIE C., 1968, " 'I Can't' Versus 'He Won't': Further Considerations of the Psychical Consequences of the Anatomic and Physiological Differences Between the Sexes," *Journal of the American Psychoanalytic Association*, 16, pp. 588–600.

BARRY, HERBERT, III, MARGARET K. BACON, and IRVIN L. CHILD, 1957, "A Cross-Cultural Survey of Some Sex Differences in Socialization," *Journal of Abnormal and Social Psychology*, 55, #3, pp. 327–332.

BAUM, MARTHA, 1971, "Love, Marriage and the Division of Labor," *Sociological Inquiry*, 41, #1, pp. 107–117.

BEACH, FRANK A., 1965, *Sex and Behavior*. New York, John Wiley.

BENEDEK, THERESE, 1949, "Psychosomatic Implications of the Primary Unit, Mother-Child," *American Journal of Orthopsychiatry*, 19, #4, pp. 642–654.

———, 1952, *Psychosexual Functions in Women*. New York, Ronald Press.

———, 1956, "Psychobiological Aspects of Mothering," *American Journal of Orthopsychiatry*, 26, pp. 272–278.

———, 1959, "Parenthood as a Developmental Phase: A Contribution to the Libido Theory," *Journal of the American Psychoanalytic Association*, 7, #3, pp. 389–417.

———, 1960, "The Organization of the Reproductive Drive," *International Journal of Psycho-Analysis*, 41, pp. 1–15.

———, 1968, "Discussion of Mary Jane Sherfey: The Evolution and Nature of Female Sexuality in Relation to Psychoanalytic Theory," *Journal of the American Psychoanalytic Association*, 16, pp. 424–448.

BENJAMIN, JOHN D., 1961, "The Innate and the Experiential in Child Development," in Henry W. Brosin, ed., *Lectures on Experimental Psychiatry*. Pittsburgh, University of Pittsburgh Press.

BENNETT, E. M., and L. R. COHEN, 1959, "Men and Women, Personality Patterns and Contrasts," *Genetic Psychology Monographs*, 59, pp. 101–155.

BENNIS, WARREN G., and PHILIP E. SLATER, 1968, *The Temporary Society*. New York, Harper and Row.

BERGER, PETER L., and HANSFRIED KELLNER, 1974, "Marriage and the Construction of Reality," pp. 157–174 in Rose Laub Coser, ed., *The Family: Its Structures and Functions*. New York, St. Martin's Press.

BERNARD, JESSIE, 1972, *The Future of Marriage*. New York, Bantam Books.

——, 1974, *The Future of Motherhood*. New York, Penguin Books.

BIBRING, GRETE, 1953, "On the 'Passing of the Oedipus Complex' in a Matriarchal Family Setting," pp. 278–284 in Rudolph M. Loewenstein, ed., *Drives, Affects, and Behavior: Essays in Honor of Marie Bonaparte*. New York, International Universities Press.

——, 1959, "Some Considerations of the Psychological Processes in Pregnancy," *Psychoanalytic Study of the Child*, 14, pp. 113–121.

BIBRING, GRETE L., THOMAS F. DWYER, DOROTHY S. HUNTINGTON, and ARTHUR VALENSTEIN, 1961, "A Study of the Psychological Processes in Pregnancy and of the Earliest Mother-Child Relationship," *Psychoanalytic Study of the Child*, 16, pp. 9–72.

BILLER, HENRY B., 1971, *Father, Child, and Sex Role*. Lexington, Mass., D. C. Heath.

BLOCH, RUTH, 1972, "Sex and the Sexes in Eighteenth-Century Magazines," unpublished paper.

BLOS, PETER, 1957, "Preoedipal Factors in the Etiology of Female Delinquency," *Psychoanalytic Study of the Child*, 12, pp. 229–249.

——, 1962, *On Adolescence: A Psychoanalytic Interpretation*. New York, Free Press.

BOOTH, ALAN, 1972, "Sex and Social Participation," *American Sociological Review*, 37, pp. 183–193.

BOTT, ELIZABETH, 1957, *Family and Social Network: Roles, Norms and External Relationships in Ordinary Urban Families*. London, Tavistock Publications.

BOWLBY, JOHN, 1951, *Maternal Care and Mental Health*. New York, Schocken Books, 1966.

——, 1969, *Attachment and Loss, Volume 1: Attachment*. London, Penguin Books, 1971.

BOWLES, SAMUEL, and HERBERT GINTIS, 1976, *Schooling in Capitalist America: Educational Reform and the Contradictions of Economic Life*. New York, Basic Books.

BREUER, JOSEPH, and SIGMUND FREUD, 1895, *Studies on Hysteria*, in *Standard Edition of the Complete Psychological Works*, vol. 2, pp. 1–319 (see Freud, Sigmund, 1900–1901).

BRODY, SYLVIA, and SIDNEY AXELRAD, 1970, *Anxiety and Ego Formation in Infancy*. New York, International Universities Press.

BROWN, JUDITH K., 1970, "A Note on the Division of Labor by Sex," *American Anthropologist*, 72, pp. 1073–1078.

BRUNSWICK, RUTH MACK, 1940, "The Preoedipal Phase of the Libido Development," in Robert Fliess, ed., *The Psychoanalytic Reader: An Anthology of*

Essential Papers with Critical Introductions. New York, International Universities Press, pp. 231–253.

BURLINGHAM, DOROTHY, 1967, "Empathy Between Infant and Mother," *Journal of the American Psychoanalytic Association,* 15, pp. 764–780.

———, 1973, "The Pre-Oedipal Infant-Father Relationship," *Psychoanalytic Study of the Child,* 28, pp. 23–47.

BURTON, ROGER V., and JOHN W. M. WHITING, 1961, "The Absent Father and Cross-Sex Identity," *Merrill-Palmer Quarterly of Behavior and Development,* 7, #2, 1961, pp. 85–95.

CALDWELL, BETTYE, LEONARD HERSHER, EARL L. LIPTON, et al., 1963, "Mother-Infant Interaction in Monomatric and Polymatric Families," *American Journal of Orthopsychiatry,* 33, pp. 653–664.

CALDWELL, BETTYE, CHARLENE WRIGHT, ALICE HONIG, and JORDAN TANNENBAUM, 1970, "Infant Day Care and Attachment," *American Journal of Orthopsychiatry,* 40, #3, pp. 397–412.

CALOGERAS, ROY C., and FABIAN X. SCHUPPER, 1972, "Origins and Early Formulations of the Oedipus Complex," *Journal of the American Psychoanalytic Association,* 20, #4, pp. 751–775.

CAMBOR, C. GLENN, 1969, "Preoedipal Factors in Superego Development: The Influence of Multiple Mothers," *Psychoanalytic Quarterly,* 38, #1, pp. 81–96.

CHASSEGUET-SMIRGEL, JANINE, 1964, "Feminine Guilt and the Oedipus Complex," pp. 94–134 in J. Chasseguet-Smirgel, ed., *Female Sexuality.* Ann Arbor, University of Michigan Press, 1970.

———, 1976, "Freud and Female Sexuality: The Consideration of Some Blind Spots in the Exploration of the 'Dark Continent,' " *International Journal of Psycho-Analysis,* 57, #3, pp. 275–286.

CHODOROW, NANCY, 1971, "Being and Doing: A Cross-Cultural Examination of the Socialization of Males and Females," pp. 173–197 in Vivian Gornick and Barbara K. Moran, eds., *Woman in Sexist Society: Studies in Power and Powerlessness.* New York, Basic Books.

———, 1974, "Family Structure and Feminine Personality," pp. 43–66 in Michelle Z. Rosaldo and Louise Lamphere, eds., *Woman, Culture and Society.* Stanford, Stanford University Press.

———, 1976, "Oedipal Asymmetries and Heterosexual Knots," *Social Problems,* 23, #4, pp. 454–468.

CLARK, ALICE, 1919, *The Working Life of Women in the Seventeenth Century.* London, G. Routledge.

COHEN, MABEL B., 1966, "Personal Identity and Sexual Identity," pp. 156–182 in Jean Baker Miller, ed., 1973, *Psychoanalysis and Women.* Baltimore, Penguin Books.

COLEMAN, R. W., E. KRIS, and S. PROVENCE, 1953, "Study of Variations in Early Parental Attitudes," *Psychoanalytic Study of the Child,* 8, pp. 20–47.

COLLIER, JANE FISHBURNE and MICHELLE ZIMBALIST ROSALDO, 1975, "Marriage, Motherhood, and Direct Exchange: Expressions of Male Dominance in 'Egalitarian' Societies." Paper presented at the 74th Annual Meeting of the American Anthropological Association, San Francisco.

CONNER, B. L., 1972, "Hormones, Biogenic Amines and Aggression," in Cymour Levine, ed., *Hormones and Behavior*, New York, Academic Press.

COSER, ROSE LAUB, 1974*a*, "Authority and Structural Ambivalence in the Middle-Class Family," pp. 362–373 in 1974*b*, *The Family: Its Structures and Functions*.

———, ed., 1974*b*, *The Family: Its Structures and Functions*. New York, St. Martin's Press.

CRANDALL, VIRGINIA C., 1972, "The Fels Study: Some Contributions to Personality Development and Achievement in Childhood and Adulthood," *Seminars in Psychiatry*, 4, #4, pp. 383–397.

D'ANDRADE, ROY, 1966, "Sex Differences and Cultural Institutions," pp. 173–204 in Eleanor E. Maccoby, ed., *The Development of Sex Differences*. Stanford, Stanford University Press.

DEUTSCH, HELENE, 1925, "The Psychology of Woman in Relation to the Functions of Reproduction," pp. 165–179 in Robert Fliess, ed., 1969, *The Psychoanalytic Reader: An Anthology of Essential Papers with Critical Introductions*. New York, International Universities Press.

———, 1930, "The Significance of Masochism in the Mental Life of Women," pp. 195–207 in Robert Fliess, ed., 1969, *The Psychoanalytic Reader: An Anthology of Essential Papers with Critical Introductions*. New York, International Universities Press.

———, 1932, "On Female Homosexuality," pp. 208–230 in Robert Fliess, ed., 1969, *The Psychoanalytic Reader: An Anthology of Essential Papers with Critical Introductions*. New York, International Universities Press.

———, 1933, "Motherhood and Sexuality," *Psychoanalytic Quarterly*, 2, pp. 476–488.

———, 1944 and 1945, *Psychology of Women*, vols. 1 and 2. New York, Grune & Stratton.

DICKS, HENRY V., 1967, *Marital Tensions*. New York, Basic Books.

EDWARDS, RICHARD C., 1975, "The Social Relations of Production in the Firm and Labor Market Structure," in Richard C. Edwards, Michael Reich, and David M. Gordon, eds., *Labor Market Segmentation*. Lexington, Mass., D. C. Heath.

EHRENREICH, BARBARA, and DEIRDRE ENGLISH, 1973, *Complaints and Disorders: The Sexual Politics of Sickness*. New York, Feminist Press.

EHRHARDT, ANKE, 1973, "Maternalism in Fetal Hormonal and Related Syndromes," in Joseph Zubin and John Money, eds., *Contemporary Sexual Behavior: Critical Issues in the 1970's*. Baltimore, Johns Hopkins University Press.

EIBL-EIBESFELDT, IRENAUS, 1970, *Ethology: The Biology of Behavior*. New York, Holt, Rinehart and Winston.

ENGELS, FREDERICK, 1884, *The Origin of the Family, Private Property, and the State*. New York, International Publishers, 1967.

ERIKSON, ERIK, 1950, *Childhood and Society*. New York, W. W. Norton.

———, 1964*a*, *Insight and Responsibility*. New York, W. W. Norton.

———, 1964*b*, "Womanhood and the Inner Space," in Robert Jay Lifton, ed., *The Woman in America*. Boston, Houghton Mifflin.

FAIRBAIRN, W. R. D., 1940, "Schizoid Factors in the Personality," pp. 3–27 in 1952, *An Object-Relations Theory of the Personality.*

———, 1941, "A Revised Psychopathology of the Psychoses and Psychoneuroses," pp. 28–58 in 1952, *An Object-Relations Theory of the Personality.*

———, 1944, "Endopsychic Structure Considered in Terms of Object-Relationships," pp. 82–136 in 1952, *An Object-Relations Theory of the Personality.*

———, 1952, *An Object-Relations Theory of the Personality.* New York, Basic Books.

———, 1954, "Observations of the Nature of Hysterical States," *British Journal of Medical Psychology,* 27, #3, pp. 105–125.

FASTEAU, MARC F., 1974, *The Male Machine.* New York, McGraw-Hill.

FERENCZI, SANDOR, 1924, *Thalassa: A Theory of Genitality.* New York, W. W. Norton, 1968.

FLIEGEL, ZENIA ODES, 1973, "Feminine Psychosexual Development in Freudian Theory: A Historical Reconstruction," *Psychoanalytic Quarterly,* 42, pp. 385–408.

FLIESS, ROBERT, 1961, *Ego and Body Ego: Contributions to Their Psychoanalytic Psychology.* New York, International Universities Press, 1970.

FORD, CLELLAN S., and FRANK A. BEACH, 1951, *Patterns of Sexual Behavior.* New York, Harper and Row.

FORTES, MEYER, 1974, "The First Born," *Journal of Child Psychology and Psychiatry,* 15, pp. 81–104.

FRANKFURT INSTITUTE FOR SOCIAL RESEARCH, 1972, *Aspects of Sociology.* Boston, Beacon Press.

FREEDMAN, DAVID, 1961, "On Women Who Hate Their Husbands," in Hendrik M. Ruitenbeek, ed., 1966, *Psychoanalysis and Female Sexuality.* New Haven, College & University Press Services.

FREEMAN, JO, 1971, "The Social Construction of the Second Sex," pp. 123–141 in Michelle Garskof, ed., *Roles Women Play.* Belmont, Calif., Brooks/Cole Publishing.

FREUD, ANNA, 1936, *The Ego and the Mechanisms of Defense.* New York, International Universities Press, rev. ed., 1966.

———, 1962, "Contribution to Discussion, 'The Theory of the Parent-Infant Relationship,' " *International Journal of Psycho-Analysis,* 43, pp. 240–242.

FREUD, SIGMUND, 1900–1901, "The Interpretation of Dreams," *Standard Edition of the Complete Psychological Works* (hereafter, *SE*), vols. 4 and 5, pp. 1–713. London, Hogarth Press and Institute of Psycho-Analysis.

———, 1905a, "Fragment of an Analysis of a Case of Hysteria," *SE,* vol. 8, pp. 3–122 ("Dora").

———, 1905b, "Three Essays on the Theory of Sexuality," *SE,* vol. 7, pp. 125–245.

———, 1908, " 'Civilized' Sexual Morality and Modern Nervousness," *SE,* vol. 9, pp. 179–204.

———, 1909, "Analysis of a Phobia in a Five-Year-Old Boy", *SE,* vol. 10, pp. 3–149 ("Little Hans").

———, 1910, "A Special Type of Choice of Object Made by Men (Contributions to the Psychology of Love I)," *SE,* vol. 11, pp. 164–175.

————, 1913, *Totem and Taboo*, *SE*, vol. 13, pp. 1–161.

————, 1914, "On Narcissism: An Introduction," *SE*, vol. 14, pp. 69–102.

————, 1917a, *Introductory Lectures on Psycho-Analysis*, *SE*, vols. 15 and 16, pp. 3–476.

————, 1917b, "Mourning and Melancholia," *SE*, vol. 14, pp. 239–258.

————, 1921, "Group Psychology and the Analysis of the Ego," *SE*, vol. 18, pp. 67–143.

————, 1923a, "The Ego and the Id," *SE*, vol. 19, pp. 3–59.

————, 1923b, "The Infantile Genital Organization (An Interpolation into the Theory of Sexuality)," *SE*, vol. 19, pp. 140–153.

————, 1924, "The Dissolution of the Oedipus Complex," *SE*, vol. 19, pp. 172–179.

————, 1925, "Some Psychical Consequences of the Anatomical Distinction Between the Sexes," *SE*, vol. 19, pp. 243–258.

————, 1926, "Inhibitions, Symptoms and Anxiety," *SE*, vol. 20, pp. 77–174.

————, 1927, "The Future of an Illusion," *SE*, vol. 21, pp. 3–56.

————, 1930, *Civilization and Its Discontents*, *SE*, vol. 21, pp. 59–145.

————, 1931, "Female Sexuality," *SE*, vol. 21, pp. 223–243.

————, 1933, *New Introductory Lectures on Psychoanalysis*, *SE*, vol. 22, pp. 3–182.

————, 1937, "Analysis Terminable and Interminable," *SE*, vol. 23, pp. 211–253.

————, 1939, *Moses and Monotheism: Three Essays*, *SE*, vol. 23, pp. 3–137.

FRIEDL, ERNESTINE, 1975, *Women and Men: An Anthropologist's View*. New York, Holt, Rinehart and Winston.

GALENSON, ELEANOR, 1971, "A Consideration of the Nature of Thought in Childhood Play," in John B. McDevitt and Calvin F. Settlage, eds., *Separation-Individuation: Essays in Honor of Margaret S. Mahler*. New York, International Universities Press.

————, 1976, "Scientific Proceedings—Panel Reports," Panels on the Psychology of Women, Annual Meeting of the American Psychoanalytic Association, 1974. *Journal of the American Psychoanalytic Association*, 24, #1, pp. 141–160.

GALENSON, ELEANOR, and HERMAN ROIPHE, 1971, "The Impact of Early Sexual Discovery on Mood, Defensive Organization, and Symbolization," *Psychoanalytic Study of the Child*, 26, pp. 195–216.

GANS, HERBERT, 1967, *The Levittowners*. New York, Vintage Books.

GARFINKEL, HAROLD, 1967, *Studies in Ethnomethodology*. Englewood Cliffs, Prentice-Hall.

GILMAN, CHARLOTTE PERKINS, 1898, *Women and Economics*. New York, Harper & Row, 1966.

GLATZER, HENRIETTE, 1959, "Notes on the Preoedipal Fantasy," *American Journal of Orthopsychiatry*, 24, pp. 383–390.

GOETHALS, GEORGE W., 1973, "Symbiosis and the Life Cycle," *British Journal of Medical Psychology*, 46, pp. 91–96.

————, 1974, "Mother-Infant Attachment and Premarital Behavior: The Contact Hypothesis," unpublished paper delivered, Grand Rounds, Harvard Medical School, Department of Psychology.

GOODE, WILLIAM J., 1963, *World Revolution and Family Patterns*. New York, Free Press.

GORDON, MICHAEL, ed., 1973, *The American Family in Social-Historical Perspective*. New York, St. Martin's Press.

GREENACRE, PHYLLIS, 1950, "Special Problems of Early Female Sexual Development," *Psychoanalytic Study of the Child*, 5, pp. 122–138.

——, 1958, "Early Physical Determinants in the Development of the Sense of Identity," *Journal of the American Psychoanalytic Association*, 6, #4, pp. 612–627.

——, 1968, "Perversions: General Considerations Regarding Their Genetic and Dynamic Background," *Psychoanalytic Study of the Child*, 23, pp. 47–62.

GREENSON, RALPH, 1968, "Dis-Identifying from Mother: Its Special Importance for the Boy," *International Journal of Psycho-Analysis*, 49, pp. 370–374.

GRUNBERGER, BELA, 1964, "Outline for a Study of Narcissism in Female Sexuality," pp. 68–83 in J. Chasseguet-Smirgel, ed., 1970, *Female Sexuality*. Ann Arbor, University of Michigan Press.

GUNTRIP, HARRY, 1961, *Personality Structure and Human Interaction: The Developing Synthesis of Psycho-dynamic Theory*. New York, International Universities Press.

——, 1971, *Psychoanalytic Theory, Therapy, and the Self*. New York, Basic Books.

HABERMAS, JURGEN, 1971, *Knowledge and Human Interests*. Boston, Beacon Press.

HAMMER, SIGNE, 1975, *Daughters and Mothers: Mothers and Daughters*. New York, Quadrangle, New York Times Book Co.

HARLOW, H. F., and R. R. ZIMMERMAN, 1959, "Affectional Responses in the Infant Monkey," *Science*, 130, pp. 421–432.

——, M. K. HARLOW, R. O. DODSWORTH, and G. L. ARLING, 1970, "Maternal Behavior of Rhesus Monkeys Deprived of Mothering and Peer Associations in Infants," pp. 88–98 in Freda Rebelsky, ed., *Child Development and Behavior*. New York, Alfred A. Knopf.

HARTMANN, HEIDI, 1976, "Capitalism, Patriarchy, and Job Segregation by Sex," *Signs*, 1, #3, part 2, pp. 137–169.

HARTMANN, HEINZ, 1939, *Ego Psychology and the Problem of Adaptation*. New York, International Universities Press, 1958.

——, ERNST KRIS, and RUDOLPH M. LOEWENSTEIN, 1951, "Some Psychoanalytic Comments on 'Culture and Personality,' " pp. 86–116 in 1964, "Papers on Psychoanalytic Psychology," *Psychological Issues*, monograph 14, vol. 4, no. 2.

——, 1964, "Papers on Psychoanalytic Psychology," *Psychological Issues*, monograph 14, vol. 4 no. 2. New York, International Universities Press.

HEIMAN, MARCEL, 1968, "Discussion of Sherfey's Paper on Female Sexuality," *Journal of the American Psychoanalytic Association*, 16, pp. 406–416.

HERSHBERGER, RUTH, 1948, *Adam's Rib*. New York, Harper & Row.

HERZOG, ELIZABETH, and CECELIA E. SUDIA, 1972, "Families Without Fathers," *Childhood Education*, January, pp. 175–181.

HETHERINGTON, E. M., 1972, "Effects of Father Absence on Personality Development in Adolescent Daughters," *Developmental Psychology*, 7, pp. 313–326.

———, 1973, "Girls Without Fathers," *Psychology Today*, 6, pp. 46–52.

HOCHSCHILD, ARLIE RUSSELL, 1975a, "Attending to, Codifying, and Managing Feelings: Sex Differences in Love," paper presented to the American Sociological Association Meetings, San Francisco, August 29.

———, 1975b, "The Sociology of Feeling and Emotion: Selected Possibilities," pp. 280–307 in Marcia Millman and Rosabeth Moss Kanter, *Another Voice*. New York, Anchor Books.

HORKHEIMER, MAX, 1936, "Authority and the Family," in 1972, *Critical Theory*. New York, Herder and Herder.

HORNEY, KAREN, 1926, "The Flight from Womanhood: The Masculinity Complex in Women as Viewed by Men and by Women," in *Feminine Psychology*, 1967, pp. 54–70.

———, 1932, "The Dread of Women," *International Journal of Psycho-Analysis*, 13, pp. 348–360.

———, 1933, "The Denial of the Vagina: A Contribution to the Problem of the Genital Anxieties Specific to Women," in *Feminine Psychology*, 1967, pp. 147–161.

———, 1967, *Feminine Psychology*. New York, W. W. Norton.

INTERNATIONAL JOURNAL OF PSYCHO-ANALYSIS, 57, part 3, 1976.

JACOBSON, EDITH, 1950, "Development of the Wish for a Child in Boys," *Psychoanalytic Study of the Child*, 5, pp. 139–152. New York, International Universities Press.

———, 1964, *The Self and the Object World*. New York, International Universities Press.

———, 1968, "On the Development of the Girl's Wish for a Child," *Psychoanalytic Quarterly*, 37, pp. 523–538.

JAY, NANCY, n.d., "The Uncertainty of Paternity," unpublished paper.

JOHNSON, MIRIAM, 1963, "Sex Role Learning in the Nuclear Family," *Child Development*, 34, pp. 319–334.

———, 1975, "Fathers, Mothers and Sex-Typing," *Sociological Inquiry*, 45, #1, pp. 15–26.

———, JEAN STOCKARD, JOAN ACKER, AND CLAUDEEN NAFFZIGER, 1975, "Expressiveness Re-evaluated," *School Review*, 88, pp. 617–644.

JONES, ERNEST, 1927, "The Early Development of Female Sexuality," *International Journal of Psycho-Analysis*, 8, pp. 459–472.

———, 1933, "The Phallic Phase," *International Journal of Psycho-Analysis*, 14, pp. 1–33.

———, 1935, "Early Female Sexuality," *International Journal of Psycho-Analysis*, 16, pp. 263–273.

———, 1961, *The Life and Work of Sigmund Freud*. New York, Anchor Books, 1963.

JOURNAL OF THE AMERICAN PSYCHOANALYTIC ASSOCIATION, 24, #1, 1976.

KAGAN, JEROME, and MARION FREEMAN, 1963, "Relation of Childhood Intelligence, Maternal Behaviors and Social Class to Behavior During Adolescence," *Child Development*, 36, pp. 899–911.

KEISER, SYLVAN, 1968, "Discussion of Sherfey's Paper on Female Sexuality," *Journal of the American Psychoanalytic Association*, 16, pp. 449–456.

KEPHART, WILLIAM M., 1967, "Some Correlates of Romantic Love," *Journal of Marriage and the Family*, 29, pp. 470–474.

KERNBERG, OTTO, 1975, *Borderline Conditions and Pathological Narcissism*. New York, Jason Aronson.

KESTENBERG, JUDITH S., 1956a, "On the Development of Maternal Feelings in Early Childhood: Observation and ·Reflections," *Psychoanalytic Study of the Child*, 11, pp. 257–291.

————, 1956b, "Vicissitudes of Female Sexuality," *Journal of the American Psychoanalytic Association*, 4, pp. 453–476.

————, 1968, "Outside and Inside, Male and Female," *Journal of the American Psychoanalytic Association*, 16, #3, pp. 457–520.

KLEIN, MELANIE, 1928, "Early Stages of the Oedipus Conflict," *International Journal of Psycho-Analysis*, 9, pp. 167–180.

————, 1932, *The Psychoanalysis of Children*. London, Hogarth Press, 1959.

————, 1937, "Love, Guilt and Reparation," in Melanie Klein and Joan Riviere, 1964, *Love, Hate and Reparation*. New York, W. W. Norton.

————, 1948, *Contributions to Psycho-analysis, 1921–1945*. London, Hogarth Press.

KLEIN, MELANIE, PAULA HEIMANN, SUSAN ISAACS, and JOAN RIVIERE, 1952, *Developments in Psycho-Analysis*. London, Hogarth Press.

KOHLBERG, LAWRENCE, 1966, "A Cognitive Developmental Analysis of Sex-Role Concepts & Attitudes," pp. 82–173 in E. Maccoby, ed., *The Development of Sex Differences*. Stanford, Stanford University Press.

KOHN, MELVIN L., 1969, *Class and Conformity*. Homewood, Ill., Dorsey Press.

KOHUT, HEINZ, 1971, "Analysis of Self: A Systematic Approach to the Psychoanalytic Treatment of Narcissistic Personality Disorders," *Psychoanalytic Study of the Child*, monograph 4. New York, International Universities Press.

KOMAROVSKY, MIRRA, 1962, *Blue-Collar Marriage*. New York, Vintage Books, 1967.

————, 1974, "Patterns of Self-Disclosure of Male Undergraduates," *Journal of Marriage and the Family*, 36, #4, pp. 677–686.

KOTELCHUCK, MILTON, 1972, "The Nature of the Child's Tie to His Father," doctoral dissertation, Harvard University.

KOVEL, JOEL, 1970, *White Racism: A Psychohistory*. New York, Vintage Books.

LAING, R. D., 1959, *The Divided Self*. London, Penguin Books.

LAMPL-DE GROOT, JEANNE, 1927, "The Evolution of the Oedipus Complex in Women," pp. 180–194 in Robert Fliess, ed., 1969, *The Psychoanalytic Reader: An Anthology of Essential Papers with Critical Introductions*. New York, International Universities Press.

————, 1933, "Problems of Femininity," *Psychoanalytic Quarterly*, 2, pp. 489–518.

————, 1952, "Re-evaluation of the Role of the Oedipus Complex," *International Journal of Psycho-Analysis*, 33, pp. 335–342.

LANCASTER, JANE BECKMAN, 1976, "Sex Roles in Primate Societies," in Michael S. Teitelbaum, ed., *Sex Differences*. New York, Anchor Books.

LASLETT, BARBARA, 1973, "The Family as a Public and Private Institution: An Historical Perspective," *Journal of Marriage and the Family*, 35, pp. 480–492.

LASLETT, PETER, 1972, *Household and Family in Past Time*. Cambridge, Cambridge University Press.

LEE, RICHARD, and IRVEN DEVORE, eds., 1968, *Man the Hunter*. Chicago, Aldine.

LEIFER, A. D., P. H. LEIDERMAN, C. R. BARNETT, and J. A. WILLIAMS, 1973, "Effects of Mother-Infant Separation on Maternal Attachment Behavior," in F. Rebelsky and L. Dormon, eds., *Child Development and Behavior*, 2nd ed. New York, Alfred A. Knopf.

LEONARD, MARJORIE R., 1966, "Fathers and Daughters: The Significance of 'Fathering' in the Psychosexual Development of the Girl," *International Journal of Psycho-Analysis*, 47, pp. 325–334.

LERNER, BURTON, RAYMOND RASKIN, and ELIZABETH DAVIS, 1967, "On the Need to Be Pregnant," *International Journal of Psycho-Analysis*, 48, pp. 288–297.

LÉVI-STRAUSS, CLAUDE, 1956, "The Family," pp. 261–285 in Harry Shapiro, ed., *Man, Culture and Society*. London, Oxford University Press.

LEVY, DAVID, 1943, *Maternal Overprotection*. New York, Columbia University Press.

LEVY, KATA, 1960, "Simultaneous Analysis of a Mother and Her Adolescent Daughter: The Mother's Contribution to the Loosening of the Infantile Object Tie," *Psychoanalytic Study of the Child*, 15, pp. 378–391.

LIDZ, THEODORE, STEPHEN FLECK, and ALICE R. CORNELISON, 1965, *Schizophrenia and the Family*. New York, International Universities Press.

LOEWALD, HANS W., 1962, "Internalization, Separation, Mourning, and the Superego," *Psychoanalytic Quarterly*, 31, pp. 483–504.

————, 1973, "On Internalization," *International Journal of Psycho-Analysis*, 54, pp. 9–17.

LYND, ROBERT S., and HELEN MERRELL LYND, 1929, *Middletown*. New York, Harcourt, Brace, 1956.

LYNN, DAVID B., 1959, "A Note on Sex Differences in the Development of Masculine and Feminine Identification," *Psychological Review*, 66, pp. 126–135.

————, 1962, "Sex Role and Parent Identification," *Child Development*, 33, pp. 555–564.

LYNN, DAVID B., and W. L. SAWREY, 1959, "The Effects of Father-Absence on Norwegian Boys and Girls," *Journal of Abnormal and Social Psychology*, 59, pp. 258–262.

MACCOBY, ELEANOR, and CAROL JACKLIN, 1974, *The Psychology of Sex Differences*. Stanford, Stanford University Press.

MAHLER, MARGARET S., 1968, *On Human Symbiosis and the Vicissitudes of Individuation. Volume 1: Infantile Psychosis*. New York, International Universities Press.

MARTIN, M. KAY, and BARBARA VOORHIES, 1975, *Female of the Species*. New York,

Columbia University Press.

MARX, KARL, 1867, *Capital*, vol. 1. New York, International Publishers.

MASTERS, WILLIAM H., and VIRGINIA E. JOHNSON, 1966, *Human Sexual Response*. Boston, Little, Brown.

MEAD, MARGARET, 1935, *Sex and Temperament in Three Primitive Societies*. New York, William Morrow.

———, 1949, *Male and Female*. New York, Dell Publishing, 1968.

———, 1954, "Some Theoretical Considerations on the Problem of Mother-Child Separation," *American Journal of Orthopsychiatry*, 24, pp. 471–483.

———, 1962, "A Cultural Anthropologist's Approach to Maternal Deprivation," pp. 237–254 in 1966, *Maternal Care and Mental Health/ Deprivation of Maternal Care*. New York, Schocken Books.

MILLER, JEAN BAKER, ed., 1973, *Psychoanalysis and Women*. New York, Penguin Books.

MISCHEL, WALTER, 1966, "A Social-Learning View of Sex Differrences in Behavior," pp. 56–81 in Eleanor E. Maccoby, ed., *The Development of Sex Differences*. Stanford, Stanford University Press.

———, 1970, "Sex Typing and Socialization," pp. 3–72 in Paul Mussen, ed., *Carmichael's Manual of Child Psychology*, 3rd ed., vol. 2.

MITCHELL, JULIET, 1974, *Psychoanalysis and Feminism*. New York, Pantheon Books.

MITSCHERLICH, ALEXANDER, 1963, *Society Without the Father: A Contribution to Social Psychology*. New York, Schocken Books, 1970.

MONEY, JOHN, and ANKE A. EHRHARDT, 1972, *Man and Woman, Boy and Girl*. Baltimore, Johns Hopkins University Press.

MOORE, BURNESS E., 1976, "Freud and Female Sexuality: A Current View," *International Journal of Psycho-Analysis*, 57, #3, pp. 287–300.

MORTON, PEGGY, 1970, "A Woman's Work is Never Done," *Leviathan*, 2, #1, pp. 32–37.

MUENSTERBERGER, WARNER, 1969, "Psyche and Environment: Sociocultural Variations in Separation and Individuation," *Psychoanalytic Quarterly*, 38, pp. 191–216.

NEWTON, NILES, 1955, *Maternal Emotions: A Study of Women's Feelings Toward Menstruation, Pregnancy, Childbirth, Breast Feeding, Infant Care, and Other Aspects of Their Femininity*. Psychosomatic Medicine Monograph. New York, Paul Hoeber, Harper and Brothers.

———, 1973, "Interrelationships Between Sexual Responsiveness, Birth, and Breast Feeding," in Joseph Zubin and John Money, eds., *Contemporary Sexual Behavior: Critical Issues in the 1970's*. Baltimore, Johns Hopkins University Press.

NEWTON, NILES, and MICHAEL NEWTON, 1972, "Psychologic Aspects of Lactation," pp. 277–284 in Judith M. Bardwick, ed., *Readings on the Psychology of Women*. New York, Harper and Row.

OLDEN, CHRISTINE, 1958, "Notes on the Development of Empathy," *Psychoanalytic Study of the Child*, 13, pp. 505–518.

ORTNER, SHERRY B., 1974, "Is Female to Male as Nature Is to Culture?" in

Michelle Z. Rosaldo and Louise Lamphere, eds., *Woman, Culture and Society*. Stanford, Stanford University Press.

PARENS, HENRI, 1971, "A Contribution of Separation-Individuation to the Development of Psychic Structure," pp. 100–112 in McDevitt and Settlage, eds., *Separation-Individuation: Essays in Honor of Margaret S. Mahler*. New York, International Universities Press.

PARSONS, TALCOTT, 1942, "Age and Sex in the Social Structure of the United States," in 1964, *Essays in Sociological Theory*. New York, Free Press.

——, 1943, "The Kinship System of the Contemporary United States," in 1964, *Essays in Sociological Theory*. New York, Free Press.

——, 1951, *The Social System*. New York, Free Press, 1964.

——, 1954, "The Incest Taboo in Relation to Social Structure and the Socialization of the Child," in 1964, *Social Structure and Personality*.

——, 1964, *Social Structure and Personality*. New York, Free Press, 1970.

PARSONS, TALCOTT, and ROBERT F. BALES, 1955, *Family, Socialization and Interaction Process*. New York, Free Press.

PARSONS, TALCOTT, with WINSTON WHITE, 1961, "The Link Between Character and Society," in Parsons, 1964, *Social Structure and Personality*.

PECK, ELLEN, and JUDITH SENDEROWITZ, eds., 1974, *Pronatalism: The Myth of Mom and Apple Pie*. New York, Thomas Y. Crowell.

PLECK, JOSEPH H., and JACK SAWYER, 1974, *Men and Masculinity*. New Jersey, Prentice-Hall.

POLATNICK, MARGARET, 1973, "Why Men Don't Rear Children: A Power Analysis," *Berkeley Journal of Sociology*, 18, pp. 45–86.

RAPAPORT, DAVID, 1960, "The Structure of Psychoanalytic Theory," *Psychological Issues*, monograph 6, vol. 2, no. 2. New York, International Universities Press.

REICH, WILHELM, 1933, *Character Analysis*. London, Vision Press.

——, 1966, *Sex-Pol*. New York, Vintage Books.

REITER, REYNA, ed., 1975, *Toward an Anthropology of Women*. New York, Monthly Review Press.

RICH, ADRIENNE, 1976, *Of Woman Born: Motherhood as Experience and Institution*. New York, W. W. Norton.

RITVO, SAMUEL, and ALBERT J. SOLNIT, 1958, "Influences of Early Mother-Child Interaction on Identification Processes," *Psychoanalytic Study of the Child*, 13, pp. 64–85.

RIVIERE, JOAN, 1937, "Hate, Greed and Aggression," in Melanie Klein and Joan Riviere, 1964, *Love, Hate and Reparation*. New York, W. W. Norton.

ROAZEN, PAUL, 1969, *Brother Animal: The Story of Freud and Tausk*. New York, Alfred A. Knopf.

ROESSLER, RICHARD T., 1971, "Masculine Differentiation and Feminine Constancy," *Adolescence*, 6, #22, pp. 187–196.

ROIPHE, HERMAN, 1968, "On an Early Genital Phase: With an Addendum on Genesis," *Psychoanalytic Study of the Child*, 23, pp. 348–365.

ROIPHE, HERMAN, and ELEANOR GALENSON, 1973, "Object Loss and Early Sexual Development," *Psychoanalytic Quarterly*, 42, pp. 73–90.

————, 1975, "Some Observations on Transitional Object and Infantile Fetish," *Psychoanalytic Quarterly*, 44, #2, pp. 206–231.

ROSALDO, MICHELE Z., 1974, "Woman, Culture, and Society: A Theoretical Overview," in M. Z. Rosaldo and Louise Lamphere, eds., 1974, *Woman, Culture and Society*.

ROSALDO, MICHELLE Z., and LOUISE LAMPHERE, eds., 1974, *Woman, Culture and Society*. Stanford, Stanford University Press.

ROSSI, ALICE S., 1968, "Transition to Parenthood," *Journal of Marriage and the Family*, 30, pp. 26–39.

————, 1977, "A Biosocial Perspective on Parenting," *Daedalus*, 106, #2, pp. 1–31.

RUBIN, GAYLE, 1975, "The Traffic in Women: Notes on the 'Political Economy' of Sex," pp. 157–210 in Reyna Reiter, ed., *Toward an Anthropology of Women*. New York, Monthly Review Press.

RUBIN, LILLIAN BRESLOW, 1976, *Worlds of Pain: Life in the Working Class Family*. New York, Basic Books.

RUBIN, ZICK, 1970, "Measurement of Romantic Love," *Journal of Personality and Social Psychology*, 6, pp. 265–273.

————, 1975, "Loving and Leaving," unpublished paper.

RUTTER, MICHAEL, 1972, *Maternal Deprivation Reassessed*. Baltimore, Penguin Books.

SARLIN, CHARLES, 1963, "Feminine Identity," *Journal of the American Psychoanalytic Association*, 11, #4, pp. 790–816.

SCHAFER, ROY, 1968, *Aspects of Internalization*. New York, International Universities Press.

————, 1974, "Problems in Freud's Psychology of Women," *Journal of the American Psychoanalytic Association*, 22, #3, pp. 459–485.

SCHAFFER, H. RUDOLPH, 1971, *The Growth of Sociability*. Baltimore, Penguin Books.

————, 1977, *Mothering*. Cambridge, Harvard University Press.

SCHAFFER, H. R., and PEGGY E. EMERSON, 1964, "The Development of Social Attachments in Infancy," *Monographs of the Society for Research in Child Development*, 29, #3.

SCHREIBER, FLORA RHETA, 1973, *Sybil*. New York, Warner Books.

SHERFEY, MARY JANE, 1966, "The Evolution and Nature of Female Sexuality in Relation to Psychoanalytic Theory," *Journal of the American Psychoanalytic Association*, 14, #1, pp. 28–128.

SHERMAN, JULIA, 1971, *On the Psychology of Women*. Springfield, Ill., Charles C Thomas.

SLATER, PHILIP E., 1961, "Toward a Dualistic Theory of Identification," *Merrill-Palmer Quarterly of Behavior and Development*, 7, #2, pp. 113–126.

————, 1968, *The Glory of Hera: Greek Mythology and the Greek Family*. Boston, Beacon Press.

————, 1970, *The Pursuit of Loneliness*. Boston, Beacon Press.

————, 1974, *Earthwalk*. New York, Bantam Books.

SPERLING, MELITTA, 1950, "Children's Interpretation and Reaction to the Unconscious of Their Mothers," *International Journal of Psycho-Analysis*, 31, pp. 36–41.

SPITZ, RENE, 1965, *The First Year of Life: A Psychoanalytic Study of Normal and Deviant Development of Object Relations*. New York, International Universities Press.

SPRINCE, MARJORIE P., 1962, "The Development of a Preoedipal Partnership Between an Adolescent Girl and Her Mother," *Psychoanalytic Study of the Child*, 17, pp. 418–450.

STACK, CAROL B., 1974, *All Our Kin*. New York, Harper and Row.

STEPHENS, WILLIAM N., 1963, *The Family in Cross-Cultural Perspective*. New York, Holt, Rinehart and Winston.

STOLLER, ROBERT J., 1964, "A Contribution to the Study of Gender Identity," *International Journal of Psycho-Analysis*, 45, pp. 220–226.

———, 1965, "The Sense of Maleness," *Psychoanalytic Quarterly*, 34, pp. 207–218.

———, 1968, "The Sense of Femaleness," *Psychoanalytic Quarterly*, 37, #1, pp. 42–55.

———, 1972, "The Bedrock of Masculinity and Femininity: Bisexuality," *Archives of General Psychiatry*, 26, pp. 207–212.

———, 1973, "Overview: The Impact of New Advances in Sex Research on Psychoanalytic Theory," *American Journal of Psychiatry*, 130, #3, pp. 241–251.

———, 1974, "Facts and Fancies: An Examination of Freud's Concept of Bisexuality," in Jean Strouse, ed., *Women and Analysis*. New York, Grossman Publishers.

STROUSE, JEAN, ed., 1974, *Women and Analysis*. New York, Grossman Publishers.

SULLIVAN, HARRY STACK, 1953, *The Interpersonal Theory of Psychiatry*. New York, W. W. Norton.

TEITELBAUM, MICHAEL S., ed., 1976, *Sex Differences: Social and Biological Perspectives*. New York, Anchor Books.

THOMPSON, CLARA M., 1964, *On Women*. New York, New American Library, 1971.

TIGER, LIONEL, 1969, *Men in Groups*. New York, Random House.

U.S. DEPARTMENT OF LABOR, EMPLOYMENT STANDARDS ADMINISTRATION, Women's Bureau, *1975 Handbook on Women Workers*, Bulletin 297.

VANEK, JOANN, 1973, "Keeping Busy: Time Spent in Housework, United States, 1920–1970," doctoral dissertation, University of Michigan.

WEISSKOPF, SUSAN C., 1972, "The Psychoanalytic Theory of Female Development: A Review and a Critique" doctoral dissertation, School of Education, Harvard University.

WEITZMAN, LENORE J., 1975, "Sex-Role Socialization," in Jo Freeman, ed., *Women: A Feminist Perspective*. Palo Alto, Mayfield Publishing.

WELLS, ROBERT V., 1971, "Demographic Change and the Life Cycle of American Families," *Journal of Interdisciplinary History*, 2, #2, pp. 273–282.

WHITING, BEATRICE, ed., 1963, *Six Cultures: Studies of Child-Rearing*. New York, John Wiley.

WHITING, BEATRICE B., and JOHN W. M. WHITING, 1975, *Children of Six Cultures*. Cambridge, Harvard University Press.

WHITING, JOHN W. M., 1959, "Sorcery, Sin and the Superego: A Cross-Cultural Study of Some Mechanisms of Social Control," pp. 147–168 in Clellan S. Ford, ed., 1967, *Cross-Cultural Approaches: Readings in Comparative Research*. New Haven, Human Relations Area Files.

———, 1960, "Totem and Taboo—A Re-evaluation," in Jules H. Masserman, ed., *Psychoanalysis and Human Values*. New York, Grune and Stratton.

———, 1971, "Causes and Consequences of the Amount of Body Contact between Mother and Infant," paper presented to the American Anthropological Association Meetings, New York.

WHITING, JOHN W. M., RICHARD KLUCKHOHN, and ALBERT ANTHONY, 1958, "The Function of Male Initiation Rites at Puberty," in Eleanor E. Maccoby, T. M. Newcomb, and E. L. Hartley, eds., *Readings in Social Psychology*. New York, Holt.

WINCH, ROBERT F., 1962, *Identification and Its Familial Determinants*. New York, Bobbs-Merrill.

WINNICOTT, D. W., 1958a, "The Capacity to be Alone," pp. 29–36 in 1965b, *The Maturational Processes and the Facilitating Environment*.

———, 1958b, *Collected Papers: Through Paediatrics to Psycho-analysis*. London, Tavistock Publications.

———, 1960, "The Theory of the Parent-Infant Relationship," *International Journal of Psycho-Analysis*, 41, pp. 585–595.

———, 1965a, *The Family and Individual Development*. New York, Basic Books.

———, 1965b, *The Maturational Processes and the Facilitating Environment*. New York, International Universities Press.

———, 1971, *Playing and Reality*. New York, Basic Books.

WOLFF, CHARLOTTE, 1971, *Love Between Women*. Harper and Row.

YOUNG, MICHAEL, and PETER WILLMOTT 1957, *Family and Kinship in East London*. London, Penguin Books, 1966.

ZARETSKY, ELI, 1976, *Capitalism, the Family and Personal Life*. New York, Harper and Row.

ZILBOORG, GREGORY, 1944, "Masculine and Feminine: Some Biological and Cultural Aspects," pp. 96–131 in Jean Baker Miller, ed., 1973, *Psychoanalysis and Women*. New York, Penguin Books.

Index

Design: Jeri Davis
Composition: Chapman's Phototypesetting
Lithography: Publisher's Press
Binder: Mountain States Bindery
Binding: Joanna Oxford 30260

Text: VIP Baskerville 10/12
Display: VIP Baskerville
Paper: Natural Book, basis 50